First World War
and Army of Occupation
War Diary
France, Belgium and Germany

14 DIVISION
Headquarters, Branches and Services
Adjutant and Quarter-Master General
1 January 1916 - 30 September 1917

WO95/1879/1

The Naval & Military Press Ltd
www.nmarchive.com
Published in association with The National Archives

Published by

The Naval & Military Press Ltd

Unit 10 Ridgewood Industrial Park,

Uckfield, East Sussex,

TN22 5QE England

Tel: +44 (0) 1825 749494

www.naval-military-press.com

www.nmarchive.com

This diary has been reprinted in facsimile from the original. Any imperfections are inevitably reproduced and the quality may fall short of modern type and cartographic standards.

© **Crown Copyright**
Images reproduced by permission of The National Archives, London, England, 2015.

Contents

Document type	Place/Title	Date From	Date To
Heading	WO95/1879 Adjt & QMG-14 Div Jan-Dec 1916 Jan-Sep 1917		
Heading	14th Division 'A' & 'Q' Branch Jan 1916-Sep 1917		
Heading	A Branch 14th Div. Vol: 4		
Heading	War Diary of Headquarters, 14th (Light) Division ("A" Branch) from 1st January, 1916 to 31st January, 1916. (Volume 9)		
War Diary	H7c7.7	01/01/1916	07/01/1916
War Diary	H7c7.7 Sheet 28	08/01/1916	13/01/1916
War Diary	H.7c.7.7	14/01/1916	20/01/1916
War Diary	H7c7.7 Sheet 28	21/01/1916	31/01/1916
Miscellaneous	Total Daily Casualties of The 14th (Light) Division. For Month Of January, 1916 Appdx XXI		
Miscellaneous	The following is the List of Promotions and Honours awarded to Officers, Warrant-Officers, Non-commissioned officers and Men of the 14th (Light) Division for services rendered in connection with Military Operations in the Field. Appdx XXII	14/01/1916	14/01/1916
Miscellaneous	14th (Light) Division. Casualties Amongst Officers For Month of January, 1916 App XXIII		
Miscellaneous	14th (Light) Division. App XXIV		
Miscellaneous	Appendix XXI Daily expenditure of Gun Ammunition.		
Heading	War Diary of "A" and "Q" Branches Headquarters, 14th (Light) Division. from 1st February, 1916 to 29th February, 1916 (Volume)		
War Diary	H 7 c 7.7 Sheet 28	01/02/1916	12/02/1916
War Diary	H 7 C 7.7 Sheet 27 Esquelbec Sheet 27	13/02/1916	13/02/1916
War Diary	Esquelbec	14/02/1916	20/02/1916
War Diary	Hesselles	20/02/1916	24/02/1916
War Diary	Doullens	24/02/1916	25/02/1916
War Diary	Sus-St-Leger	25/02/1916	28/02/1916
War Diary	Barly	29/02/1916	29/02/1916
Miscellaneous	Orders For Entrainment Appdx XXVI	17/02/1916	17/02/1916
Miscellaneous	Table of Lorries Of Extra Baggage. Appx XXVIa	17/02/1916	17/02/1916
Miscellaneous	Advance Parties Will Go In The Following Trains.	17/02/1916	17/02/1916
Miscellaneous	Entrainment Programme. 14th Division. Sheet 1. Appx XXVII		
Miscellaneous	Reserve Division Entrainment. General Instructions.		
Miscellaneous	14th Division. Table D		
Miscellaneous			
Miscellaneous	Supplies During Movement By Rail. Appx XXVIIa		
Miscellaneous			
Miscellaneous	E=Esquelbecq C=Cassel. Sheet 2.		
Miscellaneous	E=Esquelbecq C=Cassel. Sheet 3		
Miscellaneous	E=Esquelbecq C=Cassel. Sheet 4		
Miscellaneous	Expenditure of Ammunition February 1916 App XXIX		
Miscellaneous	Total Daily Casualties of The 14th (Light) Division For Month Of Appx XXX		
Miscellaneous	14th (Light) Division. Casualties Amongst Officers for the month of February, 1916 Appx XXXI		

Miscellaneous	14th (Light) Division Appx XXXII		
Miscellaneous	Appendix. Positions of Units At 11.50 P.m Appdx XXVIII		
Heading	War Diary of "A" & "Q" Branches, Headquarters, 14th (Light) Division, From 1st March, 1916 To 31st March, 1916 (Volume XIII)		
War Diary	Barly	01/03/1916	05/03/1916
War Diary	Berneville Sh 51 C V.6.d	06/03/1916	14/03/1916
War Diary	Berneville	15/03/1916	20/03/1916
War Diary	Warlus Sheet 57 C	21/03/1916	31/03/1916
Miscellaneous	14th (Light) Division.	18/03/1916	18/03/1916
Miscellaneous	Ammunition Expended during March 1916. Appx XXXIV		
Miscellaneous	Total Daily Casualties of The 14th (Light) Division. For Month Of March 1916 Appx XXXV		
Miscellaneous	14th (Light) Division. Officer Casualties For Month of March, 1916. Appx XXXVI		
Miscellaneous	14th (Light) Division. Reinforcements Received During Month of March, 1916.		
Heading	War Diary of "A" & "Q" Branches, 14th (Light) Division. From 1st April, 1916. To 30th April, 1916 (Volume XIV)		
War Diary	Warlus Sheet 57 C	01/04/1916	22/04/1916
War Diary	Warlus	23/04/1916	30/04/1916
Miscellaneous	14th (Light) Division. Ammunition Expenditure During Month of April, 1916		
Miscellaneous	Total Daily Casualties of The 14th (Light) Division. For Month Of April 1916		
Miscellaneous	14th (Light) Division. Location of Units.	09/05/1916	09/05/1916
Miscellaneous	14th (Light) Division. Reinforcements Received During Month of April 1916		
Miscellaneous	14th (Light) Division. Casualties Amongst Officers For Month of April 1916		
Heading	War Diary of "A" & "Q" Branches, 14th (Light) Division from 1st May 1916 to 31st May 1916 (Volume XV)		
War Diary	Warlus Sheet 57 C	01/05/1916	31/05/1916
Miscellaneous	14th (Light) Division. Ammunition Expended: June 1916		
Miscellaneous	14th (Light) Division. Casualties Amongst Officers For Month of May 1916 Appendix XXX		
Miscellaneous	Casualties For June. Other Ranks. Appendix XXXI		
Miscellaneous	14th (Light) Division. Reinforcements Received During The Month of May 1916		
Miscellaneous	Appendix XXXIII O.C/111/A.	02/05/1916	02/05/1916
Heading	War Diary of "A" & "Q" Branches 14th (Light) Division from 1st June, 1916 to 30th June, 1916. (Volume XVI)		
War Diary	Warlus Sheet 51 C	01/06/1916	30/06/1916
Miscellaneous	14th (Light) Division. Ammunition Expended During June, 1916 Appdx XXXIV		
Miscellaneous	Appendix. Special Allotment For Days V-Z Appdx XXXV		
Miscellaneous	14th (Light) Division. Casualties Amongst Officers For Month of June, 1916 Appdx XXXVI		

Miscellaneous	14th (Light) Division. Casualties During Month of June, 1916 Appdx XXXVII		
Miscellaneous	14th (Light) Division. Reinforcements During June, 1916 Appdx XXXVIII		
Heading	Original War Diary of "A" & "Q" Branches, 14th (Light) Division from July 1st, 1916 To July 31st, 1916. (Volume XVII)		
War Diary	Warlus Sheet 51 C	01/07/1916	27/07/1916
War Diary	Warlus	28/07/1916	30/07/1916
War Diary	Sus St Leger	30/07/1916	30/07/1916
War Diary	Sus St Leger Frohen Legrand	31/07/1916	31/07/1916
Miscellaneous	XXXVIII. A O.C./206	28/07/1916	28/07/1916
Miscellaneous	O.C./206 XXXVIII. A	28/07/1916	28/07/1916
Miscellaneous	XXXVIII. B O.C. 207	29/07/1916	29/07/1916
Miscellaneous	XXXVIII. C O.C. 208	30/07/1916	30/07/1916
Miscellaneous	XXXVIII. C O.C. 208		
Miscellaneous	14th (Light) Division. Ammunition Expended During July, 1916		
Miscellaneous	14th (Light) Division. Casualties Amongst Officers For Month of July, 1916		
Miscellaneous	14th (Light) Division. Other Ranks. Casualties During Month of July, 1916		
Miscellaneous	14th (Light) Division. Reinforcements During Month of July, 1916		
Miscellaneous	Table Showing Actual Location of Troops During Movement To Preliminary Concentration Area.		
Heading	War Diary of "A" & "Q" Branches, 14th (Light) Division. From 1st August, 1916 To 31st August, 1916. Volume XVIII		
War Diary	Frohen Le Grand Bernaville	01/08/1916	12/08/1916
War Diary	Buire Bellevue Fm	13/08/1916	31/08/1916
Miscellaneous	List of Appendices War Diary 1-8-16 To 31-8-16		
Miscellaneous	Appendix XLIII O.C. 211	31/07/1916	31/07/1916
Miscellaneous	XLIII (a) O.C. 211		
Miscellaneous	41st Infantry Bde. QH 2	31/07/1916	31/07/1916
Miscellaneous	Appendix XLIV 14th (Light) Division.	13/08/1916	13/08/1916
Miscellaneous	Appendix XLV 14th Divn. No. Q.829/2	17/08/1916	17/08/1916
Miscellaneous	Administrative Arrangements, for Move August 31st. 1916	30/08/1916	30/08/1916
Miscellaneous	Railway Time Table 31-8-16	30/08/1916	30/08/1916
Miscellaneous	14th (Light) Division. Location of Units. Appendix XLVII	03/08/1916	03/08/1916
Miscellaneous	Location of Units. 14th (Light) Division. Appendix XLVII	13/08/1916	13/08/1916
Miscellaneous	Location of Units. 14th (Light) Division Appendix XLIX	19/08/1916	19/08/1916
Miscellaneous	Location of Units. 14th (Light) Division Appendix L	26/08/1916	26/08/1916
Miscellaneous	14th (Light) Division Reinforcements. Month of August, 1916		
Miscellaneous	14th (Light) Division. Casualties During The Month of October, August, 1916		
Heading	War Diary of "A" & "Q" Branches 14th (Light) Division From 1st Sept To 30th Sept 1916 Volume XXIX		
War Diary		01/09/1916	12/09/1916
War Diary	Fricourt	13/09/1916	16/09/1916

War Diary	Buire	17/09/1916	30/09/1916
Miscellaneous	Administrative Arrangements 15th September, 1916		
Miscellaneous	Supply Arrangements, 16th & 17th. App. II	16/09/1916	16/09/1916
Miscellaneous	41st Inf Bde 42nd Inf Bde 43rd Inf Bde Appendix III	21/09/1916	21/09/1916
Miscellaneous	Administrative Arrangements for move 21st and 22nd Sept. Appendix IV	20/09/1916	20/09/1916
Miscellaneous	Administrative Arrangements. Relief of 12th Div. Appendix V	25/09/1916	25/09/1916
Miscellaneous	14th (Light) Division. Location of Units. App. VI	02/09/1916	02/09/1916
Miscellaneous	Location of Units. 14th (Light) Division. App. VII	13/09/1916	13/09/1916
Miscellaneous	14th (Light) Division. Reinforcements During Month of September, 1916 App VIII		
Miscellaneous	14th (Light) Division. Summary Of Accurate Casualties. App IX		
Heading	War Diary of Administrative Branch 14th (Light) Division From 1st October To 31st October 1916 Volume XL		
War Diary		01/10/1916	26/10/1916
War Diary	Lecauroy	27/10/1916	31/10/1916
Miscellaneous	Appendices With October War Diary, "A" & "Q" Branches, 14th (Light) Division		
Miscellaneous	14th (Light) Division. Casualties During The Month of October, 1916 Appendix I		
Miscellaneous	14th (Light) Division. Reinforcements Month of October, 1916 Appendix II		
Miscellaneous	14th (Light) Division. Location of Units. Appendix III	01/10/1916	01/10/1916
Miscellaneous	14th (Light) Division. Location of Units. Appendix IV	17/10/1916	17/10/1916
Miscellaneous	Table of Moves 25th To 30th Oct		
Heading	War Diary of 14th (Light) Division Administrative Branch From 1st November 1916 To 30th Novr 1916 (Volume 14)		
War Diary	Le Cauroy	01/11/1916	30/11/1916
Miscellaneous	14th (Light) Division. Location of Units.	01/11/1916	01/11/1916
Miscellaneous	14th (Light) Division. Location Table	08/11/1916	08/11/1916
Miscellaneous	14th (Light) Division. Location Table	24/11/1916	24/11/1916
Heading	War Diary of Administrative Branches 14th (Light) Division From 1st Dec 1916 To 31st Dec 1916 Volume 43		
War Diary	Le Cauroy	06/12/1916	19/12/1916
War Diary	Warlus	21/12/1916	31/12/1916
Miscellaneous	Administrative Arrangements In Connection With 14th Division O.O. 97	13/12/1916	13/12/1916
Miscellaneous	14th (Light) Division. Location Table	09/12/1916	09/12/1916
Miscellaneous	14th (Light) Division. Location Table	19/12/1916	19/12/1916
Miscellaneous	14th (Light) Division. Location Table	26/12/1916	26/12/1916
Heading	War Diary of 14th (Light) Division Administrative Branches From 1st Jany 1917 To 31st Jany 1917 Volume 44		
War Diary	Warlus	01/01/1917	31/01/1917
Miscellaneous	14th (Light) Division. Location Table	22/01/1917	22/01/1917
Heading	War Diary of 14th (Light) Division Administrative Branches From 1st Feby To 28th Feby 1917 Volume		
War Diary	Warlus	01/02/1917	28/02/1917
Miscellaneous	14th (Light) Division. Location Table	04/02/1917	04/02/1917
Miscellaneous	14th (Light) Division. Location Table	08/02/1917	08/02/1917
Miscellaneous	14th (Light) Division. Location Table	28/02/1917	28/02/1917

Heading	War Diary of Administrative Branch 14th (Light) Division From 1st March To 31st March 1917 Volume 46		
War Diary	Warlus	01/03/1917	31/03/1917
Miscellaneous	14th (Light) Division. Location Table	18/03/1917	18/03/1917
Heading	War Diary Administrative Branch 14th Light Division April 1st To April 30th 1917 Vol 19		
War Diary	Warlus	01/04/1917	23/04/1917
War Diary	Bailleulmont	24/04/1917	25/04/1917
War Diary	Arras	26/04/1917	30/04/1917
Miscellaneous	Supply & Transport arrangements in connection move of the Division to back area.	13/04/1917	13/04/1917
Miscellaneous	14th (Light) Division. Location Table	27/04/1917	27/04/1917
Miscellaneous	14th (Light) Division. Location Table	29/04/1917	29/04/1917
Heading	War Diary of 14th (Light) Division (Administrative Branches) For 1st May, 1917 To 31st May, 1917 Volume 47		
War Diary	Arras	01/05/1917	17/05/1917
War Diary	M 23 a 6.6 1500y N of Mercatel	18/05/1917	18/05/1917
War Diary	Camp On Beaurains Mercatel Road	19/05/1917	31/05/1917
Miscellaneous	Administrative Arrangements In Connection With O. O. 122 Of 10th May	10/05/1917	10/05/1917
Miscellaneous			
Diagram etc	Sanitary Arrangements.		
Miscellaneous	Sanitation App III	29/05/1917	29/05/1917
Miscellaneous	Salvage App 2	27/05/1917	27/05/1917
Miscellaneous	14th (Light) Division. Location Table	06/05/1917	06/05/1917
Miscellaneous	14th (Light) Division. Location Table	13/05/1917	13/05/1917
Heading	War Diary of 14th (Light) Division Administrative Branches 1st June 1917 To 30th June 1917 Volume 48		
Miscellaneous	Copies to:-		
War Diary	Divl. HQ. Camp at M 23 a 6.6. 1500x N of Mercatel	01/06/1917	09/06/1917
War Diary	Marieux	10/06/1917	30/06/1917
Miscellaneous	Handing Over App 1	06/06/1917	06/06/1917
Miscellaneous	Administrative Arrangements For The New Area App 2	08/06/1917	08/06/1917
Miscellaneous	Supply Arrangements For Rest Area App 3	08/06/1917	08/06/1917
Miscellaneous	Scheme For Destroying "Dud" Shell App 4		
Diagram etc	PIT For exploding nest of "dud" shell.		
Miscellaneous	14th (Light) Division. Schedule Of "Dud" Shell Destroyed.		
Miscellaneous	Divisional Horse Show held June 26th 1917 List of Prize Winners. App 5		
Miscellaneous	App 6 Q. 364	27/06/1917	27/06/1917
Heading	War Diary of 14th (Light) Division Administrative Branch 1st July 1917 To 31st July 1917 Volume 49		
War Diary	Marieux	01/07/1917	11/07/1917
War Diary	St Jans Capel	12/07/1917	31/07/1917
Miscellaneous	Administrative Orders For The Move App 1		
Miscellaneous	Entraining Station, Doullens (South)	09/07/1917	09/07/1917
Miscellaneous	Entraining Station-Doullens (North)		
Miscellaneous	Entraining Station, Candas		
Miscellaneous	Administrative Orders For The Move	09/07/1917	09/07/1917
Miscellaneous	Administrative Arrangements In The New Area. App II	10/07/1917	10/07/1917
Miscellaneous	In continuation of this Office No. A. 342/14 dated 18/6/17 App III	28/07/1917	28/07/1917
Miscellaneous	Fighting Strength-Infantry Brigade App 1		

Miscellaneous	Appendix II		
Miscellaneous	Appendix III		
Miscellaneous	Appendix IV		
Miscellaneous	Appendix V		
Miscellaneous	Appendix VI		
Miscellaneous	Appendix VII		
Miscellaneous	Appendix VIII		
War Diary	St Jans Capel	01/08/1917	05/08/1917
War Diary	Caestre	06/08/1917	14/08/1917
War Diary	Reninghelst	15/08/1917	17/08/1917
War Diary	Dickebusch	18/08/1917	25/08/1917
War Diary	Reninghelst	27/08/1917	28/08/1917
War Diary	Berthen	29/08/1917	31/08/1917
Miscellaneous	Reference 14th Division O.O. No. 131 Of 4/8/17	05/08/1917	05/08/1917
Miscellaneous	Reference para. 5.	05/08/1917	05/08/1917
Miscellaneous	Reference 14th Division O.O. No. 131 of 4/8/17	05/08/1917	05/08/1917
Miscellaneous	Reference para. 5.	05/08/1917	05/08/1917
Miscellaneous			
Miscellaneous	Administrative Arrangements, Reference 14th Division Warning Order No. 132		
Miscellaneous	Administrative Arrangements, Reference 14th Division Warning Order No. 132	15/08/1917	15/08/1917
Miscellaneous	Administrative Instructions. Reference 14th (Light) Division O.O. No. 133	17/08/1917	17/08/1917
Miscellaneous	A. 221/30 App IV	19/08/1917	19/08/1917
Miscellaneous	Reference 14th Divisional Warning Order No. 134 of 18/8/17 para. 7	19/08/1917	19/08/1917
Miscellaneous	14th (Light) Division Administrative Arrangements. App VI	24/08/1917	24/08/1917
Miscellaneous			
Miscellaneous	14th (Light) Division Administrative Arrangements. App VI	24/08/1917	24/08/1917
Miscellaneous			
Miscellaneous	Administrative Instructions. Reference 14th (Light) Division O.O. 138 Of Aug. 25th, 1917	25/08/1917	25/08/1917
Miscellaneous		25/08/1917	25/08/1917
Miscellaneous	Administrative Instructions. Reference 14th (Light) Division O.O. 138 Of Aug. 25th, 1917		
Miscellaneous	Administrative Instructions Move To Berthen Area.	28/08/1917	28/08/1917
Miscellaneous	Administrative Instructions Reference 14th Division O.O. 142 Of 31/8/17	31/08/1917	31/08/1917
Heading	War Diary Administrative Branch 14th Light Division September 1917 Vol 24		
War Diary	Ravelsberg 28 S 17 Central	01/09/1917	05/09/1917
War Diary	Ravelsberg	06/09/1917	30/09/1917
Miscellaneous	Regulations For 14th Divisional Trench Tramways.	06/09/1917	06/09/1917
Diagram etc	Sketch Map of Trench Tramways Heavy & Light Railways Not Shown		
Miscellaneous	Salvage. App II	07/09/1917	07/09/1917
Miscellaneous	14th (Light) Division. Scheme For Winter Hutting With 2 Brigades In Line		
Miscellaneous	C.R.A. C.R.E. 41st Infantry Bde. 42nd Infantry Bde. 43rd Infantry Bde. 11th K. Liverpool R.	14/09/1917	14/09/1917
Miscellaneous	O.C.213/1 App V	25/09/1917	25/09/1917
Miscellaneous	New Year's Honours Gazette.	18/09/1917	18/09/1917

WO95/1879

Adjt & QMG - 14 Div

Jan-Dec 1916
Jan-Sep 1917

14TH DIVISION

'A' & 'Q' BRANCH

JAN 1916-SEP 1917

"A" Branch
14th Div.
Vol: 4
Jan '16
Jan '16
Sep '17

CONFIDENTIAL.

WAR DIARY

of

HEADQUARTERS, 14TH (LIGHT) DIVISION

("A" Branch)

from 1st January, 1916   to   31st January, 1916.

(VOLUME 9).

Army Form C. 2118

Volume IX

WAR DIARY
or
INTELLIGENCE SUMMARY

(Erase heading not required.)

Instructions regarding War Diaries and Intelligence Summaries are contained in F.S. Regs., Part II. and the Staff Manual respectively. Title Pages will be prepared in manuscript.

Place	Date	Hour	Summary of Events and Information	Remarks and references to Appendices
HQ 77.	1.		Rehearsal completed. Readjustment of areas. Div. Train left Div. Area owing to interference. Army's Park relieves to Sub. Park established there & transport to ELVERDINGHE. Completed settling in huts at HOSPITAL FARM. Orders for Transfer of Cookhouse Stores to hd. Div. received.	left
	2.			(A)
	3.		Prospects forward dump of trench bridges and 15th bn. Transport convoy towards Salient areas. Trench Tramway starting points.	left
	4.		Further instructions re transfer of Stores to late place at HAZEBROUCK on 5th Jan. & cancels 1.10 a.m. this exact place for change notes for.	left
	5.		All arrangements for transfer of Stores cancelled by G.H.Q. 8.15 a.m.	left
	6.		Nothing to record.	
	7.		Nothing to record	

Army Form C. 2118

WAR DIARY
or
INTELLIGENCE SUMMARY
(Erase heading not required.)

Instructions regarding War Diaries and Intelligence Summaries are contained in F.S. Regs., Part II. and the Staff Manual respectively. Title Pages will be prepared in manuscript.

Place	Date	Hour	Summary of Events and Information	Remarks and references to Appendices
1.7.07. Hut 28	6.		Det: No definite advance from Army but movement through new line areas heartaken over. Submitted to Corps Transport Officer 15" LD in command 200 horses are handed over in exchange for 100 LD. ordered to issue for tract transport routes and times from hrs to 8.30 with RE stores & beginning of new road.	Ott. Sheet 28.
	9.		2nd LD. horses handed over to Mtd. 6th Div. Trucks again the dawn on 10th must be A. no. Sheet 28. Downwards. the exchange to WINDMILL A 23 when legt Div countermands no det:	Ott.
	10.		194 LD horses handed over to Mtd 6th Div. Trucks content with Track Duquets starts for RE New Railroad spurs Rl train late and refilling very protracted owing to thorough Road works two furrows places for vehicles. Refilling completed at 2 pm	Ott
	11.		2d names of Officers to be detailed by 10 am. to go to England on 14th called for Tactical Exercise from 1 Corps.	Ott
	12.		Commenced handing over horses to 6th Div at WATOU 192 LD handed over	Ott
	13.		Lt Col ULRIC THYNNE arrived to take Command of the BRDS vice Lt Col MACLACHLAN wounded	

Army Form C. 2118

WAR DIARY
or
INTELLIGENCE SUMMARY
(Erase heading not required.)

Instructions regarding War Diaries and Intelligence Summaries are contained in F.S. Regs., Part II. and the Staff Manual respectively. Title Pages will be prepared in manuscript.

Place	Date	Hour	Summary of Events and Information	Remarks and references to Appendices
H7c 7.7	14.		Orders received for transfer of 1 Coy Blanket wagons Vehicle only known first Echelon in Gazette. "Bleu Green" HQ Submitted.	OAR.
	15.		Drawings detachment from 16 Coy Lorry started for ammunition rations to 14th Divn. Refilling completed in 2 hrs 30 minutes.	OAR
	16.		12 LD horse handed over to 49th Divn. Refilling at A.D.V. Railhead completed in 2 hrs 15 minutes.	OAR
	17.		132 FD horses + 56 mules handed over to 14th Division. Handing over completed 3 Sept for 14 LD hupit for transfer.	all
	18.		Suggested withdrawal of horse to unit in rest. - reported all our heavy horses shortage - organs Bridles the hand horses bridlering - unserviceable accepted.	OAR.
	19.		Overall for scouts received orders trip 23 for trial report issue to Captain Reichen not 4.30 pm 19th	OAR.
	20.		Broken drag nets taken over from C.E. VI Corps. 1000 rounds of Ammunition S.A.A. received for trial. Smith 415 SAA for trial report.	OAR.

1875 Wt. W593/326 1,000,000 4/15 J.B.C. & A. A.D.S.S./Forms/C. 2118.

WAR DIARY
or
INTELLIGENCE SUMMARY
(Erase heading not required.)

Army Form C. 2118

Instructions regarding War Diaries and Intelligence Summaries are contained in F. S. Regs., Part II. and the Staff Manual respectively. Title Pages will be prepared in manuscript.

Place	Date	Hour	Summary of Events and Information	Remarks and references to Appendices
47c77. Shut 28	21st		Nothing to record	
	22nd		BRIELEN dugouts occupied by one company detailed by 4th Rif Bde	Began C. Rut X
	23rd		Nothing to record -	Appx
	24th		Nothing to record.	
	25th		14th D.A. to move to new localities by 1st of Feb. Lt Col N. THYNNE handed over command to Major SEYMOUR, of 4 R.B. and London Scots pending further instructions	Appx.
	26th		Overall to scouts reported very useful but changes proposed. Smaller Sizes	Appx.
	27th		Nothing to record.	

WAR DIARY
INTELLIGENCE SUMMARY
(Erase heading not required.)

Army Form C. 2118

Place	Date	Hour	Summary of Events and Information	Remarks and references to Appendices
47c7.7 Sheet 28.	28th		Report on enemy piercing S.A.A. at 10 yards. Pieces w/clean hole. German topplate. Tried in places in frame lines for fragments. Ascertain but is stopped all sniping. For this represented to the war Office.	Appx
	29th		14th D.A. until further notice hoping new location (49th Div'n Counterbarrage lines) New head and loading place to be made at the new location. of AM and D.A.C.	Appx.
	30th		Nothing to record.	
	31st		Capt. W.H. BECKWITH left division and handed over duties of ADDOL to L.M. Seale and proceeded to 17th Corps. Appendices:— XXI Casualties:— XXII Honours Rewards XXIII Officers Casualties:— XXIV Total Reinforcements XXV Expenditure of gun ammunition.	Col Hammerton Lt Col ADDSMy 14 K Dn

Jan 1 1916

Appdx XXI.

TOTAL DAILY CASUALTIES OF THE 14TH (LIGHT) DIVISION.
FOR MONTH OF January, 1916.

24 hours ending	Killed		Wounded		S.Wounded		Gassed		Missing		Total		Gd.Total	
	O.	O.R	O.	O.R	O.	O.R	O.	O.R	O.	O.R	O.	O.R	O.	O.R
1st		1		5						1		7		7
2nd		1	1	10							1	11	1	18
3rd		2		15								17	1	35
4th		5		22								27	1	62
5th		10		41								51	1	113
6th		4		12								16	1	129
7th		4		12								16	1	145
8th		3	1	9							1	12	2	157
9th		7	1	6		1					1	14	3	171
10th	1	4	1	14							2	18	5	189
11th		5		25								30	5	219
12th	1	3		17							1	20	6	239
13th		9		16								25	6	264
14th		7	1	9							1	16	7	280
15th		12		11		1						24	7	304
16th		3		11								14	7	318
17th		7		21								28	7	346
18th		4	1	25							1	29	8	375
19th		1		14								15	8	390
20th	1	10	2	21	1	2					4	33	12	423
21st		2	1	16							1	18	13	441
22nd		3	1	14							1	17	14	458
23rd		5	1	39							1	44	15	502
24th		2	2	7							2	10	17	511
25th		8		19								27	17	538
26th	1	3		10							1	13	18	551
27th		4		5								9	18	560
28th		5		12		4				1		22	18	582
29th		4		15		1						20	18	602
30th			1	13						1		13	19	615
31st		2	1	16	1						2	18	21	633
Total for Month.	4	140	15	482	2	9				2	21	633		

App^x XXII.

The following is the List of Promotions and Honours awarded to Officers, Warrant-Officers, Non-commissioned officers and Men of the 14th (Light) Division for services rendered in connection with Military Operations in the Field.

London Gazette of 14th Jan. 1916.

STAFF. To be Major-General.

    Colonel (Temp.Major-General) V.A.Couper.
    Colonel (Temp.Major-General) O.S.W.Nugent,D.S.O.,A.D.C.

To be Companions of the Distinguished Service Order.

    Major (Temp. Lt-Colonel) L.J.Comyn, Connaught Rangers.
    Major J.A. Hartigan,M.B.,R.A.M.C., D.A.D.M.S.

14th Signal Co.

To be Companion of the Distinguished Service Order.

    Major E.F.W.Barker,   K.O.Y.L.I.

Awarded the Military Cross.

    Temp. 2nd Lieut. C.M. Kay, R.E.

Awarded the Distinguished Conduct Medal.

    No. 47871. Pioneer W.G.Crutchley, R.E.
    40031   —   C.F. MALDEN, R.E.

Royal Field Artillery.

Awarded the Military Cross.

    Captain C.E. Walker,   48th Brigade.

Awarded the Distinguished Conduct Medal.

    No. 96248. Sergeant M. Kelly,   47th Brigade.
    11809. Corporal T. Hayes,   47th Brigade.
    11973. Bombardier H. Saunders,48th Brigade.
    6185. Bombardier P. Wilson, 48th Brigade.
    84007. A/Bombardier F. Walker,49th Brigade.

11th Bn. The King's (Liverpool Regiment) (Pioneers).

To be a Companion of the Distinguished Service Order.

    Major (Temp.Lieut-Colonel) V.T. Bailey.

6th Bn. The Somersetshire Light Infantry.

To be a Companion of the Distinguished Service Order.

    Major T.F. Ritchie.

Awarded the Distinguished Conduct Medal.

    No. 7395. Sergeant E. Williams,
    11224. Corporal H.W. Webb,
    10296. Private J.J. Miller.

- 2 -

5th Bn. Oxfordshire & Buckinghamshire Light Infantry.

Awarded the Military Cross.

Temp. Captain N.F. Barwell.

Awarded the Distinguished Conduct Medal.

No. 10247. Sergeant N. Tarr,
7664. Sergeant W. Adams.
10910. A/Corporal A. Smart.

8th Bn. King's Own Yorkshire Light Infantry.

Awarded the Distinguished Conduct Medal.

No. 11351. Lance-Sergeant H. Buckley.

King's Royal Rifle Corps.

To be a Companion of the Distinguished Service Order.

Major C.H.N. Seymour,   8th Bn.

Awarded the Military Cross.

Captain H.M.B.de S.La Terriere,   7th Bn.
Temp. Captain J. Christie,   9th Bn.
Temp. Captain E.W. Benson,   9th Bn.
Temp. Captain M. Mallalue,   9th Bn.
Temp. 2nd Lieut. C.D. Lacey,   9th Bn.

Awarded the Distinguished Conduct Medal.

No. 3315. Sergeant W.H. Wallington, 9th Bn.
8049. Lance-Corporal E. Vickers, 9th Bn.

10th Bn. Durham Light Infantry.

Awarded the Military Cross.

Temp. Captain C.E. Pumphrey.

Awarded a clasp to his Distinguished Conduct Medal.

No. 12901. R.S.M. A. Nobel.

Awarded the Distinguished Conduct Medal.

No. 12707. Lance-Corporal E. Chicken.

6" DCLI
11650, Pte A G GITTINS

- 3 -

The Rifle Brigade (The Prince Consort's Own)

Awarded the Military Cross.

Temp. Captain L. Woodroffe,	8th Bn.
Temp. Lieut. C.R.Gorell-Barnes,	8th Bn.
Temp. 2nd Lieut. R.H. Lawson,	7th Bn.
Temp. 2nd Lieut. R.E. d'Erlanger,	9th Bn.
No. 25, C.S.M. G.Goodey,	9th Bn.

Awarded the Distinguished Conduct Medal.

No. 3450. R.S.M. H.Wilkins,	9th Bn.
R.N/8005 C.S.M. H.Harwood,	8th Bn.
R.N/3469.Sergeant G.Jackson,	8th Bn.
B/1058.Sergeant A.E.Taylor,	9th Bn.
B/2867.Corporal B. Wooding,	8th Bn.
2065.A/Corporal C.H.Pearce,	7th Bn.
B/ 309.Rifleman W.Searle,	7th Bn.
3484.Rifleman H.Nash,	7th Bn.
1652.Rifleman W.Hobday,	8th Bn.
B/3164.Rifleman L.Schofield,	8th Bn.
3308.Rifleman N.Wood,	9th Bn.
B/2314.Rifleman F.Sheppard,	9th Bn.

14th Divisional Cyclist Company.

Awarded the Distinguished Conduct Medal.

Lance-Corporal B. Shaw.

Royal Army Medical Corps.

Awarded the Military Cross.

Captain S. Miller, M.B. (S.R.)

Chaplains Department.

Awarded the Military Cross.

Rev. J.C. Kinnear, M.A., C.F.(4th Class)

==================

Issued with D.R.O. No. 1134 dated 20th January, 1916.
==================

Headquarters,
 14th (Light) Division.
  20th January, 1916.

App.ᵈˣ XXIII

14TH (LIGHT) DIVISION.

CASUALTIES AMONGST OFFICERS FOR MONTH OF JANUARY, 1916.

January.

2nd.	2/Lieut. D.M. MacKinlay, 8th Bn. K.R.R.C.		Wounded.
8th.	2/Lieut. C.B. Wood, 8th Bn. R.B.		Wounded.
9th.	2/Lieut. J.R. Paris, 10th D.L.I.		Accidentally by Bayonet.
10th.	2/Lieut. K.V. Carter, 5th Ox & Bucks L.I.		Wounded.
10th.	2/Lieut. R.A. Butt, 5th K.S.L.I.		Killed.
12th.	2/Lieut. J. H. Hudson, 49th Bde R.F.A.		Wounded. (since died)
14th.	2/Lieut. W.R.A Wareing, 11th L'pool R		Wounded.
18th.	2/Lieut. R.C. Browne, 7th Bn. R.B.		Wounded. (Grenade Accident)
20th.	Capt. G.R.R.Colman, H.Q.Staff, 41st Inf.Bde. (Bde M.G.Officer)		Wounded.
20th.	2/Lieut. C.S. Underhill, 5th K.S.L.I.		Wounded. (since died).
20th.	2/Lieut. E. Barlow, 9th K.R.R.C.		Wounded. (slightly, at duty)
20th	2/Lieut. C.F. Batty, 10th Durham L.I.		Killed.
21st.	2/Lieut. J.R. Grantham, 9th Bn. R.B.		Wounded.
22nd.	2/Lieut. E.H. Krause, 10th Durham L.I.		Wounded.
23rd.	2/Lieut. C.E. Winter, 7th Bn. R.B.		Wounded.
24th.	2/Lieut. R.H.M. Lewis, 7th K.R.R.C.		Wounded.
24th.	Lieut. D. Higgins, 5th Ox & Bucks L.I.		Wounded.

(over)

January.

26th.   2/Lieut. T. J. McLaren,   Killed.
           47th Bde R.F.A.

30th.   2/Lieut. A.C. Heberden,   Wounded.
           7th K.R.R.C.

31st.   2/Lieut. W. H. Butland,   Wounded.
           10th Durham L.I.

==========

14TH (LIGHT) DIVISION.

Total number of reinforcements arrived during the month of January 1916.

Officers. 19.
Other Ranks. 930.

Appendix ~~V~~ XXV

Daily expenditure of Gun Ammunition.

Date	A	AX	B	BX
1	101	-	-	24
2	189	4	-	99
3	154	-	-	31
4	145	10	-	53
5	136	10	-	35
6	135	44	-	74
7	196	36	-	70
8	168	24	1	22
9	206	11	1	42
10	107	74	1	13
11	143	213	1	96
12	153	336	1	143
13	392	195	-	40
14	177	88	1	23
15	247	125	-	92
16	244	55	-	94
17	121	41	-	41
18	45	4	-	18
19	164	11	-	25
20	146	180	-	69
21	220	79	-	29
22	86	251	-	40
23	122	80	-	-
24	109	46	-	20
25	110	120	-	54
26	248	599	-	163
27	192	24	-	5
28	58	124	-	38
29	84	52	-	19
30	47	-	-	5
31	79	17	-	-

CONFIDENTIAL.

WAR DIARY

of

"A" and "Q" Branches

HEADQUARTERS, 14TH (LIGHT) DIVISION.

from 1st February, 1916   to 29th February, 1916.

(Volume ~~III~~).

* * * * * * *

Army Form C. 2118

Volume XII

WAR DIARY
or
INTELLIGENCE SUMMARY
(Erase heading not required.)

Instructions regarding War Diaries and Intelligence Summaries are contained in F. S. Regs., Part II. and the Staff Manual respectively. Title Pages will be prepared in manuscript.

Place	Date 1916	Hour	Summary of Events and Information	Remarks and references to Appendices
H 7 c 7.7 Sheet 28	1 Feb.		Nothing to record.	A
	2 Feb.		Returning Surplus Camp Equipment	A
	3rd Feb.		D.D.R. 2nd Army inspected Regimental first line Transport Animals	A
	4th		Transport for Brigade's machine gun companies and Lewis Guns completed. Lewis Guns being issued to Battalions. The Division came under the orders of the XIV Corps.	A
	5th	12 m	Ration for trails and Ordnance changes from GODEWAERSVELDE to Advanced Railhead PESELHOEK. No facilities for settling and no notice given – fix reported in Barn occupied by R.E. in Train Camp.	A
	6th		Court of Enquiry held on Fire	A

Army Form C. 2118

WAR DIARY
or
INTELLIGENCE SUMMARY
(Erase heading not required.)

Instructions regarding War Diaries and Intelligence Summaries are contained in F.S. Regs., Part II. and the Staff Manual respectively. Title Pages will be prepared in manuscript.

Place	Date	Hour	Summary of Events and Information	Remarks and references to Appendices
H7c7.7 Sheet 28	5/2/15	7th	Orders received for relief of this Division by 20th Sth. Division to move into Rest prior to Entrainment on the 19th to join XI Corps in 2nd Army Area.	
	8th		Orders for handing over Camps, Huts, tents and horse lines. Extra Transport indented for to carry Blankets and kit. 45 motor lorries & 13 lorries daily.	
	9th		Programme of Entrainment issued. Times of relief known —	
	10th		H.Q. Div. come out of the line into billets preparatory to moving to new area. WINNEZEELE - OUDEZEELE and BRIEL	
	11th		H.Q. Div. posted to new area. 2nd Bde Headquarters to WINNEZEELE. 4th Inf. Bde Hd. Qrs. move towards to HOUTKERQUE. 5th Inf. Bde Hd. Qrs. move towards to HOUTKERQUE. Entrainment completed at STEENVOORDE. Railhead changed to STEENVOORDE. 9th K.R.R.C. ordered to entrain at OR — out-movement to WORMHOUDT.	
	12th	5.30am	5th K.S.L.I. to HOUTKERQUE 9th R.B. to HOUTKERQUE	movement by Road to STEENVOORDE commenced

1875 Wt. W593/826 1,000,000 4/15 J.B.C. & A. A.D.S.S./Forms/C. 2118.

Army Form C. 2118

WAR DIARY
or
INTELLIGENCE SUMMARY
(Erase heading not required.)

Instructions regarding War Diaries and Intelligence Summaries are contained in F. S. Regs., Part II. and the Staff Manual respectively. Title Pages will be prepared in manuscript.

Place	Date Feby.	Hour	Summary of Events and Information	Remarks and references to Appendices
H.Q. 77 Sheet 57	13th	8am	Divnl H.Q. to ESQUELBEC. 20th Div G.O.C. assumed command of the line. Relief being complete.	Sheet 27.
ESQUELBEC Sheet 27		9am	Wksg of Kents 2nd Reg. & Redoubt Lines of 76 Inf Bde completed.	
ESQUELBEC	14th		Hrs of Infy & Artillery commenced. 2 F.C. & ARNEKE. Bngdrs to reconnoitre line in the vicinity.	
	15th		Lines of R.A. completed. 14th Division now in Corps Reserve.	
	16th		Orders for Entrainment issued. Arrangements proceeding for H.Q. of Division billeting area & breakaway onwards for detraining at LONGUEAU.	App XXVI
	17th		Arranging Blanket Transport, Entrainment programme Accounts. Instructions to Entrainment & Advanced Parties. R.A. despatched to LONGUEAU	App XXVII A

WAR DIARY
or
INTELLIGENCE SUMMARY
(Erase heading not required.)

Army Form C. 2118

Place	Date	Hour	Summary of Events and Information	Remarks and references to Appendices
ESQUELBEC	Feb 18		Completion of Return went arrangements. Final Awards Table taken to M.D.R.T.N.R.	App XXVII
	19		Entrainment of Division commenced at ESQUELBEC - CASSEL orders and programme attached. Division detrained at LONGUEAU suburb of AMIENS. Capt VYVYAN DAVIES Superintended entrainment at ESQUELBEC and Major STERICKER 950 seagrass at CASSEL Such minutiae by our Regimental Officer. Capt PARSONS D.A.D.M.S. was assisted by 1st S.A. Subordinates Detrain went at LONGUEAU. Officers from 14th D.A. during journey attacked in taking blankets. Note Butties had strong arrows & knives from blanket. 1st During arrival from billets and town into baggage & between meals. Platoons from WATOU, LEDRINGHEM were kept by 11th Inniskilling Regt the remainder from ZUYDSCHOTE by the 1/20th London Regt. Train went hill took from train wait Station baggage Stand by... Convoy of D.S.C. arrived at MONTON VILLERS and first Convoy of D.S.C. arrived at ST.OUEN.	App XXVIII a Sheet LENS 11 AMIENS 17
ESQUELBEC	20.		Div. HQ. closed at ESQUELBEC at 8 am. Reopened at HESCELLES at 9pm. G.O.C. & Staff by Motor to HESCELLES. Entraining detraining & billets G.O.C. Staff by Motor. 14 D.S.C. at ST.OUEN 14 D.A.S.P. arrived + kept baggage 2nd convoy of 14 D.S.C. 3rd convoy of railway station & billets. 8th Army Sigs. by road to HESCELLES. Troops from Train to billets. Mobile Ambulances assembled at ESQUELBEC.	
HESCELLES	21	8pm	Entrainment + Detrainment continued. Convoy of Mobile Ambulances arrived 4 new area. Rlhd to Divs. 2 F.A.N.U. 3rd Convoy of 14 D.S.C. arrived ST.OUEN	

WAR DIARY or INTELLIGENCE SUMMARY

Army Form C. 2118

(Erase heading not required.)

Instructions regarding War Diaries and Intelligence Summaries are contained in F. S. Regs., Part II. and the Staff Manual respectively. Title Pages will be prepared in manuscript.

Place	Date	Hour	Summary of Events and Information	Remarks and references to Appendices
HESDIGNEUL	22nd		Entrainment & Detrainment continued. 1st Convoy of D.S.C arrived at HOUVEN. Entrainment completed according to programme.	
	23rd		Detrainment completed. Platform clear by 1 p.m. Trained a very heavy load through the frost, but lorries were over horses late owing to snow. Horses, bedding, gun-harness was carried to Front line autospot. One company of 9th Scots Fusiliers in train. No 3 lorries of MT. Blanket lorries at entraining Station carried out their programme successfully. At Detraining Station. 8 army lorries waited. However the station actually detailed, arriving MT Baggage of MT at 9 lorries until lorries from incoming troops became available. Enough lorries held spare. 12 trained to arrive to proper place of troops. Distance to billets approximately:	
			1st Army 15th. 10 miles	
			43 "	15 "
			42 "	"
			43 "	2 "
			All units of 12 J.B. were carried in lorries on leaving entraining stations. Other units marched to their own billets to which baggage had been sent forward to follow the lorries. It was a few hours after ... were concerned in to follow up in as long ... until rendezvous in the following morning.	
	24th		The Division moved into DOULLENS-CANDAS area. H.Q. at DOULLENS. 9 Blanket lorries from D.A.S by 3rd Army supplemented by D.A.P which half moved to DOULLENS. Refilling took place in the previous day. Supply section had difficulty with their convoys in reaching the Division.	

WAR DIARY
or
INTELLIGENCE SUMMARY

Army Form C. 2118

(Erase heading not required.)

Place	Date	Hour	Summary of Events and Information	Remarks and references to Appendices
HESSELIN	24.	(6am)	Conference with 110th Inf. Brigade upon the route the Division should follow, & finally reached the decision made by the Brig. They were ordered to march to HESSELIN from HESSELIN in front of their line of march.	A.
DOULLENS.		6pm	Reached SAULTY. Everywhere congestion & difficulties were being already experienced. 110th Bde Gp. arrived at LUST-LEGER at 2 AM.	Appx XXVIII A.
DOULLENS	25		Division started to move to LUST-LEGER. A good deal of snow had fallen during the night and roads in consequence were treacherous. 110th French troops they became sheets of ice. A French motor lorry firing up to LUST-LEGER going towards DOULLENS made very small progress. Our first touch of the 47th Division was in the morning at DOULLENS. Troops were highly disorganised. Several stragglers were met leaving DOULLENS from the front & others in small parties. On arrival in DOULLENS we met the traffic in confusion & chaos from every direction. About 12 noon Col. R. when traffic slowly disappeared to still the situation & eventually got things in hand & with help of the Military Police finally reached DOULLENS. The whole then transferred to our Mobile R.F. Corps Farm. RA's into Cantonments of the Train were much billeted in the destinations and bivouacs this billeting along the road following days heard bombing by enemy	A.
SUS-ST LEGER		2am		
SUS-ST LEGER	26		Division completed its move into LUST-LEGER which only reached DOULLENS. Refilling in transport to start Area began returning towards midnight. Orders received for taking over frontage of 33 French Div.	E.

Army Form C. 2118

WAR DIARY
or
INTELLIGENCE SUMMARY
(Erase heading not required.)

Instructions regarding War Diaries and Intelligence Summaries are contained in F. S. Regs., Part II. and the Staff Manual respectively. Title Pages will be prepared in manuscript.

Place	Date	Hour	Summary of Events and Information	Remarks and references to Appendices
SUS-ST-LEGER	Feb 27th		DAC moved up into Bivouac at Pr. Barriers close by Poroi of 14th Div. Examples from lies trains on the road. Rations & Supplies at NIENCOURT. Refilling at SHORTY Station except Pr. in 2 groups which Refilled at NIENCOURT	I.
	28th		43 coys AM moved to DAINVILLE BERNEVILLE SIMENCOURT with 43 at BERNEVILLE. On Return of such pr batteries moved forward from No at BERNEVILLE with 4/50, 28/29, 15 Feb 16. Leave and wagons and a proportion of B.M.Cs. kept at supply heads & Refill locally by emplacements of Rear artillery in WARLUS BERNEVILLE SIMENCOURT. horse transport from D.A.L.P. Refilling at or 27th	I.
	29th		DWL & Q. EARLY. A/51 J.A. LARRAS DAINVILLE and BERNEVILLE Enon Riechofski. 145 in EN COURT with D. Leve. 4th Ox Bucks L1	I.
BARLY		10am	SOMBRIN Belin SUS-ST-LEGER. Battalions moving to DAINVILLE BERNEVILLE SIMENCOURT lost went to AGNY & DA. Clear billets. 4/3 DA. marched up after dark into AGNY the HICOURT section of the line. D.A.C. Supplies as yesterday. Supplying Pr. billets. Refilling as in previous day.	I.

The following appendices are attached

Am. Expdn.	App xx/x
Cavalry or	" xxx
Officers	" xxx/
Reinforcements	" xxx"

P.Freeman Capt.
D.A.D.Q
14/3 Div 4

1375 Wt. W593/826 1,000,000 4/15 J.B.C. & A. A.D.S.S./Forms/C. 2118.

Appx XXVI

SECRET.   S.Q.18/XIV.

ORDERS FOR ENTRAINMENT.

1. The Division will entrain in accordance with the attached Time Table "A".

2. Units will arrive at their entraining station as follows:-

    Infantry Battalions.

    The transport, one Company and all baggage will be at the entraining station 3 hours and the remainder will arrive one hour before the train is due to start.

    Other Units.

    Will arrive 3 hours before their trains are due to start.

    The entrainment must be completed half an hour before the departure of the train.

3. Troops will halt outside the entraining station yard until permitted by the R.T.O. to enter. No troops or transport will enter the station yard without his permission.

4. The R.T.O. is in charge of the entraining and railway arrangements. His orders are to be complied with by all Staff and Regimental Officers.

5. A Staff Officer from Divisional Headquarters will be present at each entraining station.

6. The A.P.M. will detail 3 Mounted Policemen to be on duty at each entraining station throughout the entrainment. These policemen will be sent forward on the last train.
    Each Unit on arrival will detail 3 picquets of 1 N.C.O. and 3 men who will be posted under direction of the Staff Officer on duty at the station to prevent men leaving the station premises.

7. Parties for loading horses and vehicles and fatigue parties for loading baggage are to be told off before the troops arrive at the station. The Officer in charge will report to the Staff Officer on duty who will show them where to put down their arms and equipment. They will pile arms and put down their equipment, leaving a guard on them and will then proceed with their work till finished. They will then assemble at the place where their equipment is, put it on and fall in with their arms ready to be marched to the train.

8. Lorries will be provided for extra transport in accordance with the attached table "B".

9. Supply wagons will be sent to the Units whose supplies they carry the night before entrainment and will entrain with them.

10. Baggage wagon horses will be sent to Units the day before entrainment.

11. Billeting parties will proceed as in attached table "C".

12. Breast ropes for horse trucks must be provided by the Units themselves. Ropes for lashing vehicles on the flat trucks will be provided by the Railway.

13. During the journey, picquets must be provided at all stops for each end of the train to prevent troops leaving. These picquets will be told off beforehand and entrained in trucks near the ends of the train.

14. No personnel or stores will be allowed in the brake vans.

15. On arrival at the detraining station the R.T.O. there will take charge of the detrainment.

16. All Units will entrain with the Iron Ration on the man, the current day's food and the supply section wagons of the Train loaded with the rations for the following day. This will be used on the journey.

17. O.C. Units will be informed at the detraining station of the refilling point to which supply section wagons of the Train are to be sent to draw rations for the day following detrainment. These wagons will be attached to Units until the arrival of the Train Companies to which they belong.

17th February, 1916.

Lieut Colonel.
A.A. & Q.M.G., 14th (Light) Division.

App XXVIa

TABLE OF LORRIES OF EXTRA BAGGAGE.

An officer from each unit will meet lorries at the times and places shown for reporting.

Unit.	No of lorries.	Report at Place.	Time	Date.	Remarks.
47th F.A.Bde,	3	ESQUELBECQ	4 p.m.	18th	) To be handed over at
49th F.A.Bde,	3	"	4 p.m.	18th	) 12 noon after dumping whole of Bde Baggage at railway Str
11th L'pool R	3	LEDRINGHEM,	9 a.m.	19th	
48th F.A.Bde,	3	RUBROUCK,	6 p.m.	19th	Must complete dumping of baggage by 10.30 a.m. 20th and be handed over.
Div'l H.Qrs,	2	ESQUELBEC	4 p.m.	19th	
R.A. H.Qrs,	1	ZEGGARS CAPELL	4 p.m.	19th	
Div.Signal Co.	1	ESQUELBEC,	2 p.m.	19th	
Div.Cyclists,	1	ESQUELBEC,	2 p.m.	19th	
Div.Train,H.Q.Coy,	1	ESQUELBEC,	2 p.m.	19th	Must complete dumping at Railway Stn by 12 noon 20th in
43th F.A.Bde,	3	ESQUELBEC,	4 p.m.	19th	
8th R.B.	3	OUDEZEELE,	9 a.m.	20th	
9th R.B.	3	WORMHOUDT,	9 a.m.	20th	
7th K.R.R.C.	3	WINNEZEELE,	11 a.m.	20th	
5th Ox & Bucks,	3	WORMHOUDT,	12 noon,	20th	
8th K.R.R.C.	3	WINNEZEELE,	2 p.m.	20th	
5th K.S.L.I.	3	WORMHOUDT,	4 p.m.	20th	
7th R.B.	3	WINNEZEELE,	10 p.m.	20th	
9th K.R.R.C.	3	HERZEELE,	6 a.m.	21st	
41st Bde H.Qrs,	1	WINNEZEELE,	6 a.m.	21st	
42nd Bde H.Qrs,	1	WORMHOUDT,	9 a.m.	21st	
61st Field Co.R.E.	1	OUDEZEELE,	9 a.m.	21st	
62nd Field Co.R.E.	1	HERZEELE.	9 a.m.	21st	
44th Field Amblce	1	WINNEZEELE,	9 a.m.	21st	
No.2 Coy.Div.Train,	1	WINNEZEELE,	9 a.m.	21st	
42nd Field Amblce,	1	WORMHOUDT,	2 p.m.	21st	
No.3 Coy.Div.Train,	1	WORMHOUDT,	2 p.m.	21st	
89th Field Co.R.E.	1	HERZEELE,	2 p.m.	21st	
6th Somerset L.I.	3	WORMHOUDT,	10 a.m.	21st	
43rd Field Amblce,	1	WORMHOUDT,	4 p.m.	21st	
No.4 Coy.Train,	1	WORMHOUDT,	4 p.m.	21st	
6th D.C.L.I.	3	WORMHOUDT,	10 p.m.	21st	
D.L.O.Y.	1	ESQUELBEC,	10 p.m.	21st	
6th K.O.Y.L.I.	3	WORMHOUDT,	4 a.m.	22nd	
43rd Bde H.Qrs,	1	WORMHOUDT,	6 a.m.	22nd	
D.A.C.	2	ARNEKE,	9 a.m.	22nd	

PLACES OF MEETING ARE :-
ESQUELBEC,	=	Square,
LEDRINGHEM,	=	Church,
RUBROUCK,	=	Church,
ZEGGARS CAPPEL,	=	Square,
OUDEZEELE,	=	Square,
WINNEZEELE,	=	Church,
HERZEELE,	=	Square,
ARNEKE,	=	Church.

Headquarters,
14th Division,
17th February, 1916.

ADVANCE PARTIES WILL GO IN THE FOLLOWING TRAINS.

41st Infantry Bde Group,	10.31 a.m.	19th from	CASSEL.
42nd " " "	12.10 p.m.	19th "	ESQUELBEC.
43rd " " "	10.31 a.m.	20th "	CASSEL.
D. L. O. Y.	3.10 p.m.	20th "	ESQUELBEC.
Mobile Vety Section,	3.10 p.m.	20th "	ESQUELBEC.

Other Units have been ordered to send parties by ordinary train :

STRENGTH OF ADVANCED PARTIES.

	Officers.	N.C.Os and Men.
Field Coys R.E.		2
Infantry Bde H.Qrs,	1	2
Battalions,	1	9
Div. Train, per Company,		3.
Field Ambulances,		3.

==========

Headquarters,
   14th (Light) Division.
      17th February, 1916.

Appx XXVII

E = Esquelbecq.
G = Gässel.

ENTRAINMENT PROGRAMME.   14TH DIVISION.   Sheet 1.

Date.	Train No.	Type	Serial No.	NAME OF UNIT.	Entraining Station.	Train leaves	Marche Due Destination	Remarks.
Feb. 19th.	1	T.C.	1451 1455.	A Battery 47th Bde R.F.A. ½ Bde Ammn Column,	E	9.10	H.T.13.	
	2	T.C.	1472 1475.	B Battery, 49th Bde R.F.A. 1/3rd Bde Ammn Column,	G	10.51	H.T.14.	
	3	T.C.	1452 1455.	B Battery,47th Bde R.F.A. ½ Bde Ammn Column,	E	12.10	H.T.16.	
	4	T.C.	1473 1475	C Battery, 49th Bde R.F.A. 1/3rd Bde Ammn Column,	G	13.51	H.T.17.	
	5	T.C.	1440 1460 1460 1470	H.Q.46th Bde R.F.A. H.Q.,47th Bde R.F.A. H.Q.,48th Bde R.F.A. H.Q.,49th Bde R.F.A.	E	15.10	H.T.19.	
	6	T.C.	1404(Pt)	11th Liverpool Regt.	G	16.41	H.T.20.	
	7	T.C.	1453. 1455.	C Battery,47th Bde R.F.A. ½ Bde Ammn Column,	E	18.10	H.T.22.	
	8	T.C.	1474. 1475.	D Battery 49th Bde R.F.A. 1/3rd Bde Amm. Column,	G	19.51	H.T.23.	
	9	T.C.	1454. 1455.	D Battery 47th Bde R.F.A. ½ Bde Ammn Column,	E	21.20	H.T. 1.	
	10	T.C.	1405. 1403. 1404(Rdr)	Div'l Cyclist Co. H.Q.& No.1 Section Sig.Co. 11th Liverpool Regt.	G	22.51	H.T. 2.	Less 1 Co.,6 G.S.Wagons,12 H.D.M.(See No.10 Train).
Feb. 20th	11	T.C.	1401 1402. 1437.	Div'l Headquarters, H.Q.,Div'l R.A. H.Q.& H.Q.Co.Div'l Train,	E	0.10	H.T. 4.	

RESERVE DIVISION ENTRAILMENT.   GENERAL INSTRUCTIONS.

1. Entraining Stations will be   CASSEL
                                 ESQUELBECQ

   Regulating Station ~~was.~~ ST. OMER

2. A Staff Officer should be detailed for duty at the ~~R.S.~~ to keep in touch with ~~D.A.D.R.~~ R.T.O. there and the Division.

3. Arrangements should be made by the Division to control traffic on the road approaches to the entraining stations, and no troops or transport should be allowed to enter the station yards until the R.T.O. is ready.

4. (a) Each train of a " Combattant " type (C) consists of 1 Officer's carriage: 13 flat trucks: 34 covered trucks.

   (b) Each train of a " Parc " type (P) consists of 1 Officer's carriage: 23 flat trucks: 24 covered trucks.

   (c) Each flat truck will take an average of 4 axles.
       Each covered truck will take 6 H.D.Horses.   )
                                   or 8 L.D.Horses or mules.)
                                   or 40 Men.   )

   (d) No personnel or stores will be allowed in the brake vans at each end of the train.

5. Orders will be issued to Units to cover the following points:-

   1. (a) INFANTRY BATTALIONS.   The transport and 1 Company will
          --------------------- arrive at the entraining station
                                 three hours before the departure
                                 of the trains and the remaining
                                 3 Companies one hour.

      (b) OTHER UNITS   Will arrive three hours before the
          -----------   departure of the trains.

   2. The entrainment of all Units must be completed half an hour before the time of departure of train.

   3. Breast ropes for horse trucks must be provided by the Units themselves: ropes for lashing vehicles on the flat trucks will be provided by the Railway.

   4. Pickets must be provided at all stops for each end of the train to prevent troops leaving.

                                            Lieut. Col.
                                            A.D.R.T. (N.R.)

14TH DIVISION.   TABLE   D.

UNIT.	Serial No.	DESCRIPTION.
14th Divisional Units.	1401	Divisional Headquarters.
	1402	H.Q. Divisional Artillery.
	1403	Squadron D.L.O.Y.
	1404	11th Liverpool Reg't. (Pioneers)
	1405	Divisional Cyclist Co.
	1406	H.Q., & No. 1 Section Divisional Signal Co.
41st Infantry Brigade.	1410	Brigade Headquarters.
	1411	7th K.R.R.C.
	1412	8th K.R.R.C.
	1413	7th Rifle Brigade.
	1414	8th Rifle Brigade.
	1415	No. 2 Section Signal Co.
	1416	Brigade Machine Gun Co.
42nd Infantry Brigade.	1420	Brigade Headquarters.
	1421	5th Ox. & Bucks L.I.
	1422	5th K.S.L.I.
	1423	9th K.R.R.C.
	1424	9th Rifle Brigade.
	1425	No. 3 Section Signal Co.
	1426	Brigade Machine Gun Co.
43rd Infantry Brigade.	1430	Brigade Headquarters.
	1431	6th Somerset L.I.
	1432	6th D.C.L.I.
	1433	6th K.O.Y.L.I.
	1434	10th Durham L.I.
	1435	No. 4 Section Signal Co.
	1436	Brigade Machine Gun Co.

UNIT.	Serial No.	DESCRIPTION.
46th Brigade R.F.A.	1440	Brigade H.Q.
	1441	A. Battery.
	1442	B. Battery.
	1443	C. Battery.
	1444	D. Battery.
	1445	Brigade Ammunition Column.
47th Brigade R.F.A.	1450	Brigade H.Q.
	1451	A. Battery.
	1452	B. Battery.
	1453	C. Battery.
	1454	D. Battery.
	1455	Brigade Ammunition Column.
48th Brigade R.F.A.	1460	Brigade H.Q.
	1461	A. Battery.
	1462	B. Battery.
	1463	C. Battery.
	1464	D. Battery.
	1465	Brigade Ammunition Column.
49th Brigade R.F.A.	1470	Brigade H.Q.
	1471	
	1472	B. Battery.
	1473	C. Battery.
	1474	D. Battery.
	1475	Brigade Ammunition Column.
Divisional Ammunition Column.	1478	Headquarters.
	1479	No. 1 Section 2/3rds.
	1479A	No. 1 Section 1/3rd.
	1480	No. 2 Section 2/3rds.
	1480A	No. 2 Section 1/3rd.
	1481	No. 3 Section 2/3rds.
	1481A	No. 3 Section 1/3rd.

UNIT.	Serial No.	DESCRIPTION.
Divisional Engineers.	1483	Headquarters.
	1484	61st Field Co. R.E.
	1485	62nd Field Co. R.E.
	1486	89th Field Co. R.E.
Divisional Train (less transport with Troops)	1487	H.Q. and No. 1 Company (100th)
	1488	No. 2 Company. (101st)
	1489	No. 3 Company. (102nd)
	1490	No. 4 Company. (103rd)
Medical Units.	1491	44th Field Ambulance.
	1492	42nd Field Ambulance.
	1493	43rd Field Ambulance.
	1494	25th Sanitary Section.
Veterinary Unit.	1495	26th Mobile Veterinary Section.

Appx XXVII a.

SUPPLIES DURING MOVEMENT BY RAIL.

On February 18th D.S.C. refilled Div.Train as usual with supplies for consumption 19th and then refilled for a 2nd time the supply wagons of those units which were to go by train on 19th before 6 p.m. D.S.C. then loaded up the supplies for the same units for consumption 21st.

On February 19th D.S.C. convoy consisting of lorries loaded with supplies for 21st for units entraining before 6 p.m. that day went by road to ST. OUEN, remainder of D.S.C. refilled Supply wagons for all remaining units with supplies for 20th and refilled with supplies for 21st Supply wagons of units entraining before 6 p.m. 20th. Lorries were then reloaded with supplies for those units for 21st.

On 20th D.S.C. 1st convoy refilled supply wagons of first units to arrive on the way to their billets reloaded at railhead CANDAS and returned to ST. OUEN.

This system was continued throughout the move.

After arrival at destination refilling for each Group took place in or near the village where it was billetted.

Unit					
H.Q.Div'l Artillery	DOULLENS.	SUS ST.LEGER.	SUS ST.LEGER.	SUS ST.LEGER.	SUS ST.LEGER. BARLY.
46th F.A.Bde.	LONGUEVILLETTE.	)Roadside	(LIENCOURT.	LIENCOURT.	LIENCOURT. LIENCOURT
47th F.A.Bde.	CANDAS	)between DOULLENS	(DENIER.	DENIER & BERLENC.	DENIER. DENIER.
48th F.A.Bde.	CANDAS.	)and LUCHEUX.	(LE CAUROY.	LE COUROY. COURT.	LIGNEREUIL. LIGNEREUIL.
49th F.A.Bde.	FIENVILLERS.		(SARS LE BOIS.	SARS LE BOIS.	SAR LE BOIS SARS LE BOIS
D.A.C.	BEAUVAL	BEAUVAL	DOULLENS.	ETREE WANIN	Partly in action. Partly in action. LIGNEREUIL. LIGNEREUIL.
Trench Mortar Btts.	YSEUX	YSEUX	BEAUVAL	"	"
H.Q. Div.Engineers,	DOULLENS.	SUS ST.LEGER.	SUS ST.LEGER.	SUS ST.LEGER.	SUS LT.LEGER. BARLY.
61st Fd.Coy.R.E.	OCCOCHES.	"	"	SUS ST.LEGER.	FOSSEUX. FOSSEUX.
62nd Fd.Coy.R.E.	GEZAINCOURT.	LUCHEUX	"	"	" BARLY.
89th Fd.Coy.R.E.	FRESCHWILLERS.	HUMBERCOURT.	HUMBERCOURT.	HUMBERCOURT.	" FOSSEUX.
H.Q.Div.Train,	DOULLENS.	SUS ST.LEGER.	SUS ST.LEGER.	SUS ST.LEGER.	SUS ST.LEGER. BARLY.
H.Q.Coy.Div.Train,	HARDINVAL	CANDAS	HEM	LIENCOURT.	LIENCOURT. LIENCOURT.
No.2 Coy.Div.Train,	DOULLENS,	WARLUZEL,	BLAVINCOURT.	WARLUZEL	WARLUZEL BAVINCOURT.
" 3 " "	HEM	4th VISEE	SUS ST.LEGER.	SUS ST.LEGER.	SUS.ST.LEGER. APPEGRENEC.
" 4 " "	BEAUVAL	GROUCHES.	COULLEMONT.	COULLEMONT.	COULLEMONT. BARLY.
42nd Fd.Ambice.	GEZAINCOURT.	LUCHEUX	SUS ST.LEGER.	SUS ST.LEGER.	WANQUETIN. WANQUETIN.
43rd Field Ambice.	BEAUVAL.	COULLEMONT.	COULLEMONT.	COULLEMONT.	COULLEMONT. BARLY.
44th Field Ambice	DOULLENS.	SOMBRIN	SOMBRIN	SOMBRIN	SOMBRIN. SOMBRIN.
25th Sanitary Section,	DOULLENS.	SUS ST.LEGER.	SUS ST.LEGER.	SUS ST.LEGER.	SUS ST.LEGER. BARLY.
14th F.A.N.U.	FLESSELLES.	FLESSELLES.	DOULLENS.	DOULLENS.	DOULLENS. DOULLENS.
26th Mob.Vet.Section,	BEAUVAL	BEAUVAL	DOULLENS.	ETREE WANIN	LIGNEREUIL LIGNEREUIL.
14th Div.Supply Column.	CANDAS	SOMBRIN	SOMBRIN	SOMBRIN	SOMBRIN SOMBRIN
14th Div.Amm.Sub.Park,	DOULLENS.	GRAND RULLECOURT.	GRAND RULLECOURT.	GRAND RULLECOURT.	LUCHEUX. LUCHEUX.

E = Esquelbecq   C = Cassel.   Sheet 2.

Date.	Train No.	Type	Serial No	NAME OF UNIT.	Entraining Station.	Train leaves	Marche Due Destination	Remarks.
Feb. 20th	12.	T.C.	1431. 1435	A Battery 46th Bde R.F.A.	C	1.31	R.T.5.	
	13.	T.C.	1441 1445	A Battery 46th Bde R.F.A. ¼ Bde Ammn Column.	E	9.10	R.T.13.	
	14.	T.C.	1432 1435	B Battery 46th Bde R.F.A. ¼ Bde Ammn Column.	C	10.31	R.T.14.	
	15.	T.C.	1442 1445	B Battery 46th Bde R.F.A. ¼ Bde Ammn Column.	E	12.10	R.T.15.	
	16.	T.C.	1433.	C Battery 46th Bde R.F.A. ¼ Bde Ammunition Column.	C	13.31	R.T.17.	
	17.	T.C.	1443 1445	C Battery 46th Bde R.F.A. ¼ Brigade Ammn. Column.	E	15.10	R.T.19.	
	18.	T.C.	1434 1435	D.Battery 46th Bde. R.F.A. ¼ Bde. Ammn. Column.	C	16.41	R.T.20.	
	19.	T.C.	1444 1435	D.Battery 46th Bde. R.F.A. ¼ Bde Ammn. Column.	E	18.10	R.T.22.	
	20.	T.C.	1414	8th Rifle Brigade.	C	19.31	R.T.23.	Less 1 Platoon.
	21.	T.C.	1424	9th Rifle Brigade.	E	21.20	R.T.1.	Less 3 Platoons.
	22.	T.C.	1411	7th K.R.R.C.	C	22.31	R.T.2.	Less 1 Platoon.
Feb. 21st.	23.	T.C.	1421	5th Ox. A. Bucks L.I.	E	0.10	R.T.4.	Less 1 Platoon.
	24.	T.C.	1412	8th K.R.R.C.	C	1.31	R.T.5.	Less 3 Platoons.

E = Esquelbecq.   C = Cassel.   Sheet 3.

Date.	Train No.	Type.	Serial No.	Name of Unit.	Ent'g Station.	Train leaves	Marche.	Bus Destination.	Remarks.
Feb. 21st.	25	T.C.	1422	5th K.S.L.I.	E	9.10	H.T.13.		Less 5 Platoons.
	26	T.C.	1413	7th Rifle Brigade.	C	10.31	H.T.14.		Less 5 Platoons.
	27	T.C.	1423	9th K.R.R.C.	E	12.10	H.T.15.		Less 1 Platoon.
	28	T.C.	1410 1415 1418	H.Q. 41st Infantry Bde. No. 2 Section Signal Coy. Brigade Machine Gun Coy.	C	13.31	H.T.17.		Plus 8 Platoons, as shown above of 41st Inf.Bde.
	29	T.C.	1420 1425	H.Q. 42nd Infantry Bde. No. 3 Sec Divisional Coy. Divisional Mach [?]	E	15.10	H.T.19.		Plus 9 Platoons,as shown above of 42nd Bde.
	30	T.C.	1434	81st Field Coy. R.E.	C	16.41	H.T.20.		
	31	T.C.	1433 1435	H.Q. Div. R.E. 82nd Field Coy. R.E.	E	18.10	H.T.22		
	32	T.C.	1491 1488	44th Field Ambulance No. 2 Co. Div'l Train	C	19.31	H.T.23		
	33	T.C.	1492 1489	45nd Field Ambulance No. 3 Co. Div'l Train	E	21.20	H.T.1		
	34	T.C.	1436	89th Field Co. R.E.	C	22.31	H.T.2		
Feb. 22nd	35	T.C.	1431	8th Somerset L.I.	E	0.10	H.T.4		Less 5 platoons.
	36	T.C.	1493 1490	43rd Field Ambulance No. 4 Co. Div'l Train	C	1.31	H.T.5		
	37	T.C.	1432	8th D.C.L.I.	E	9.10	H.T.13		Less 5 platoons

Sheet 4.

E = Esquelbecq.   C = Cassel

Date.	Train No.	Type.	Serial No.	Name of Unit.	Ent'g Station.	Train leaves.	Due Marche. Destination.	Remarks.
Febr 2nd.	38	T.C.	1403. 1494 1495	Squadron D.L.O.Y. Sanitary Section. Mobile Veterinary Section.	C	10.31	H.T.14.	
	39	T.C.	1433	6th K.O.Y.L.I.	E	12.10	H.T.16.	Less 1 platoon.
	40	T.C.	1434	10th Durham L.I.	C	13.31	H.T.17	Less 3 platoons.
	41	T.C.	1430 1435 1436	H.Q.,43rd Infantry Bde. No.4 Section Signal Coy. Brigade Machine Gun Coy.	E	15.10	H.T.19	Plus 10 platoons as shown above of 43rd Infantry Brigade.
	42	T.P.	1478 1479A	H.Q., Divn Ammun Column. 1/3rd No. 1 Section	C	16.41	H.T.20	
	43	T.P.	1479	2/3rds No. 1 Section	E	18.10	H.T.22	
	44	T.P.	1480	2/3rds No. 2 Section	C	19.31	H.T.23	
	45	T.P.	1481	2/3rds No. 3 Section	E	21.20	H.T.1	
	46	T.P.	1480A 1481A	1/3rd No. 2 Section 1/3rd No. 3 Section	C	22.31	H.T.2	

Appx XXIX

EXPENDITURE OF AMMUNITIONN
FEBRUARY 1916.

Date.	A.	A.X.	B.	B.X.
1st	65	12	-	-
2nd	637	578	-	100
3rd	368	248	-	112
4th	242	24	-	-
5th	112	162	-	16
6th	308	152	-	34
7th	150	296	-	82
8th	171	105	-	34
9th	118	58	-	74
10th	175	152	-	28
11th	287	578	-	10
12th	952	566	-	146
29th	476	93	-	24

appx. XXX

TOTAL DAILY CASUALTIES OF THE 14TH (LIGHT) DIVISION.

FOR MONTH OF ....

24 hours ending	Killed		Wounded		S.Wounded		Gassed		Missing		Total		Gd.Total	
	O.	O.R	O.	O.R	O.	O.R	O.	O.R	O.	O.R	O.	O.R	O.	O.R
1st		1		7								8		8
2nd	1	8	1	20		1					2	29	2	34
3rd		13		12		1					1	25	3	62
4th		1		18								19	3	81
5th		3		9								12	3	93
6th		2	1	15		1					1	18	4	111
7th	1	5	3	8		3					4	16	8	124
8th	1	1	-	23							1	24	9	151
9th		4		15								19	9	170
10th		7	1	6		1					1	14	10	184
11th		4	1	13	-	1					1	18	11	202
12th		13	1	33	2	-					3	45	14	248
13th		12	1	19	-	2	-	1			1	35	15	283
14th														
15th														
16th														
17th														
18th														
19th														
20th														
21st														
22nd														
23rd														
24th														
25th														
26th														
27th														
28th														
29th														
30th														
31st														
Total for month.	3	74	9	198	3	9	-	1			15	282		

14TH (LIGHT) DIVISION.

CASUALTIES AMONGST OFFICERS FOR THE MONTH OF FEBRUARY, 1916.

2-2-16.	2/Lieut. B.M. Arnold, 7th K.R.R.C.	Wounded.
2-2-16.	2/Lieut. A.W. Smith, 5th Ox & Bucks L.I.	Killed.
3-2-16.	2/Lieut. A.F.McC Riggs, 7th K.O.Y.L.I. 20th Divn. attached 5th K.S.L.I.	Slightly wounded (at duty).
6-2-16.	2/Lieut. M.A. Young, 9th R.B.	Wounded.
7-2-16.	Major C.H.N. Seymour, 8th K.R.R.C.	Wounded.
7-2-16.	Capt. A.C. Sheepshanks, 8th R.B.	Wounded.
7-2-16.	2/Lieut. F.G. Davies, 9th R.B.	Killed.
7-2-16.	Capt. H. Dunkerley, R.A.M.C. att. 8th R.B.	Wounded.
8-2-16.	Capt. F.B. Roberts, 9th R.B.	Killed.
10-2-16.	Capt. A.P. Forster, 7th K.R.R.C.	Wounded.
11-2-16.	2/Lieut. W.J. Milton, 5th K.S.L.I.	Wounded.
12-2-16.	2/Lieut. T.B. Jolly, 5th K.S.L.I.	Wounded (slightly at duty).
12-2-16.	2/Lieut. J.S. Tatham, 9th K.R.R.C.	Wounded.
12-2-16.	2/Lieut. E. Barton, 9th K.R.R.C.	Wounded (slightly at duty).
13-2-16.	Lieut. D.J.A. Kerr, 49th Bde R.F.A.	Wounded.

======

appx XXXII

14TH (LIGHT) DIVISION.

REINFORCEMENTS JOINED THE DIVISION DURING THE MONTH OF FEBRUARY, 1916.

Officers, 50.

Other Ranks, 1141.

Appx. XXVIII

APPENDIX.
POSITIONS OF UNITS AT 11.50 p.m.

	24th	25th	26th	27th	28th	29th
Divisional H.Qrs.	DOULLENS.	SUS ST.LEGER.	SUS ST.LEGER.	SUS ST.LEGER.	SUS ST.LEGER.	BARLY.
14th Signal Co.	"	"	"	"	"	"
Div. Cavalry.	GEZAINCOURT.	GRAND RULLECOURT.	GRAND RULLECOURT.	GRAND RULLECOURT.	FOSSEUX.	FOSSEUX.
Div. Cyclists.	"	SUS ST.LEGER.	SUS ST.LEGER.	SUS ST.LEGER.	BARLY.	BARLY.
8th M.M.G.Battery.	MONTPLAISIR,	MONTPLAISIR.	BERLENCOURT.	BERLENCOURT.	BLAVINCOURT.	BLAVINCOURT.
H.Q.,41st Inf.Bde.	GEZAINCOURT.	WARLUZEL	WARLUZEL	WARLUZEL	WARLUZEL	ARRAS.
41st I.B.M.G.Coy.	"	"	"	"	"	"
7th K.R.R.C.	DOULLENS.	SOMBRIN	SOMBRIN	SOMBRIN	SOMBRIN	BERNEVILLE.
8th K.R.R.C.	"	"	"	"	"	ARRAS
7th R.B.		WARLUZEL	WARLUZEL	WARLUZEL	WARLUZEL	ARRAS
8th R.B.		SOMBRIN	SOMBRIN	SOMBRIN	SOMBRIN	DAINVILLE.
H.Q.,42nd Inf.Bde.	GEZAINCOURT,	GRAND RULLECOURT.	GRAND RULLECOURT.	GRAND RULLECOURT.	GRAND RULLE-	SOMBRIN.
42nd Bde M.G.Coy.	"	"	"	"	COURT,	"
5th Ox & Bucks L.I.	GEZAINCOURT	"	"	"	"	SIMENCOURT.
5th K.S.L.I.	OCCOCHES	"	"	"	"	SOMBRIN.
9th K.R.R.C.	and	SUS ST.LEGER.	SUS ST.LEGER.	SUS ST.LEGER.	SUS ST.LEGER.	"
9th R.B.	HEM.	GRAND RULLECOURT.	GRAND RULLECOURT.	GRAND RULLECOURT.	GRAND RULLE- COURT.	"
H.Q. 43rd Inf.Bde.		HUMBERCOURT.	HUMBERCOURT.	HUMBERCOURT.	DAINVILLE.	⎫
43rd Bde M.G.Coy.		"	"	"	BERNEVILLE.	⎬
6th Somerset L.I.		"	"	"	"	⎭ Trenches
6th D.C.L.I.	BEAUVAL.	COULLEMONT.	COULLEMONT.	COULLEMONT.	SIMONCOURT.	⎫
6th K.O.Y.L.I.		HUMBERCOURT.	HUMBERCOURT.	HUMBERCOURT.	DAINVILLE.	⎬
10th Durham L.I.		COULLEMONT.	COULLEMONT.	COULLEMONT.	SIMONCOURT.	⎭
11th L'pool Regt.	ANTHEULE.	WARLUZEL	FOSSEUX	FOSSEUX	FOSSEUX	FOSSEUX.

C O N F I D E N T I A L.

WAR DIARY

of

"A" & "Q" Branches,

HEADQUARTERS, 14TH (LIGHT) DIVISION,

From 1st March, 1916   To   31st March, 1916.

(Volume XIII)

Army Form C. 2118

Volume XIII

WAR DIARY
or
INTELLIGENCE SUMMARY
(Erase heading not required.)

Place	Date	Hour	Summary of Events and Information	Remarks and references to Appendices
BARLY	1Mn		4/0 J.A. Lent 5th Bn Bucks Ll & SIMENCOURT and BERNEVILLE with 1/2 at SIMENCOURT his 1/2 J.S. Bucks Ll (Pros Bucks L) attached (been) hab ARRAS shelling of the line. Town inhabitants appealed to BERNEVILLE & SIMENCOURT in order to take over from French Mayor the Emblomment. Refilling as in previous day. 1/4th of 3rd Div. reinforced Bn Lls in VILLERVAL from in then relief.	✗
	2nd.		In DAINVILLE HdQ to BERNEVILLE. Gve. warned. Commando of westfront at 10 a.m. Remainder of Batteries despatch of U/74 J. R/2 J.A. Came up in relief of French and entered into position afterdark. Refilling as in previous day.	✗ ✗
	3rd.		Division adjusted to battle. Refilling on road FOSSEUX—WANQUETIN	✗
	4th.		Division continues readjusting its battle refilling as for 3rd. Division arrangement to satisfactory and will be continued. 1050 Rumours arrived shortly are that some mines have exploded. Prisonencourume caused by this jointly arrangement.	✗
	5th.		Administrative command are attended to DAINVILLE FOSSEUX—BARLY Area of Division very crowded	✗

Army Form C. 2118

WAR DIARY
or
INTELLIGENCE SUMMARY

(Erase heading not required.)

Instructions regarding War Diaries and Intelligence Summaries are contained in F. S. Regs., Part II. and the Staff Manual respectively. Title Pages will be prepared in manuscript.

Place	Date	Hour	Summary of Events and Information	Remarks and references to Appendices
BERNEVILLE Sh. 51C V.6.d.	6 Mar		Bath's started at BERNEVILLE and JIMENCOURT	
	7th		All lorry traffic to be reduced supply lorries to run by night	
	8th		Nothing to record	
	9th		Roads breaking up rapidly BARLY-SOMBRIN - FOSSEUX Road closed.	
			Decided to refill on the NOYELETTE - WANQUETIN Road and lorries and refilling take place tomorrow on the HABARCQ - WANQUETIN Road. Lorries to go to Rations by day but return to AVESNES by night. Refilling as above - nothing further to record	
	10th		Road from HABARCQ - WANQUETIN reported as giving slightly	
	11th			
	12.		Nothing to record	
	13th		Restrictions on traffic during thaw removed. Billeting reconnaissance of WARLUS with a view to Div H.Q. moving on	
	14th		departure of 8th Div. Billeting Reconnaissance of HAUTEVILLE	

Army Form C. 2118

WAR DIARY
or
INTELLIGENCE SUMMARY
(Erase heading not required.)

Instructions regarding War Diaries and Intelligence Summaries are contained in F. S. Regs., Part II. and the Staff Manual respectively. Title Pages will be prepared in manuscript.

Place	Date	Hour	Summary of Events and Information	Remarks and references to Appendices
BERNEVILLE	May 15		Watering facilities very limited owing to breakage of water pump BERNEVILLE. Great difficulty in obtaining properly filled rations. Shortage of rations again, too much unloading in area. Have slept and most of the horses no transport	
	16		Shortage again at Railhead. Increase in Divisional pack difficult to procure. There is a depot at Railhead holding over 200 thousand Rations would stand the difficulty. Most French inhabitants of this village return and notifies all arrangements were discovered that 3 troops after working last bought and lost night any entrenchments of billets enjoying to the limit no extrication from into a French Army beyond to the limit	※
	17		Divisional H.Q. moves to WARLUS from BERNEVILLE	※
	18		Orders received to leave BARLY by 1pm tomorrow 19th to unit.	※
	19		Move of units from BARLY and readjustment of area consequent on HAUTEVILLE MANQUETIN coming into Divisional area as per appendix	App. No. XXXIII ※
	20.		Nothing to record	※

1875 Wt. W593/826 1,000,000 4/15 J.B.C. & A. A.D.S.S./Forms/C. 2118.

WAR DIARY

Army Form C. 2118

Place	Date	Hour	Summary of Events and Information	Remarks and references to Appendices
WARLUS HUTS	21		Took over the DECAUVILLE light Railway from SAULTY-LARBRET to WANQUETIN. Unit left loading at 8am finished 11am left loading at WANQUETIN not completed till 7pm. Railway very unreliable possibly due to inexperience of railway personnel who are taken over from the French. 1 section and 2nd Battery Anti aircraft Rail gun'ts accommodated by rly in WARLUS. Refilling completed.	A.
	22		Refilling at Commune of DECAUVILLE at WANQUETIN. Refilling completed till 7pm. By 10 am. but dumping lorries supplies not completed train cannot get up the railway again. Much very difficult to load train commanding officers.	A.
	23		Recommenced fatigue of officer 1 N.C.o. & 57 men detailed for loading supplies at SAULTY-SAFORT on the 25th inst. Post Office closed.	A.
	24		Nothing to Record.	A.
	25		March of 2/6th Durh. L.I. attached for instruction 13/- 2 cpls & 25 others 1 W.O/ful. Lieun. Smee of - Ratenes Sands 26th Entraining Batt's Divisions. Post officer reopened.	A.
	27		Nothing to Record.	A.

WAR DIARY
INTELLIGENCE SUMMARY

Army Form C. 2118

Place	Date	Hour	Summary of Events and Information	Remarks and references to Appendices
WARLUS Sheet 57.C	March 28		Nothing to record	
	29		Major ANSTERICKER left to take over duties of G.S.O 3 Third Army. Captain G.E.R. PRIOR 1st Bn DEVONSHIRE Regt. to take on duties G.S.O. 3 i/c Div. Capt. G.E. MITCHELL attached from Canadian M. STONVILLE 110 Reinforcements arrived at SAULTY	
	30.		Visited C.in C. Army Comdr.	
	31.		Visit from Lord KITCHENER. Attached Appendix XXXIV. Army List September for the month Casualties. " XXXV " XXXVI Officers " XXXVII Reinforcements	

Stringer Capt
for A.A. & Q.M.G.

Appx XXXIII

14TH (LIGHT) DIVISION.

The following moves will take place tomorrow, 19th instant :-

UNIT.	FROM.	TO	Billeting representatives:-	To be clear of
D.A.C.	BARLY	HAUTEVILLE.	Meet D.A.A.&Q.M.G. at Church, HAUTEVILLE, 5 p.m. today.	BARLY by 1 p.m.
H.Q.,14th Div.Train.	BARLY,	WARLUS,	Arranged	ditto.
2 Coys Div.Train.	HAUTEVILLE.	WANQUETIN,	To communicate with Administrative Comdt. WANQUETIN as soon as possible.	HAUTEVILLE by noon.
1st Line Transport of 41st Inf.Bde. H.Q. & 3 Battns. 1 Battn.	SIMENCOURT. BERNEVILLE.	WARLUS.	Arranged.	Move to be completed by 5 p.m. 20th inst., to fit in with relief of units in trenches.
14th Div.Cyclist Co.	BARLY.	FOSSEUX.	} To communicate with Administrative Command, as soon as possible.	} BARLY by 1 p.m.
Mobile Vety.Section,	BARLY,	FOSSEUX,		

Administrative Commdts:-
BARLY,
FOSSEUX
WANQUETIN
BERNEVILLE
SIMENCOURT.

Copies to
41st Inf.Bde.
B.T.O., 41st Inf.Bde.
14th Div.Artillery.
14th Div.Train.
14th Cyclist Co.
A.D.V.S., 14th Divn.
"G" Branch

for information. Camp Commdt.14th Divn.
A.P.M.,14th Divn.
        }For information.

18th March, 1916.

Captain,
for A.A.&Q.M.G.
14th (Light) Division.

Appendix XXXIII

AMMUNITION EXPENDED during MARCH 1916.

Date	A	A.X	B	B.X	F	A.P	N. Stokes	Trench Mortar 3.7"	2"
1st	476	93	-	24					
2nd	398	125	-	58					
3rd	94	-	-	15					
4th	350	-	-	-					
5th	90	-	-	78					
6th	221	24	-	32					
7th	104	48	-	71					
8th	185	51	-	38					
9th	129	36	-	30					
10th	241	22	-	30					
11th	119	38	-	-					
12th	301	58	-	-					
13th	194	19	-	15					
14th	232	54	-	8					
15th	165	4	-	3					
16th	175	19	-	22	9	-	15	-	-
17th	207	61	-	-	14	-	19	-	-
18th	266	69	-	36	4	-	-	3	-
19th	227	49	-	229	-	-	4	-	-
20th	323	99	-	67	49	1	-	-	-
21st	145	38	-	10	-	16	-	3	-
22nd	109	48	-	-	16	16	-	-	-
23rd	194	83	-	-	-	-	-	8	-
24th	134	57	-	19	9	16	-	-	4
25th	96	11	-	-	8	-	-	-	-
26th	118	41	13	12	40	6	-	4	5
27th	188	135	11	23	-	-	-	10	-
28th	163	127	4	16	2	3	-	6	3
29th	60	25	-	-	-	-	-	6	6
30th	175	139	-	-	18	-	18	12	7
31st	88	42	1	94	28	-	-	29	7

MARCH 1916.

TOTAL DAILY CASUALTIES OF THE 14TH (LIGHT) DIVISION.
FOR MONTH OF March 1916.

Appx XXXV

24 hours ending	Killed O.	Killed O.R	Wounded O.	Wounded O.R	S.Wounded O.	S.Wounded O.R	Gassed O.	Gassed O.R	Missing O.	Missing O.R	Total O.	Total O.R	Gd.Total O.	Gd.Total O.R
1st				2							–	2	–	2
2nd											–	–	–	2
3rd		1		4							–	5	–	7
4th		5	1	8							1	13	1	20
5th		1	–	23		1					–	25	1	45
6th				4							–	4	1	49
7th				6							–	6	1	55
8th		1		11							–	12	1	67
9th		1		3							–	4	1	71
10th			1	2							1	2	2	73
11th				7							–	7	2	80
12th				14								14	2	94
13th	1	4		5	1						2	9	4	103
14th				1		4					–	5	4	108
15th				4		1					–	5	4	113
16th				2							–	2	4	115
17th		1	1	4							1	5	5	120
18th	1	3		18		1					1	22	6	142
19th		2	2	14		2					2	18	8	160
20th	2	12	2	17							4	29	12	189
21st				11							–	11	12	200
22nd				8							–	8	12	208
23rd		1		6							–	7	12	215
24th			1	3					1	2	2	5	14	220
25th				3							–	3	14	223
26th		2		3		1					–	6	14	229
27th			1	13							1	13	15	242
28th				5		4					–	9	15	251
29th		2	1	5							1	7	16	258
30th		1		2							–	3	16	261
31st		1		4							–	5	16	266
Total for month	4	38	10	212	1	14			1	2			16	266

Appx XXXVI

14TH (LIGHT) DIVISION.

OFFICER CASUALTIES FOR MONTH OF MARCH, 1916.

Date.	Rank, Name, & Unit.	Casualty.
4-3-16.	2/Lieut. H.G. Howard, 47th Bde R.F.A.	Wounded.
10-3-16.	Capt. C.A.F. Fowke, 5th Ox & Bucks L.I.	Wounded.
12-3-16.	Lieut. R.P. Hayes, 43rd Bde M.G. Company,	Killed. (Accidentally).
12-3-16.	Capt. J. Benskin, 89th Field Co. R.E.	Accidentally injured.
17-3-16.	Lieut. H.G. Rowley, 61st Field Co. R.E.	Died.
17-3-16.	2/Lieut. G.H. Bailey, 7th K.R.R.C.	Wounded.
17-3-16.	2/Lieut. F.C. Stoer, 6th D.C.L.I.	Killed.
19-3-16.	2/Lieut. W.S.M. Brady, 9th K.R.R.C.	Wounded.
19-3-16.	2/Lieut. A.E.J. McLean, 9th K.R.R.C.	Wounded.
19-3-16.	Capt. G.B.S. Walrond, 6th Somerset L.I.	Killed.
19-3-16.	Lieut. C.E.R. Heaton Ellis, 6th K.O.Y.L.I.	Killed.
20-3-16.	2/Lieut. D.Y.B. Tanqueray, 9th K.R.R.C.	Wounded.
20-3-16.	2/Lieut. V.C. Clarke, 10th Durham L.I.	Wounded.
24-3-16.	2/Lieut. D.H. Miller, 8th R.B.	Missing.
24-3-16.	Capt. N.A.G. Quicke, 6th D.C.L.I.	Wounded.
27-3-16.	2/Lieut. R.B. Barker-Mill, 9th R.B.	Wounded.
29-3-16.	2/Lieut. A.C. Lawson, 7th R.B.	Wounded.

* * * * * * * * * * * *

Appx XXXVII.

14TH (LIGHT) DIVISION.

REINFORCEMENTS RECEIVED DURING MONTH OF MARCH, 1916.

Officers   63.

Other Ranks, 1136.

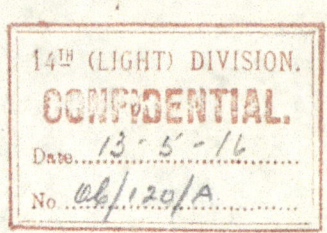

CONFIDENTIAL.

WAR DIARY

of

"A" & "Q" Branches, 14th (Light) Division.

From 1st April, 1916.   To 30th April, 1916.

(Volume XIV).

Army Form C. 2118

WAR DIARY
or
INTELLIGENCE SUMMARY
(Erase heading not required.)

Volume XIV

Instructions regarding War Diaries and Intelligence Summaries are contained in F. S. Regs., Part II. and the Staff Manual respectively. Title Pages will be prepared in manuscript.

Place	Date	Hour	Summary of Events and Information	Remarks and references to Appendices
WARLUS Nr 57C.	April 1st		Refilling as for last week. DECAUVILLE Railway working better.	Off
	2.		Nothing to record.	
	3.		Orders received & transmitted for return of winter Clothing as laid down by the Army Commander.	Off
	4.		Summer Scale of Fuel brought into force.	Off
	5.		Notified that the supply of No 3 Scale rifle grenades now ample.	Off
	6.		Alterations in the Ration from 2nd/4/16 and 10/4/16	GRO page 9. Off
	7.		Purchase of Straw again allowed Summer scale of Fuel cancelled as from 6/4/16.	Off
	8.		Nothing to record.	Off

Army Form C. 2118

WAR DIARY
or
INTELLIGENCE SUMMARY
(Erase heading not required.)

Instructions regarding War Diaries and Intelligence Summaries are contained in F. S. Regs., Part II, and the Staff Manual respectively. Title Pages will be prepared in manuscript.

Place	Date	Hour	Summary of Events and Information	Remarks and references to Appendices
WARLUS Sheet 57C	April 9th		Nothing to record.	
	10th		Sent party [Proceed partly via BOULOGNE] partly via HAVRE 39 and 15 respectively.	Appx.
	11th		D.A.A. and 57th Divn. sent for 3 days attachment.	Appx.
	12th		68th section Anti Aircraft arrived & was accommodated at WARLUS. Joined 39th DAC section. Left 57th after 16th April.	Appx.
	13th		Line cancelling all leave from troops destined a leave. Wire to Motor Trans. 18/15	Appx.
	14th		Nothing to record.	
	15th		D.A. and 57th Divn. left for England on completion of attachment.	Appx.

Army Form C. 2118

WAR DIARY
or
INTELLIGENCE SUMMARY
(Erase heading not required.)

Instructions regarding War Diaries and Intelligence Summaries are contained in F.S. Regs., Part II. and the Staff Manual respectively. Title Pages will be prepared in manuscript.

Place	Date	Hour	Summary of Events and Information	Remarks and references to Appendices
WARLUS Sheet 57C	April 16th		Nothing to record	
	17th		Nothing to record.	AA
	18th		Arrival of Indians recalled from Issus & Kokine to St Pol only so thinned up	AA
	19th		Further arrivals from Issus only 2-3 at St Pol remainder apparently sent on to AUBIGNY. Claims paid in THESSELLES, VILLERS BOCAGE area.	AA
	20th		Appear to serving 56th Divn units dro & newcomer part of the area.	AA
	21st		Nothing to record	
	22nd		Remark to open 26th inst	AA

1875 Wt. W593/826 1,000,000 4/15 J.B.C. & A. A.D.S.S./Forms/C. 2118.

WAR DIARY
or
INTELLIGENCE SUMMARY

Army Form C. 2118

Place	Date	Hour	Summary of Events and Information	Remarks and references to Appendices
WALRUS	April 23		Brigadier General Lord BINNING left for ENGLAND on 4 days surgery. Command to Lt-Col SKINNER, who takes over Command at midnight.	GHt
	24		Nothing to report.	
	25		Nothing to report.	
	26		Nothing to Report	
	27		Nothing to Report	
	28		Nothing to Report	
	29		Nothing to Report.	
	30		Nothing to Report.	GHt

14TH (LIGHT) DIVISION.

Appx XXXIV

AMMUNITION EXPENDITURE DURING MONTH OF APRIL, 1916.

Date.	"A"	"Ax"	"B"	"Bx"	"F"	"Ap"	"Q"	"Qx"	"N"	"STOKES"	"3.7"	"2-in"
1st	79	77	-	43	-	-	-	-	-	-	10	13
2nd	189	157	-	125	14	-	-	-	12	-	30	16
3rd	212	51	1	79	-	-	-	-	-	-	40	13
4th	137	183	19	76	6	-	-	-	-	-	39	21
5th	140	59	4	35	-	-	-	-	-	5	23	-
6th	69	43	40	19	33	-	-	-	-	-	10	6
7th	45	21	-	48	-	-	-	-	-	15	12	18
8th	105	64	-	78	17	13	-	-	-	-	31	22
9th	91	60	42	11	23	-	-	-	-	1	74	14
10th	90	83	21	16	-	-	-	-	-	4	10	14
11th	98	88	11	68	-	-	-	-	-	-	50	12
12th	172	30	25	17	-	-	-	-	-	8	20	18
13th	96	6	6	8	-	-	-	-	-	-	-	-
14th	142	77	-	-	-	-	-	-	-	-	46	7
15th	205	82	17	5	4	-	-	-	-	-	38	24
16th	195	81	2	65	73	-	78	-	-	-	25	23
17th	149	91	8	201	20	-	-	-	-	22	53	31
18th	76	37	-	39	-	-	-	-	-	-	20	-
19th	213	29	-	40	-	-	-	-	-	16	7	21
20th	204	40	15	46	15	-	-	-	-	5	2	2
21st	287	132	2	51	17	-	273	-	-	4	16	9
22nd	67	126	-	19	2	-	-	-	-	-	3	-
23rd	54	191	-	156	20	-	7	-	-	28	25	27
24th	18	55	-	41	16	-	193	-	-	35	32	14
25th	60	209	-	119	4	-	63	-	-	48	40	57
26th	46	95	-	109	13	-	-	112	-	6	17	3
27th	50	70	-	25	19	-	4	105	-	9	61	13
28th	93	176	28	46	6	-	-	169	-	38	74	43
29th	74	124	-	86	10	-	185	97	-	23	21	6
30th	205	65	15	36	3	-	1	10	-	66	1	8

App XXXV

TOTAL DAILY CASUALTIES OF THE 14TH (LIGHT) DIVISION.
FOR MONTH OF April 1916

24 hours ending	Killed O.	Killed O.R	Wounded O.	Wounded O.R	S.Wounded O.	S.Wounded O.R	Gassed O.	Gassed O.R	Missing O.	Missing O.R	Total O.	Total O.R	Gd.Total O.	Gd.Total O.R	
1st		1		8							-	9	-	9	
2nd				7		2					-	9	-	18	
3rd	1	1		6							2	6	2	24	
4th				3							-	3	2	27	
5th		1		3		3					-	7	2	34	
6th			2	9		1					2	10	4	44	
7th		1		2							-	3	4	47	
8th			1	5							1	x5	5	52	x1 accidental
9th		2		x8							-	10	5	62	x1 accidental
10th				2		1					-	3	5	65	
11th		1		1		1					-	3	5	68	
12th	1			5							1	5	6	73	
13th		1		2							-	3	6	76	
14th				4							-	4	6	80	x1 accidental
15th		1				1					-	2	6	82	
16th				3							-	3	6	85	
17th	1	1		5							1	6	7	91	
18th				3							-	3	7	94	
19th		1		3							-	4	7	98	
20th				5		1					-	6	7	104	
21st	1	1		8		4					1	13	8	117	
22nd			x1	x1							1	1	9	118	x accidental
23rd				x3							-	x3	9	121	x1 accidental
24th		3		x7							-	10	9	131	x1 accidental
25th			1	13							1	13	10	144	
26th		1		x3							-	4	10	148	x1 accidental
27th				3							-	3	10	151	
28th		5	1	x14							1	19	11	170	x4 accidental
29th		1		14	x1	x1					1	16	12	186	x accidental
30th		1	1	8		2					1	11	13	197	
31st															
Total for Month	2	22	10	158	1	17	-	-	-	-	13	197	13	197	

Appx XXXVI

SECRET.   14TH (LIGHT) DIVISION.   O.C.61/A.

LOCATION OF UNITS.

		Wagon & Tpt. Lines.
H.Q., 14th (Light) Division.	WARLUS,	
14th Div. Cyclist Coy.	IZEL-LES-HAMEAU.	
H.Q., 14th Div'l Artillery,	WARLUS,	
46th Bde R.F.A. & H.Qrs.		WANQUETIN.
Bde Ammn. Col.	BERNEVILLE	LATTRE ST. QUENTIN
47th Bde R.F.A.		
Bde Ammn. Col.	BERNEVILLE.	WANQUETIN.
48th Bde R.F.A.		
Bde Ammn. Col.	BERNEVILLE.	WANQUETIN.
49th Bde R.F.A. & H.Qrs,		
Bde Ammn. Col.	BERNEVILLE.	
14th D.A.C.	HAUTEVILLE.	
14th D.A.C. Advanced Dump,	BERNEVILLE.	
H.Q. Divisional R.E.	DAINVILLE.	
61st Field Co. R.E.	DAINVILLE.	
62nd Field Co. R.E.	DAINVILLE.	
89th Field Co. R.E.	DAINVILLE.	
14th Signal Co. R.E.	WARLUS.	
8th M.M.G. Battery,	IZEL-LES-HAMEAU,	
H.Q., 41st Inf. Bde,	SAVY.	SAVY.
1 Battalion,	SAVY	SAVY.
1 "	CHELERS,	CHELERS.
1 "	MAROEUIL,	MAROEUIL.
1 "	MONT ST. ELOY,	ACQ.
Bde M.G. Company,	AUBIGNY,	AUBIGNY
H.Q., 42nd Infantry Bde,	Rue des Fours, ARRAS,	BERNEVILLE.
1 Battalion,	ARRAS.	BERNEVILLE.
1 "	BERNEVILLE	BERNEVILLE.
1 "	(In the	BERNEVILLE.
1 "	(Line,	BERNEVILLE.
Bde M.G. Company,		BERNEVILLE.
H.Q., 43rd Infantry Bde.	DAINVILLE(L.35.b.4.6 Sheet 51c.)	WARLUS.
1 Battalion,	AGNY,	WARLUS.
1 "	DAINVILLE,	WARLUS.
1 "	(In the	WARLUS.
1 "	(Line.	WARLUS.
Bde M.G. Company,		DAINVILLE.
11th Bn. King's L'pool Regt (Pioneers)	ARRAS.	
H.Q., 14th Div'l Train,	BERNEVILLE.	
No.1 Company,	HAUTEVILLE.	
No.2 "	SAVY.	
No.3 "	HAUTEVILLE.	
No.4 "	WANQUETIN.	
14th Div'l Supply Column,	AVESNES.	
42nd Field Amblce,	Convent St. Sacrement, Rue d'Amiens, ARRAS and WANQUETIN.	
43rd Field Amblce,	LIGNEREUIL.	
44th Field Amblce, (Div'l Rest Station)	LIENCOURT.	
25th Sanitary Section,	WARLUS.	
26th Mobile Veterinary Section,	FILESCAMP FARM,	
Div'l Ordnance Stores,	WARLUS.	
Refilling Point,	J.18.c. Sheet 51c.	
SCHOOLS:- Div. School,)		
Grenade School,)	HAUTEVILLE.	
Anti-Gas School)		
Machine-gun School,	IZEL-LES-HAMEAU.	

****

Headquarters,
 14th Division,
  9th May, 1916.

Appx XXXVII

14TH (LIGHT) DIVISION.

REINFORCEMENTS RECEIVED FURING MONTH OF APRIL 1916.

Officers,   54.

Other Ranks,   874.

14TH (LIGHT) DIVISION.

Appx XXXVIII

CASUALTIES AMONGST OFFICERS FOR MONTH OF APRIL 1916.

Date.	Rank, Name & Unit.	Remarks.
2-4-16.	2/Lieut. H.G.H. Dorrell, 10th Durham L.I.	Killed.
3-4-16.	2/Lieut. J.F. Egerton, 8th K.R.R.C.	Wounded.
6-4-16.	2/Lieut. S.D. Roddick, 41st Bde M.G. Company.	Wounded.
6-4-16.	2/Lieut. A.D. Rodway, 41st Bde M.G. Company,	Wounded slightly at duty, evacuated next day.
8-4-16.	Lieut. E.T. Dobbie, B/46 Bde R.F.A.	Wounded.
12-4-16.	Lieut-Col. H.M Packard, D.S.O. 46th Brigade, R.F.A.	Killed.
17-4-16.	2/Lieut. C. D. Pyne, 9th K.R.R.C.	Wounded.
21-4-16.	2/Lieut. P.H.G. Pye-Smith, 11th Bn. The King's.	Wounded (accidentally)
21-4-16.	2/Lieut. S.V. Batcher, 6th Somerset L.I.	Wounded.
25-4-16.	2/Lieut. S.C. Hebard, 7th K.R.R.C.	Wounded.
28-4-16.	2/Lieut. H. Daws, 10th Durham L.I.	Wounded.
29-4-16.	2/Lieut. E.E. Canney, 10th Durham L.I.	Wounded (accidentally at duty)
30-4-16.	Lieut. L.C. Heygate, 6th D.C.L.I.	Wounded.

CONFIDENTIAL

WAR DIARY

of

"A" & "Q" Branches, 14th (Light) Division

from 1st May 1916   to   31st May 1916.

(volume XV)

Army Form C. 2118

WAR DIARY
or
INTELLIGENCE SUMMARY
(Erase heading not required.)

Instructions regarding War Diaries and Intelligence Summaries are contained in F.S. Regs., Part II. and the Staff Manual respectively. Title Pages will be prepared in manuscript.

Place	Date	Hour	Summary of Events and Information	Remarks and references to Appendices
WARLUS Huts etc.	1st May		Nothing to report.	Ctt/A
	2.		Orders received for relief of 41st Inf Bde on 4/5/15.	Ctt/A
	3.		Nothing to report.	Ctt/A
	4.		Relief of 41st Inf Bde commenced by the 95th Inf Bde.	Ctt/A
	5.		Relief completed. One Batt. accommodated in HORRES/huts in L'HAQUETIN + one in HABARCQ. Bdy HQ & B'Mg Coy at AGNEZ-LES-DUISANS. T.M. Batteries ARRAS. Including H.Q. Coy HABARCQ. Relief of 161 Fld Coy & DANVILLE Change in Divisional AREA takes place. SIMENCOURT & FOSSEUX handed over to 6th Div. Change in location after HQ at 3/3 London Fld Coy RE and 1/5 & 9 London Regt reserves this Division from DANVILLE	App 14 XXXIII OS/III/A Ctt/A
	6.		More of 1st + 2nd Inf Bde from SIMENCOURT to BERNEVILLE (Rodrig huts) & 3rd Inf Bde to IZEL-LES-HAMEAU	Ctt/A

Army Form C. 2118

WAR DIARY
or
INTELLIGENCE SUMMARY
(Erase heading not required.)

Place	Date	Hour	Summary of Events and Information	Remarks and references to Appendices
WARLUS Sus 57C	7 Aug		Change of Headquarters from SAULTY to TINCQUES – DECAUVILLE Rail laid down by 13th Dn – in short of supply now becomes normal	Appx
	8"		8th/R.B. & 7th KRRC moved into XVII Corps area & harassive & dangerous at NEUVILLE-ST-VAAST respectively relieved trains for 9th	Appx
	9"		7th KRRC moved into XVII Corps area w/ 7th/RB & 7th Cav 7th/R.B. H.Q. returned to hpr 16-70-A – 7th KRR – R/B H.Q. m.S.Cy	Appx
	10"		KRRC – 7th/RB L. CHELERS Sappers Battalion Dn't arrived for attachment from England. Also G.T. Train g't staff officers attached Sandhurst School Bombing Throwing Return furnish Corp of MONTIGNY for amalgamation Divl Cavalry Leave 7th Corps to PDY.	Appx
	11"		Divl Cyclists move to MANIN come under IVth Corps. All Divisions ul Mounted Troops now come under 1st C Corps. Cyclist Companies to be formed into Corps Cyclist Battalion. Capt M.A. TOWLER Commands it.	Appx
	12"		Attached officers from "London" left for England. Further measures for reorganising Div Artillery received.	Appx
	13"		Major J.B. BARING. Rifle Brigade reported for Duty as Adjutant	Appx

Major J.B. BARING

Army Form C. 2118

WAR DIARY
or
INTELLIGENCE SUMMARY

(Erase heading not required.)

Instructions regarding War Diaries and Intelligence Summaries are contained in F. S. Regs., Part II. and the Staff Manual respectively. Title Pages will be prepared in manuscript.

Place	Date	Hour	Summary of Events and Information	Remarks and references to Appendices
WARLUS Sheet 57C.	14th May		Reorganisation of Divl. Artillery indefinite. Brigades and one 18 pdr Brigade and one K battery annexed by 99 Indo pre gun. to take place at once. Returns of 18 pdr ammn to by 99 Indo pre gun.	Appx.
	15.		Reorganization proceeding 61 LD to be Transferred to the 50th Divn.	Appx.
	16.		Nothing to report	
	17.		Reports rendered to Corps showing proposed numbers & surplus horses/saddles and riders & horses.	Appx.
	18.		Nothing to report.	
	19.		Nothing to report	
	20.		Nothing to report.	
	21.		Transfer of L.D. horses to 50th Divn. arranged for. Nos. 2 & 1 S.S.R. batteries.	Appx.
	22.		Nothing to report	
	23.		Transfer of LD horses to the 50th Divn. only 17 taken.	Appx.

WAR DIARY
or
INTELLIGENCE SUMMARY

Army Form C. 2118

Place	Date	Hour	Summary of Events and Information	Remarks and references to Appendices
WAR LYS. Sheet 17C	24		Most of R.A. surplus vehicles personnel horses & transport to reach ABBEVILLE by June 3 further change possible	OJA.
	25		Nothing to report	
	26		Orders for march of R.A. surplus personnel horses vehicles & transport to BOUQUEMAISON today. Orders received in Mafors moon party left at 5.10pm. Halts BOUQUEMAISON night of 26/7. 1st R.M. on night of 27/28. ABBEVILLE 28th. Party consisted of 10 officers 107 OR & Riding 1st R.D. animals 17 wagons G.S. leaving 27 G.S. wagons & 3 under carts dg. by rail. Returns handed in 29th taken.	OJA.
	27		Reorganisation of Dis. Artillery completed.	OA.
	28		Nothing to report	
	29		Nothing to report	

WAR DIARY
or
INTELLIGENCE SUMMARY
(Erase heading not required.)

Army Form C. 2118

Instructions regarding War Diaries and Intelligence Summaries are contained in F. S. Regs., Part II. and the Staff Manual respectively. Title Pages will be prepared in manuscript.

Place	Date	Hour	Summary of Events and Information	Remarks and references to Appendices
WARLUS Sr. G. °	May. 30		Army Commander inspected No.s 1, 2, & 3 Coys of the Divisional Train	app.
"	31st		Lt Col. J. D. BRUCE arrived & took over S.Co. 1 vice Lt Col KCH SACKE. L.t Col R. G. G.S.H Staff Dublin India.	
			Appendix XXIX — Extendedin of Ammunition	
			" XX — Casualties Officers during month	
			" XXXI — O.R. "	
			" XXXII — Reinforcements "	
			" XXXIII — Movement Order OC III/A	

O.C. Hamilton
Lt Col.
A.A.Q.M.E.
14th Division

5/6/16.

Appendix XXIX

14th (Light) Division.

AMMUNITION EXPENDED : JUNE 1916.

Date.	A.	A.X.	B.	B.X.	F.	A.P.	Q.	Q.X.	Stokes.	3"7"	2"
1st	153	108	-	47	9	-	-	17	26	13	28
2nd	190	9	10	72	22	-	-	-	43	82	25
3rd	161	105	4	29	5	-	-	-	6	32	12
4th	330	117	15	83	16	-	-	-	33	42	24
5th	150	85	-	88	1	10	-	51	64	50	35
6th	39	19	2	40	2	-	-	38	69	66	31
7th	507	198	2	98	20	-	-	-	85	2	45
8th	29	28	-	29	42	-	-	-	-	6	-
9th	133	90	-	58	15	-	-	-	37	20	20
10th	45	52	7	49	-	-	-	-	15	1	12
11th	23	27	-	31	-	-	10	2	15	37	10
12th	16	15	13	1	13	10	-	-	94	45	14
13th	50	7	-	231	18	18	-	6	33	24	-
14th	58	96	-	46	12	7	-	-	6	-	4
15th	51	50	-	-	-	-	-	-	9	32	5
16th	63	42	-	27	-	-	44	71	14	14	27
17th	94	90	-	83	10	-	10	41	43	26	25
18th	143	219	-	86	-	-	-	-	74	15	32
19th	57	80	8	23	15	15	58	82	7	9	-
20th	7	62	12	48	-	20	229	14	69	40	-
21st	42	267	-	108	15	-	8	-	63	31	13
22nd	44	72	-	19	-	-	34	-	45	23	17
23rd	35	58	2	26	39	-	1	-	42	10	2
24th	24	93	9	44	5	-	-	-	13	9	-
25th	65	112	-	4	15	-	-	-	-	4	-
26th	30	195	-	74	-	20	-	-	51	44	15
27th	101	112	-	58	15	19	221	-	43	35	17
28th	9	280	-	323	65	36	-	-	81	68	35
29th	19	80	-	46	71	-	92	-	44	69	22
30th	406	574	-	255	29	-	-	-	50	56	29
31st	360	214	-	72	-	-	15	-	5	17	2

Appendix XXX

14TH (LIGHT) DIVISION.

CASUALTIES AMONGST OFFICERS FOR MONTH OF MAY 1916.

Date	Rank, Name & Unit	Remarks
3-5-16	Lieut. K.W. Ramsay 7th K.R.R.C.	Killed
8-5-16	2/Lieut. G.E.S. Sewart 10th Durham L.I.	Killed
10-5-16	2/Lieut. E.P. Jones 9th Rifle Brigade.	Wounded
10-5-16	2/Lieut. R.T. Cherry 9th Rifle Brigade.	Wounded
14-5-16	2/Lieut. B.H. Farmer 5th Ox. & Bucks. L.I.	Wounded (Accidentally)
19-5-16	2/Lieut. A.E. Saxton 6th D.C.L.I.	Wounded (Accidentally)
19-5-16	Lieut. P.K. Haworth 7th K.R.R.C.	**Wounded** (Accidentally)
21-5-16	Lieut. O.P. Churchyard 7th Rifle Brigade	Wounded
27-5-16	2/Lieut. W.J. Bell 6th D.C.L.I.	Wounded

Appendix XXXI

CASUALTIES FOR JUNE.
OTHER RANKS.

	Killed	Wounded
7th K.R.R.C.	5	13
8th K.R.R.C.		9
7th R.B.	5	45
8th R.B.	3	7
41/Bde M.G.Coy.	-	-
5th Ox & Bucks L.I.	1	2
5th K.S.L.I.	2	6
9th K.R.R.C.	3	20
9th R.B.	12	34
42/Bde M.G.Coy.	-	-
6th Somerset L.I.	2	4
6th D.C.L.II.		14
6th K.O.Y.L.I.	6	22
10th Durham L.I.	3	8
43/Bde M.G.Coy.		4
11th Liverpool Regt.		10
R.F.A.	3	6
R.E.		2
Div'l Troops.	1	8
	46	212

14TH (Light) DIVISION.

REINFORCEMENTS
RECEIVED DURING THE MONTH OF MAY 1916.

Officers   59

Other Ranks   1045

Appendix XXXIII

SECRET.

O.C/111/A.

In consequence of a change of Divisional Area, the following moves will take place on the dates specified :-

46th Bde Wagon Lines,	SIMENCOURT to WANQUETIN,	On 5th May.
47th B.A.C.	SIMENCOURT to BERNEVILLE,	" " "
49th B.A.C.	SIMENCOURT to BERNEVILLE,	" " "
Transport Lines, 42nd Inf.Brigade,	SIMENCOURT to BERNEVILLE,	" " "
Infantry Battn., 42nd Inf.Brigade, Transport Lines,	SIMENCOURT to BERNEVILLE,	On 6th May.
43rd Inf.Brigade, Infantry Battn.	BERNEVILLE to WARLUS,	On 5th May.
43rd Inf.Brigade, Transport Lines,	BERNEVILLE to DAINVILLE,	On 6th May
41st Inf.Brigade, Transport of M.G.Coy,	WARLUS to HA' BAROQ,	On 5th May.
41st Inf.Brigade,	BERNEVILLE to HA' BAROQ,	" " "
47th Bde R.F.A.Wagon Lines,	FOSSEUX to LATTRE ST.QUENTIN,	" " "
Div'l Cavalry,	FOSSEUX to FILESCAMP FARM,	" " "
Div'l Cyclists,	FOSSEUX to IZEL LES HAMEAU,	" " "
8th M.M.G.Battery,	FOSSEUX to IZEL LES HAMEAU,	On 6th May.
44th Field Ambulance, (Div.Rest Station)	FOSSEUX to LIENCOURT.	Date not fixed.

The Town Commandants have been warned and Billeting Parties must report to them in good time.

The present billets must be vacated in each case by 12 noon.

Application for extra Transport must be sent to Divisional Headquarters by noon on the 4th instant. Extra Transport must be kept as low as possible.

C.C.Hamilton
LIEUT-COLONEL,
A.A.&.Q.M.G.
14TH (LIGHT) DIVISION.

2nd May, 1916.

C O N F I D E N T I A L.

WAR DIARY OF

"A" & "Q" BRANCHES 14TH (LIGHT) DIVISION.

from 1st June, 1916 to 30th June, 1916.

(Volume XVI.).

Army Form C. 2118

WAR DIARY
or
INTELLIGENCE SUMMARY
(Erase heading not required.)

Instructions regarding War Diaries and Intelligence Summaries are contained in F. S. Regs., Part II. and the Staff Manual respectively. Title Pages will be prepared in manuscript.

Place	Date	Hour	Summary of Events and Information	Remarks and references to Appendices
WARLUS Sheet 51.C	June 1st		Corps Commander inspected the 14th D.A.C. Ammtn Echelons to be at Joyeuse C.ing up to Enghs, Benj inspected on C.io, 1st half of 2nd half for Boune. Nothing to report	
"	2nd			
	3		Corps Commander inspected 43rd army D.S.A., Beaufort and 61st 63rd 7th Field Corps R.E.	
	4		Battery inspect Capt C.H. MANGER Staff Rept joined DSA & Dr & triangles attachment to B brawn of staff.	
	5.		Nothing to report	
	6.		Corps Commander inspected corps lines of 46K 47 t 48 t 49 t D.A. Notes.	
	7.		ditto to report	
	8.		Practice of Divisional staffs in and control Posts. Railway & A.P.M. routes all posts before dismissal.	
	9.		Nothing to report.	
	10.		Nothing to report.	
	11.		Nothing to report	

WAR DIARY
or
INTELLIGENCE SUMMARY.

Army Form C. 2118.

(Erase heading not required.)

Place	Date	Hour	Summary of Events and Information	Remarks and references to Appendices
WARLUS - SHURST?	June 12.		Lt Col C.G. RAWLING. C.M.G. CIE promoted Temp. B. Gen. & Comd. 62nd Inf. Bde. to join forthwith	
	13.		B. Gen C.G. RAWLING Cmg. CIE. left Command 62 Bde & 1st Div. Major T-J RITCHIE took over Command of 1/6 SOMERSET. L.I. in consequence. Nothing to report. Divnl Inf returned - broke up 10, no Inf Bdes. 3rd " " 4.5 2nd " " 2/7TH	
	14		Nothing to report.	
	15.		Nothing to report.	
	16		New Divisional Mtrs allotted 6 Divn. (4.500 Black B4).	
	17.		Nothing to Report.	
	18.		Nothing to Report. Aeroplane & Sound & movements observed in B.K.	GHA
	19	6am mid	H1 & Sqdn A/c came back under orders of No 14 tr Div. 42 Sqdn HQ entrained its front to left on relieved take over from it Tenders. Div attached to Div. occupied Winds ie BERNEVILLE	GHA

1577 Wt. W10791/1773 500,000 1/15 D. D. & L. A.D.S.S./Forms/C. 2118.

WAR DIARY
or
INTELLIGENCE SUMMARY.

(Erase heading not required.)

Army Form C. 2118.

Place	Date	Hour	Summary of Events and Information	Remarks and references to Appendices
	June 20th		42? Infy Bde. had one Co. [illegible] 33rd L.Bn. and took over [illegible] Intelligence Sk Bn in left of 142 Infy Bde. Both 33rd Bn. & H.B. 104th Infy Bde. occupied billets	Appx.
DAINVILLE	21		H.W. [illegible] took over new positions from Sk Bn in left of 42 Infy Bde. Sk Bn as in when relieving 142 Bn - Two battalions Sk Bn occupied billets ← DAINVILLE battery of report.	Appx.
	22?		42nd Infy Bde relieved twice. The [illegible]	Appx.
	23?		on [illegible] night. Rain fallen & to continue.	Appx.
	24th		No 2 Thursday lorry as Rest & Thursday lorry a fairly straight Divn. No 2 Coy Divn Train lorries appears to 41st Infy Bde Am. wildn'd releasing lorries to take Rgs from Transport lines	Appx.
			HQ ARRAS — A day to [illegible] operation — [illegible] Ammunition amount for Rgs U - Z	Appx. XXXV
	25th		Additional Left Flags taken in perfect attempt.	App.
	26th		doing to report.	App.

Army Form C. 2118.

WAR DIARY
or
INTELLIGENCE SUMMARY.
(Erase heading not required.)

Instructions regarding War Diaries and Intelligence Summaries are contained in F. S. Regs., Part II. and the Staff Manual respectively. Title pages will be prepared in manuscript.

Place	Date	Hour	Summary of Events and Information	Remarks and references to Appendices
	27th		8th Army Group of batteries heavy & SUCRERIE lower. Proportion of premature reduced to 75%.	OdA
	28th		Activity & report	Cdt.
	29th		Activity & report. Special extract of ammunition Report.	Cdt
	30th		Activity & report. At.Cdt. XXIV Expenditure of Ammn. V Special allotment for days U – Z. XXVI Casualties officers O.R. XXVII " XXVIII Reinforcement.	dA

O.H. Hammersley Lt.
de jung 14 F Bri
4/7/16

1577 Wt. W10791/1773 500,000 1/15 D. D. & L. A.D.S.S./Forms/C. 2118.

14TH (LIGHT) DIVISION.

AMMUNITION EXPENDED DURING JUNE, 1916.

Date.	"A"	"AX"	"B"	"BX"	"F"	"AP"	"Q"	"QX"	Stokes.	"3.7"	"2""	Toby.
June												
1.	71	41	-	62	35	-	281	31	33	20	6	-
2.	5	31	-	12	23	-	119	-	1	35	-	4
3.	22	215	-	138	1	-	26	-	42	37	9	4
4.	66	270	-	172	5	-	109	-	10	6	7	-
5.	46	109	-	43	12	-	-	-	-	8	9	-
6.	29	130	-	28	14	-	-	-	-	25	12	-
7.	69	109	-	39	12	-	-	-	3	9	-	2
8.	62	161	-	21	18	-	511	-	15	18	27	-
9.	45	108	-	26	24	-	-	-	-	18	3	1
10.	81	264	2	114	13	-	84	-	50	58	43	-
11.	54	185	-	209	65	-	34	-	27	34	13	2
12.	38	137	-	39	11	-	-	-	47	63	55	-
13.	81	93	-	6	-	-	-	-	-	2	-	4
14.	37	33	-	31	-	-	1	-	-	23	7	-
15.	131	55	-	73	-	-	-	-	8	17	15	4
16.	56	75	-	38	-	-	-	-	-	28	-	-
17.	107	71	-	41	-	-	42	-	-	36	36	6
18.	28	46	-	21	-	-	546	2	13	5	-	8
19.	46	104	2	29	302	25	362	25	51	19	21	9
20.	58	109	-	59	-	-	30	52	12	20	25	8
21.	62	113	-	26	-	-	-	-	3	208	-	6
22.	65	128	-	5	-	-	-	-	-	-	-	-
23.	125	63	-	100	-	-	65	36	3	-	3	-
24.	194	99	-	41	-	-	-	-	12	-	5	-
25.	382	88	-	53	-	-	109	50	143	-	27	- noon,
	231	204	-	108	-	-	-	-	-	-	-	- 8 p.m.
26th.	860	148	-	178	-	-	281	96	196	-	27	4 noon,
	656	263	-	61	-	-	-	-	117	-	32	- 8 p.m.
27.	707	230	-	72	-	-	11	-	12	-	2	- noon,
	1943	454	25	109	-	-	-	-	320	-	119	- 8 p.m.
28.	827	110	-	79	-	-	-	-	-	-	290	- noon,
	2117	929	-	122	-	-	-	-	439	-	193	- 8 p.m.
29.	496	229	-	172	-	-	-	-	8	-	-	- noon,
	226	88	-	14	-	-	-	-	84	-	100	- 8 p.m.
30.	752	94	-	-	-	-	-	-	380	-	5	- noon,
	73	41	-	--	-	-	-	-	20	-	-	- 8 p.m.

App'dx XXXV

APPENDIX.

SPECIAL ALLOTMENT FOR DAYS Y - Z.

18-pounder	9000
4.5" Howitzer,	500
2" Trench Mortar,	2000
Stokes Trench Mortar,	9000

14TH (LIGHT) DIVISION.

CASUALTIES AMONGST OFFICERS FOR MONTH OF JUNE, 1916.

1-6-16.	2/Lieut. C.R. Selwyn, 6th Somerset L.I.	Wounded.
1-6-16.	Capt. L. Woodroffe, 8th R.B.	Wounded. (since died).
4-6-16.	2/Lieut. H.G. Thomas, 11th L'pool R	Wounded.
26-6-16.	2/Lieut. H.R. Hartley, 8th R.B.	Wounded.
27-6-16.	2/Lieut. W.J.R. Moseley, 7th R.B.	Killed.
27-6-16.	2/Lieut. G.D. Ferard, 9th K.R.R.C.	Wounded.
28-6-16.	Lieut. J.C.B. Firth, 5th K.S.L.I.	Wounded.
30-6-16.	Lieut. P.E. Hobhouse, 6th Somerset L.I.	Wounded.

14TH (LIGHT) DIVISION.

CASUALTIES DURING MONTH OF JUNE, 1916.

Other Ranks.

	Killed.	Wounded.	Missing.
7th K.R.R.C.	2	22	
8th K.R.R.C.	5	18	
7th R.B.	1	7	
8th R.B.	2	15	
41st Bde M.G.Coy.	-	-	
5th Ox & Bucks L.I.	1	7	
5th K.S.L.I.	4	15	
9th K.R.R.C.	15	35	3
9th R.B.	6	37	1
42nd Bde M.G.Coy,	-	-	
6th Somerset L.I.	3	4	
6th D.C.L.I.	4	12	
6th K.O.Y.L.I.	5	15	
10th Durham L.I.	1	11	
43rd Bde M.G.Coy,	-	-	
11th King's L'pool Regt.	3	10	
R.F.A.	1	2	
R.E.		4	
Div'l Troops,	2	4	
	55	218	4

14TH (LIGHT) DIVISION.

REINFORCEMENTS DURING JUNE, 1916.

```
Officers,           31.
Other Ranks,       900.
                   ----
                   931.
                   ====
```

CONFIDENTIAL.

ORIGINAL WAR DIARY OF

"A" & "Q" BRANCHES, 14TH (LIGHT) DIVISION.

from July 1st, 1916 to July 31st, 1916.

(Volume XVII).

WAR DIARY
or
INTELLIGENCE SUMMARY

Army Form C. 2118.

Place	Date	Hour	Summary of Events and Information	Remarks and references to Appendices
WARLUS	July 1st		42nd Infantry Brigade Transport moved to DUISANS - Liverpool transport moved to WARLUS	CRA
	2nd		Battn's to work	CRA
	3rd		Battn's to work	CRA
	4th		Battn's inspected by ACKERMAN. Return 41 standard & 8 officers 35 & 8 for instruction	CRA
	5th		Heavy Artillery Offr. fourth Reg. Inspection and army instructions to fwd by Corps Troops Supply Col.	CRA
	6th		Battn's to report return 41 & 7 had returned return 41 & 7 had to return and lorries PICK ARRAS – No 1 Coy 43rd 7 hadn moved to AMMACQ and equip. 42nd 8 said moved to LIGNEREUIL	CRA
	7		No 2 Coy 43 Tn. moved to AGNEZ LES DUISANS – CRE moved to Briquetterie ST QUENTIN – HARLUS road – Tunnelly Coy attached 55 Div. took up billets at AGNEZ. Lt Col Cyril Bs. attended to 41 & Infantry Bde. to ARRAS and DUISANS. 4 – 9th Trench Mortar revised to learn from TM School.	CRA

WAR DIARY
or
INTELLIGENCE SUMMARY.
(Erase heading not required.)

Army Form C. 2118.

Place	Date	Hour	Summary of Events and Information	Remarks and references to Appendices
	8th		95th Rfa Hals forth march for Coy + T.M Battery also one battalion no Company RE and one company Div Train also of S.K.Di reached BERNAVILLE. Two battalion SK Div took up billets in UANQUETIN. One T.M battalion SK Di. relieved one battalion 33K Di. in UANQUETIN.	OAA
	9th		H.Q. Cos 32nd Rfa (11 K Bi) Hqr up billets at DUISANS. 1 Battalion 17th Coy 17th Battalion 11 K Di took up billets in AGNEZ — 1 battalion 11 K Di relieved 1 battalion SS K Bi in DAINVILLE. 1 Battalion 11 K Di took up billets in ARRAS — 1 battalion SK Bi took up billets in DAINVILLE. 1 Coy SK Di Tn. SK Di moved to UANQUETIN from ABBEVILLE — Bath at AGNEZ LES DUISANS opened E/14 K Bi & 1/1 km rear	OAA
	10th		Nothing to report.	OAA

Army Form C. 2118.

WAR DIARY
or
INTELLIGENCE SUMMARY.
(Erase heading not required.)

Place	Date	Hour	Summary of Events and Information	Remarks and references to Appendices
	11th		1/2 Batterie SK Div moved into BERNEVILLE in billets & kept ready to move	OBA
	12th		Nothing to report.	ODN
	13th		SK Div moved out of 14 K Div area. Nearing to LOYEZ etc. Same Duties & Programme Secret for Same attack on 14th.	OBA
	14th		Artillery fr Support 1st ndr for 1th at 10.45 pm 4.5" How used.	OBA
	15th		32 Bty 74th Fld Art Bg by C & 5th Fr RE moved BERNEVILLE - Field Cultur fr AGNEZ and BLANQUETIN, also batteries fr AGNEZ. 33 Bty 74th Fld moved at DOISANS into the trenches on hill by C & 1 hill below the hy at AGNEZ, on batteries BLANQUETIN - 11 Ath discipants behind new Supportments - C. batteries 11 k Div.	OBA

Army Form C. 2118.

WAR DIARY
or
INTELLIGENCE SUMMARY.
(Erase heading not required.)

Place	Date	Hour	Summary of Events and Information	Remarks and references to Appendices
	16th		32 S.H/Y/M & the road to DAINVILLE and keep y the R.H. left BEAUVILLE - 32 w.ty/M.B. road from DUISANS to BEAUVILLE - w 2 by for BEAUVILLE joins it. 11 B.T.B. remained DUISANS.	GHN
	17th		Moving to upor	R.H
	18th		Moving to upor	R.H
	19th		Administrator of Reservists handed over to 11 K Div. - In Div. line Ark Hels & 2 upt for un Filhers, bivours - AGNEZ.	R.H

Army Form C. 2118.

WAR DIARY
or
INTELLIGENCE SUMMARY.
(Erase heading not required.)

Instructions regarding War Diaries and Intelligence Summaries are contained in F. S. Regs., Part II. and the Staff Manual respectively. Title pages will be prepared in manuscript.

Place	Date	Hour	Summary of Events and Information	Remarks and references to Appendices
	20th		north of Ypres	[illeg.]
	21st		north of Ypres	[illeg.]
	22nd		north of Ypres	[illeg.]
	23		north of Ypres	[illeg.]
	24th		north of Ypres	[illeg.]

Army Form C. 2118.

WAR DIARY
or
INTELLIGENCE SUMMARY.
(Erase heading not required.)

Place	Date	Hour	Summary of Events and Information	Remarks and references to Appendices
	25th		Operation Orders received for the Brigade for Turco Line. It turns the Brigade over to 11th Bde night 26/27 and JK Division successively a following night. Division to march to area round BAILY (similar N.H. of DOULLENS) —	
	26th		Have standing orders for tour to Division issued. Hospitalar received that Div has not will move into the Division he had been associated for on its arrival, Division, Div has expressed to perform charge of D.H.E. January company should object to keep up certain supply. No circular manufacture from there. to Division to LONGUEVILLE —	
	27th		Reply of A Arm Bde 11th Div. Willing to get a 6 batteries Div Arties moved [?] home ready to relieve 2 batt.	

WAR DIARY
or
INTELLIGENCE SUMMARY.

(Erase heading not required.)

Army Form C. 2118.

Place	Date	Hour	Summary of Events and Information	Remarks and references to Appendices
WARLUS	28/5		Relief of J sector by 21st Div - to be 21st Div moved to ARRAS - [illegible] orders to [illegible] hour of Division - See Appendix XXXVIII Orders no = Appendix XXXVIII	
	29/5		Relief of K sector by 21st Div. hour of Division to be Appendix XXXVIII A Orders no = Appendix XXXVIII A. January showers [illegible]	
WARLUS	30/5	10 p	Completed relief of J and K sectors handed over to 21st Div. 14th Div. Remains in [illegible] position 21st Div. Division then has moved their of area.	
SUS ST LEGER	10		[illegible] of Div. [illegible] hand of Division no = Appendix XXXVIII A. address = Appendix XXXVIII B.	

Army Form C. 2118.

WAR DIARY
or
INTELLIGENCE SUMMARY.
(Erase heading not required.)

Place	Date	Hour	Summary of Events and Information	Remarks and references to Appendices
SOS METER	31	9.30	D.S.H.R. closed & moved to FROHEN LE GRAND	
FROHEN LE GRAND		9.20	to H.Q. opens.	
			March of units as in Appendix XXVIII. Orders as in Appendix XXVIII C	
			Appendices XXVIII march + orders for 28th	
			A " 29th march for 30th	
			B " orders for 30th	
			C " " 31st.	
			XXXIX. Amm. + spare drivers for the records to date of transfer to A.	
			XL Officers Casualties	
			L O.R. "	
			LI Reinforcements	
			LII Daily locations of Units during Retirement.	

SECRET.   O.O./206.

Reference to 1/100,000, Sheet 11.

The Division will move into the area BARLY – OCCOCHES (North Bank) – OUTREBOIS (North Bank) – MEZEROLLES – FROHEN LE GRAND – VILLERS L'HOPITAL – BONNIERES.

March Table up to 30th inst is attached.

2.   G.O.C., Infantry Brigades will command Groups as shewn in the March Table.

3.   Roads north of the GRAND RULLECOURT – BEAUDRICOURT – IVERGNY – BOUQUEMAISON are not to be used.

Roads through LUCHEUX or DOULLENS are not to be used.

4.   Baggage Sections of the Train will march with Units, Supply Sections with their Companies.

5.   As other troops are marching across the route of the Division the following time table for the use of roads will be strictly kept.

29th: Start from IVERGNY,   11 a.m.
       Clear IVERGNY,   1 p.m.
       Clear ST.POL – DOULLENS Road,   2.30 p.m.

30th: Start from IVERGNY,   10.30 a.m.
       Clear IVERGNY,   12 noon.
       Clear ST.POL – DOULLENS road,   1.30 p.m.

6.   Advanced Div'l Headquarters will close at WARLUS at 10 a.m. 30th Instant and Div'l Headquarters will open at SUS-ST.LEGER at the same hour.

                                            C.L. Hamilton
                                            Lt Col
                                            A.A.&.Q.M.G.
28th July, 1916.   14th (Light) Division.
Copies to:-
  41st Inf.Bde.   O.C. Train,
  42nd Inf.Bde.   Supply Column.
  43rd Inf.Bde.   A.D.M.S.
  L'pool R   A.D.V.S.
  R.A.   D.A.D.O.S.
  R.E.   A.P.M.
  Signal Co.   Camp Commandant.
  8th M.M.G.Bty.   VI Corps.

XXXVIII A.

S E C R E T.   O.C./206.

Unit.	29th Billets	30th Billets	Group.
Div'l Headquarters,	WARLUS.	SUS ST. LEGER.	
Section D.A.C.	HAUTEVILLE,	IVERGNY.	43rd Bde.
8th M.M.G. Battery,	HAUTEVILLE,	FROHEN LE GRAND,	42nd Bde.
Liverpool Regt.	(MEZEROLLES		
Mobile Vety Section,	(FROHEN LE GRAND,	Probably halt.	42nd Bde.
H.Q., 41st Infantry Bde.	SUS ST. LEGER,	FROHEN LE GRAND,	43rd Bde.
One Battn.	AGNEZ,	G. RULLECOURT,	)
One Battn.	SUCRERIE,	G. RULLECOURT	)
One Battn.	AGNEZ,	G. RULLECOURT	)
One Battn.	DUISANS,	SUS ST. LEGER.	) 41st Bde.
89th Field Co.R.E.	WANQUETIN,	BEAUDRICOURT,	)
No.2 Coy, Train,	BRIQUETERIE,	SOMBRIN,	)
44th Field Ambulance,	AGNEZ	SUS. ST. LEGER,	)
H.Qrs, 42nd Infantry Bde.	LIENCOURT,	IVERGNY,	)
	(OCCOCHES,)		
One Battn.	(MEZEROLLES,)		)
One Battn.	OCCOCHES,		)
One Battn.	MEZEROLLES,		)
One Battn.	BARLY,	} Probably	) 42nd Bde.
62nd Field Co.R.E.	BARLY,	} halt.	)
No.3 Coy.Train,	BARLY,		)
42nd Field Ambulance,	BARLY,		)
H.Qrs, 43rd Infantry Bde.	BARLY		)
One Battn.	WARLUZEL,	REMAISNIL,	)
One Battn.	SUS ST. LEGER	BONNIERES,	)
One Battn.	SOMBRIN,	BONNIERES,	)
One Battn.	WARLUZEL,	VILLERS L'HOPITAL	)
61st Field Co. R.E.	WARLUZEL,	VILLERS L'HOPITAL	) 43rd Bde.
No.4 Coy. Train,	SUS ST. LEGER,	BONNIERES,	)
43rd Field Ambulance,	SOMBRIN,	BONNIERES,	)
Supply Column,	SOMBRIN,	VILLERS L'HOPITAL	)
	AVESNES	VILLERS L'HOPITAL	)

Headquarters,
  14th Division,
    28th July, 1916.

XXXVIII.B

SECRET.

O.C.207.

1.   42nd Infantry Brigade Group will halt on 30th in the billets occupied on 29th.

   43rd and 41st Infantry Brigade Groups will march as ordered.

2.   On 31st, 42nd and 43rd Infantry Brigade Groups will adjust their areas to admit of the 41st Infantry Brigade Group being billeted in the same space with the addition of certain villages allotted today by Third Army.

   41st Infantry Brigade Group will march into the space cleared and extra villages.

   Details of moves for 31st will be issued as soon as practicable.

                                        [signature]
                                        A.A.&.Q.M.G.
29th July, 1916.   14th (Light) Division.

XXXVIII.C

SECRET.   O.O. 208.

Reference to 1/100.000 Sheet 11.

1. The Division will move on 31st inst. as in the accompanying table.

2. Two lorries per battalion will be provided for 41st and 42nd Infantry Brigades for packs.

One lorry each will be provided for 41st Inf.Bde T.M. Battery and 42nd Inf.Bde T.M.Battery.

One lorry will be provided for Divl. Headquarters for packs.

3. Refilling points will be :-

41st Inf.Bde between OCCACHES and RISQUETOUT 9.0.a.m.
42nd Inf.Bde between MEZEROLLES and FROHEN LE GRAND 8.0.a.m.
43rd Inf.Bde between MEZEROLLES and FROHEN LE GRAND 8.0.a.m.

4. Divl. Headquarters will close at SUS ST LEGER at 9.0.a.m. and reopen at FROHEN LE GRAND at 10.0.a.m.

signature

LIEUT.Col.
A.A.&.Q.M.G.
14th (Light) Division.

30th July 1916.

Copies to :-
41st Inf.Bde.   O.C.Train.
42nd Inf.Bde.   Supply Column.
43rd Inf.Bde.   A.D.M.S.
E'pool R.   A.D.V.S.
R.A.   D.A.D.O.S.
R.E.   A.P.M.
Signal Coy.   Camp Commandant.
8th M.M.G.Bty   VI Corps.

XXXVIII C.

O.C.208.

Unit.	From.	To	Special Instructions
Div'l Headquarters,	SUS ST.LEGER,	FROHEN LE GRAND,	Dismounted party to start at 7 a.m. under Capt.Waithman Long; Transport and Mounted men to start at 8.30 am and to clear IVERGNY cross-roads by 9.15 am in rear of Section D.A.C.
Section D.A.C.	IVERGNY.	BOISBERGUES,	March independantly starting from IVERGNY at 9 a.m. not to halt until clear of ST.POL-DOULLENS Road.
8th M.M.G.Bty.	Halt at FROHEN LE GRAND.		comes under 43rd Inf. Bde Group from 12 noon.
11th L'pool R	Halt at (OUTREBOIS (FROHEN LE GRAND.		do. do.
Mobile Vet.Sectn.	Halt at FROHEN LE GRAND.		
Supply Column,	VILLERS L'HOPITAL,	BERNEUIL,	moves independantly comes under 42nd Inf. Bde on arrival in new billets.
41st Inf.Bde H.Q.	GRAND RULLECOURT,	OCCOCHES,	) March under orders
One Battn.	-do-	BARLY,	) of Brig.Genl.Comdg.
One Battn.	-do-	BARLY,	) Inf.Bde. Will pass
One Battn.	SUS-ST-LEGER,	MEZEROLLES	) IVERGNY cross roads
One Battn.	BEAUDRICOURT,	OCCOCHES (both banks of river)	) between 10 and 11.30) am and will cross
89th Field Co.	SOMBRIN	BARLY.	) main ST.POL - DOU-) LLENS road between
H.Q.No.2 Co.Train	SUS ST.LEGER	"	) 2 and 3.30.p.m.) Supply Section of) No. 2 Coy. Div. Train
44th Fd.Ambce.	IVERGNY	"	) will march independ-) antly
42nd Inf.Bde H.Q.	OCCOCHES MEZEROLLES	FIEMVILLERS.	) March under orders of
One Battn.	OCCOCHES,	"	) Br-Genl Comdg.42nd Inf.) Bde.
One Battn.	BARLY	CANDAS	) Will not pass the
One Battn.	BARLY	CANDAS	) river L'AUTHIE before
One Battn.	MEZEROLLES	BERNEUIL,	) 7 a.m.
62nd Fd.Coy.	BARLY	ST.HILAIRE,	)
No.3 Co.Train,	BARLY,	BERNEUIL,	) Will clear present
42nd Fd.Amb,	BARLY,	ST.HILAIRE,	) billets before 4 p.m.

43rd Inf.Bde Group: Halt at present billets.

AMMUNITION EXPENDED DURING JULY, 1916.
14TH (LIGHT) DIVISION.

XXXIX

Date.	A	AX	B	BX	BPF	15-pdr.	Q	QX	NA	NXA	F	Stokes.	2"	3.7"	L:	1½" H:	Toby.
1st Noon.	819.	531	-	190	-	-	266	114	-	-	-	463	191	-	-	-	1
8 pm	130	465	-	27	-	-	-	-	-	-	-	250	31	-	-	-	-
2nd Noon.	419	596	-	132	-	-	188	48	-	-	-	363	7	-	-	-	2
8 pm.	95	11	-	-	-	-	-	-	-	-	-	135	-	-	-	-	-
3rd	11	109	-	6	-	-	-	-	-	-	-	185	6	-	-	-	-
4th	130	221	-	183	-	-	364	533	-	-	-	321	-	-	-	-	-
5th	157	105	-	25	-	-	38	46	-	-	-	140	9	-	-	-	3
6th	225	373	-	28	-	-	93	51	-	-	-	222	39	-	-	-	9
7th	136	161	-	100	-	-	-	-	-	-	-	48	-	-	-	-	-
8th	141	242	-	33	-	-	-	-	-	-	-	133	41	-	-	-	4
9th	95	252	-	110	-	-	20	18	-	-	-	245	46	-	-	-	4
10th	153	112	65	27	-	-	8	8	-	-	-	40	-	-	-	-	-
11th	184	320	-	85	-	-	-	20	-	-	-	-	31	-	-	-	-
12th	300	259	-	201	-	-	-	-	-	-	-	559	110	-	-	-	-
13th	188	156	-	143	48	-	-	-	-	-	-	363	76	-	-	-	-
14th	2778	709	54	591	-	-	-	-	-	-	-	921	126	-	-	-	-
15th	862	81	-	18	-	-	57	2	-	-	-	153	-	-	-	-	-
16th	190	201	-	73	-	-	-	-	-	-	50	227	102	-	-	-	-
17th	548	233	-	254	-	-	-	-	-	-	13	166	53	-	-	-	-
18th	187	226	-	27	-	21	-	-	-	-	-	59	23	-	-	-	-
19th	132	74	-	60	-	-	27	24	-	-	-	199	57	-	-	-	-
20th	246	353	-	225	-	-	-	-	-	-	53	180	101	11	-	-	-
21st	169	104	39	123	-	-	185	44	-	34	-	349	23	36	-	-	-
22nd	167	225	-	49	-	-	1	7	-	-	33	111	38	39	-	-	-
23rd	227	345	-	142	-	-	2	2	-	-	-	105	74	52	-	-	-
24th	1260	337	-	262	-	-	-	-	-	-	-	213	113	38	18	-	-
25th	95	440	-	183	-	-	-	-	-	-	90	581	93	22	-	-	-
26th	89	281	-	282	-	-	-	-	-	-	-	24	36	18	-	-	-
27th	71	51	-	25	13	-	-	-	-	-	-	46	18	-	16	-	-
28th	98	201	-	46	-	-	104	-	-	-	-	130	46	-	-	-	-
29th	91	175	-	87	-	-	-	65	1	38	20	183	34	-	-	-	-

14TH (LIGHT) DIVISION.

CASUALTIES AMONGST OFFICERS FOR MONTH OF JULY, 1916.

July:

1st	2/Lt. R.L. Hardy,	8th K.R.R.C.	Wounded.
1st	2/Lieut. C.E. Scott,	8th K.R.R.C.	Wounded. (At duty).
1st	2/Lieut. M.T. Sampson,	8th K.R.R.C.	Wounded.
1st	2/Lieut. A. Rhode,	6th K.O.Y.L.I.	Wounded.
2nd	2/Lieut. R.E.D. Sassoon,	7th K.R.R.C.	Wounded.
2nd	2/Lieut. R.M. Rogers,	8th K.R.R.C.	Missing.
4th	2/Lieut. C.V. Sandeman,	184 Tunnelling Coy, R.E.	Killed.
11th	Captain S.E. Birrell,	6th Somerset L.I.	Wounded and Missing.
14th	2/Lieut. H.C.G. Newton,	184th Tunnelling Co. R.E.	Wounded (Gassed)
14th	2/Lieut. F.H. Walrond,	5th Ox & Bucks L.I.	Wounded.
15th	2/Lieut. J.C.V. Polgreen,	9th R.B.	Wounded. (accidentally)
16th	2/Lieut. H.D.W. Puller,	68th Field Co. R.E.	Killed.
19th	2/Lieut. T.W. Kirkpatrick,	7th R.B.	Wounded.
21st	2/Lieut. C.A.M. Van Millingen,	7th R.B.	Wounded.
24th	Captain H.M. Gosling,	7th K.R.R.C.	Wounded.
24th	Captain E. Fairlie,	7th K.R.R.C.	Wounded.
24th	Lieut. J.M. Martin,	7th K.R.R.C.	Wounded.
23rd	Lieut. F. Roberts,	6th K.O.Y.L.I.	Killed.
23rd	2/Lieut. H.W. Hayward,	6th K.O.Y.L.I.	Missing (believed Killed)
27th	2/Lieut. H. Furze,	6th K.O.Y.L.I.	Wounded (accidentally)
27th	2/Lieut. N.F.H. Mather,	8th R.B.	Wounded.

14TH (LIGHT) DIVISION.

OTHER RANKS.

CASUALTIES DURING MONTH OF JULY, 1916.

	Killed.	Wounded.	Missing.
7th K.R.R.C.	2	15	-
8th K.R.R.C.	10	45	8
7th R.B.	3	12	-
8th R.B.	6	29	-
5th Ox & Bucks L.I.	5	23	5
5th K.S.L.I.	3	22	-
9th K.R.R.C.	4	30	-
9th R.B.	3	11	-
42nd M.G.Company,	-	3	-
6th Somerset L.I.	-	11	-
6th D.C.L.I.	2	12	-
6th K.O.Y.L.I.	12	48	8
10th Durham L.I.	4	18	-
11th L'pool R	-	11	-
R. F. A.	2	2	-
R. E.	1	8	-
	57	300 ?	16.

14TH (LIGHT) DIVISION.

REINFORCEMENTS DURING MONTH OF JULY, 1916.

Officers   67

Other Ranks,   168.

               235.
               =====

TABLE SHOWING ACTUAL LOCATION OF TROOPS DURING MOVEMENT TO PRELIMINARY CONCENTRATION AREA.

Group:	Unit.	26/27	27/28	28/29	29/30	30/31
	42nd Inf.Bde H.Q.	ARRAS	AGNEZ-LES-DUISANS	GRAND RULLECOURT	OCCOCHES-MEZEROLLES	OCCOCHES-MEZEROLLES
	5th Ox & Bucks L.I.	AGNEZ-LEZ-DUISANS	SUS-ST-LEGER,	SUS-ST-LEGER,	OCCOCHES	OCCOCHES
	9th K.R.R.C.	Brigade Reserve	WANQUETIN.	BEAUDRICOURT,	MEZEROLLES,	MEZEROLLES.
	9th R.B.	Trenches,	LOUEZ,	GRAND RULLECOURT,	BARLY,	BARLY.
A.	5th K.S.L.I.	Trenches,	AGNEZ-LEZ-DUISANS	GRAND RULLECOURT,	BARLY,	BARLY.
	62nd Fd.Coy.R.E.	ARRAS.	Briqueterie,K.28.d.	IVERGNY,	BARLY,	BARLY.
	11th L'pool R	WANQUETIN.	IVERGNY.	IVERGNY,	OUTREBOIS-FROHEN-LE-GRAND	OUTREBOIS-FROHEN-LE-GRAND.
	No.3 Coy.Train,	HAUTEVILLE,	HAUTEVILLE,	GRAND RULLECOURT,	BARLY,	BARLY.
	42nd F.Amb,	LIGNEREUIL,	LIGNEREUIL,	GRAND RULLECOURT,	BARLY,	BARLY.
	43rd Inf.Bde H.Q.	ARRAS	ARRAS	AGNEZ-LEZ-DUISANS	WARLUZEL,	REMAISNIL.
	6th Som.L.I.	AGNEZ-LEZ-DUISANS	AGNEZ-LEZ-DUISANS	WARLUZEL,	WARLUZEL,	VILLERS L'HOPITAL.
	10th D.L.I.	Brigade Reserve	Brigade Reserve	WANQUETIN N	SUS-ST-LEGER.	VILLERS L'HOPITAL.
B.	6th D.C.L.I.	Trenches,	Trenches,	LOUEZ.	SOMBRIN.	BONNIERES.
	6th K.O.Y.L.I.	Trenches,	Trenches,	AGNEZ-LEZ-DUISANS	WARLUZEL,	VILLERS L'HOPITAL.
	61st Fd.Coy.R.E.	ARRAS	ARRAS	Briqueterie,K.28.d.	SUS-ST-LEGER.	BONNIERES.
	43rd F.Amb,	HABARCQ,	HABARCQ,	HABARCQ,	SOMBRIN,	VILLERS L'HOPITAL.
	No.4 Coy.Train,	WANQUETIN.	WANQUETIN.	WANQUETIN,	SOMBRIN,	BONNIERES.
	Mob.Vet.Section	FILESCAMP Fm.	FILESCAMP Fm.	FILESCAMP Fm.	SUS-ST-LEGER.	FROHEN-LE-GRAND.
	41st Inf.Bde H.Q.	ARRAS,	ARRAS,	ARRAS,	AGNEZ-LEZ-DUISANS	GRAND RULLECOURT.
	7th H.B.	DUISANS,	DUISANS,	DUISANS,	WANQUETIN,	BEAUDRICOURT.
	7th K.R.R.C.	Brigade Reserve	Brigade Reserve	Brigade Reserve,	DUISANS,	SUS-ST-LEGER.
C.	8th K.R.R.C.	Trenches,	Trenches,	LOUEZ.	LOUEZ.	GRAND RULLECOURT.
	8th R.B.	Trenches,	Trenches,	Trenches,	AGNEZ-LEZ-DUISANS,	GRAND RULLECOURT.
	89th Fd.Coy.R.E.	ARRAS,	ARRAS,	Briqueterie,K.28.d.	Briqueterie,K.28.d.	SOMBRIN.
	No.2 Coy.Train,	AGNEZ-LEZ-DUISANS	AGNEZ-LEZ-DUISANS	AGNEZ-LEZ-DUISANS,	AGNEZ-LEZ-DUISANS,	SUS ST.LEGER.
	44th F.Amb,	LIENCOURT,	LIENCOURT,	LIENCOURT,	LIENCOURT,	IVERGNY.
	8th M.M.G.Bty,	HAUTEVILLE,	HAUTEVILLE,	HAUTEVILLE,	HAUTEVILLE,	FROHEN-LE-GRAND.
	Div'l Headquarters	WARLUS,	WARLUS,	WARLUS,	WARLUS,	SUS ST.LEGER.
	D.A.C.Detachment,	BERNEVILLE.	BERNEVILLE,	BERNEVILLE,	BERNEVILLE.	IVERGNY.
	14th Supply Column	AVESNES,	AVESNES,	AVESNES,		SUS ST.LEGER.
	43rd M.G.Coy.		To WARLUS.			To WARLUZEL.
	42nd M.G.Coy,		Direct to Gd.RULLECOURT			
	42nd T.M.Bty,		Direct to Gd.RULLECOURT			
	43rd T.M.Bty,			To WARLUZEL,		

CONFIDENTIAL.

WAR DIARY

of

"A" and "Q"   Branches, 14th (Light) Division.

From 1st August, 1916 To 31st August, 1916.

Volume   XVIII

****

Army Form C. 2118.

WAR DIARY
or
INTELLIGENCE SUMMARY.
(Erase heading not required.)

Instructions regarding War Diaries and Intelligence Summaries are contained in F. S. Regs., Part II. and the Staff Manual respectively. Title pages will be prepared in manuscript.

Place	Date	Hour	Summary of Events and Information	Remarks and references to Appendices
FROHEN LE GRAND	August 1st	9.30 a.m	A.H.Q. Closed & moved to BEANVILLE — Order Issued as Appendix — (see A.H.Q Journal).	
BEANVILLE		9.30		
	2.		Arrangements made to open laundry on 3rd at ST OUEN. Not arranged with the ARREVILLE Laundry for staff training 3rd. Took 1000 box blankets &	
	3		Nothing to report.	

Army Form C. 2118.

WAR DIARY
or
INTELLIGENCE SUMMARY.
(Erase heading not required.)

Instructions regarding War Diaries and Intelligence Summaries are contained in F. S. Regs., Part II. and the Staff Manual respectively. Title pages will be prepared in manuscript.

Place	Date	Hour	Summary of Events and Information	Remarks and references to Appendices
	4		Nothing to report	
	5		Gen Antonny reported and occupied billets along R. L'AUTHIE.	
	6		D/K RE transport marched to new about RAINEVILLE. RAINEVILLE, 4/C CARDONNETTE, 43 CORSY, DSML party marched to le JENAS RE RAINNEVILLE. Divis Transport [?] marched to Villa CANDAS. [illegible] D/K RE to the Divisional trops entrained at tactical train for MERICOURT. H.Q. Hd. & dis apart led horse & cavalry transports to CANDAS station. Sir Arty marched to RAINEVILLE are HQ marched to camp near l BUIRE.	
	7		typists etc arrived MERICOURT & took up billets in camp 10 ft therein	

1577 Wt. W10791/1773 500,000 1/15 D. D. & L. A.D.S.S./Forms/C. 2118.

WAR DIARY
INTELLIGENCE SUMMARY

Army Form C. 2118.

Place	Date	Hour	Summary of Events and Information	Remarks and references to Appendices
	8		41st Brigade Group DERNANCOURT 43rd Brigade Group N. of DERNANCOURT. 42nd Brigade Group in BULLS camp N. of DERNANCOURT. Transport moved up to billets Richard Ave of Du Trois to Sqdn at BRIKEMONT. Railhead ALBERT. XV Corps lent 15 lorries & supply lot & route of heavy lorries at DERNANCOURT & for troops & RF SA as to transport of TM batteries. Div. hdrs moved to camp N.H. of DERNANCOURT - RAHA joined Div. Hdrs.	
	9		Instructions began to arrive 51st Divl. Artillery relieve the one of our 15th Div.	

Army Form C. 2118.

WAR DIARY
or
INTELLIGENCE SUMMARY.
(Erase heading not required.)

Instructions regarding War Diaries and Intelligence Summaries are contained in F.S. Regs., Part II. and the Staff Manual respectively. Title pages will be prepared in manuscript.

Place	Date	Hour	Summary of Events and Information	Remarks and references to Appendices
	10		17th Bde Artk completed relief of 51st Bde Artk.	
	11	9 am	41st and 43rd Hows. Btys Bde began movements to take over frontage of 17th Bde. CRA 17th Bde ordered Btys covered by one section of Div Coy 35th Bde Hows to remain front to cover.	
	12	9 am	42nd Hows Bde moved to Bricourt. Sent to FRICOURT on Div Reserve. Rts. and dispatches took over new camps of newly-formed units 17 Bde. Communications between batteries and HQ 17 Bde.	

1577 Wt.W10791/1773 500,000 1/15 D.D. & L. A.D.S.S./Forms/C. 2118.

Army Form C. 2118.

WAR DIARY
or
INTELLIGENCE SUMMARY.
(Erase heading not required.)

Place	Date	Hour	Summary of Events and Information	Remarks and references to Appendices
BUIRE	13	10 c	Stiff hard chord low bones ground low temps now for 17 KOS - still frost - wind by 35KPH at 17 kts. Ran are shower at 14 kts.	
BELLEVUE Fm		10 c	Section left to store 2 BUIRE. Capt DELANEY 1 SERGT. wt 2 New trucks at 2 in 2 trucks to transport corps. Capt. Stewart NCC(T) first to lorry 7 note many out of service. 1/3 week longer when should be down to reserve - had to use cold Res Bdn to kill a 45° Pardennen	M.R.H.
	14		Nothing to report.	

1577 Wt. W10791/1773 500,000 1/15 D. D. & L. A.D.S.S./Forms/C. 2118.

Army Form C. 2118.

WAR DIARY
or
INTELLIGENCE SUMMARY.

(Erase heading not required.)

Instructions regarding War Diaries and Intelligence Summaries are contained in F. S. Regs., Part II. and the Staff Manual respectively. Title pages will be prepared in manuscript.

Place	Date	Hour	Summary of Events and Information	Remarks and references to Appendices
	15		Nothing to report.	
	16		Nothing to report.	
	17		Nothing to report.	
	18		Attack by 41st & 43rd Divisions on enemy's trenches captured 158 Officers & 1455 other Ranks. Casualties 2 Officers 198 O.R's.	

Army Form C. 2118.

WAR DIARY
or
INTELLIGENCE SUMMARY.
(Erase heading not required.)

Instructions regarding War Diaries and Intelligence Summaries are contained in F. S. Regs., Part II. and the Staff Manual respectively. Title pages will be prepared in manuscript.

Place	Date	Hour	Summary of Events and Information	Remarks and references to Appendices
	1/9		Supplying the 41st & 63rd Syph. Abbs by rail between ALBERT & FRICOURT Dumps. Three of this Transport. Am't the Transport moved to FRICOURT, kept 1/2 Syph. unit & 63° Syph. Abbs by M.T. on 2/9 to relieved by 1st & 10th & 32° Div.	A.M.
	20		Supplying of M.D.S. of 41st and 63rd Syph. Abbs. troops of FRICOURT. Stats moved to Dump except removal of for which is asking to BELLEVUE FARM.	
	26th		Whole unit now employed by 41st Syph. 63 guards by headquarters and horse lines.	

WAR DIARY
or
INTELLIGENCE SUMMARY.

Army Form C. 2118.

Place	Date	Hour	Summary of Events and Information	Remarks and references to Appendices
	22		Batt. at VIVIER Mill hut by 15 R.E.I. 50 ML other supplied by M.K.S.I.	
	23		Batt. at VIVIER Mill march by 45 Infantry.	
	24		March by W. & A.C. 2nd Field hosp DEVILLE MOD. Casualties evacuated Sh offrs & 1050 m. Prisoners with 8/10 Batt. 4 offrs 179 men.	

Army Form C. 2118.

WAR DIARY
or
INTELLIGENCE SUMMARY.
(Erase heading not required.)

Instructions regarding War Diaries and Intelligence Summaries are contained in F. S. Regs., Part II. and the Staff Manual respectively. Title pages will be prepared in manuscript.

Place	Date	Hour	Summary of Events and Information	Remarks and references to Appendices
	25th		Refy. rept 25k/26k M & 45° 2pm Mr. & 45° 2pm Mr. dismd. send up from the outft. the hope Runell NSW inter type trenches from bkkoqu in dft. contents.	
	26th		Nothing to report	
	27th		Nothing to report	
	28th		Census of tents in XI Corps area.	

1577 Wt. W10791/1773 500,000 1/15 D. D. & L.   A.D.S.S./Forms/C. 2118.

Army Form C. 2118.

WAR DIARY
or
INTELLIGENCE SUMMARY.
(Erase heading not required.)

Instructions regarding War Diaries and Intelligence Summaries are contained in F. S. Regs., Part II. and the Staff Manual respectively. Title pages will be prepared in manuscript.

Place	Date	Hour	Summary of Events and Information	Remarks and references to Appendices
	29th		Nothing to report	
	30th		Relief of 42nd & 43rd Inf Bdes in line by 24th Divn. 44th Inf Bde entrained at EDGE HILL and detrained at AIRAINES.	
	31st		Divl Hqrs close at Bellevue Farm & reopen at BELLOY-ST-LEONARD. Division less Artillery and 44th Inf Bde entrained at EDGE HILL and ALBERT and detrained at AIRAINES. 42nd Bde in AUESNE area. 43rd Bde killed in HEUCOURT area and MERICOURT area.	

1577 Wt.W10791/1773 500,000 1/15 D. D. & L. A.D.S.S./Forms/C. 2118.

LIST OF APPENDICES WAR DIARY 1-8-16 to 31-8-16.

XLIII   Administrative orders for march of Division 1-8-16.

XLIV.   Reinforcements.

XLV.   Modification of Div'l Supply System.

XLVI.   Administrative arrangements for move 31-8-16.

XLVII.   Location of Units 3-8-16.

XLVIII. Location of Units 13-8-16

XLIX.   Location of Units 19-8-16.

L.   Location of Units 26-8-16.

LI.   Reinforcements joined during the month.

LII.   Casualties during the month.

-*-*-*-*-*-*-

Appendix XLIII

SECRET.   O.O.211.

Reference to Sheet 11, 1/100,000:

1. The Division will move on 1st August as in the accompanying table.

2. Two lorries per battalion will be provided for 43rd Infantry Bde for packs.

One lorry each will be provided for 41st Inf.Bde T.M. Battery and 43rd Inf.Bde T.M. Battery.

Two lorries will be provided for Div'l Headquarters for packs.

3. Refilling Points will be :-

41st Inf.Bde between OCCOCHES and HEM, north of River L'AUTHIE at 9 a.m.

42nd Inf.Bde 1 mile South of BERNAVILLE on the road thence to CANAPLES at 9 a.m.

43rd Inf.Bde between FROHEN LE GRAND and MEZEROLLES at 9 a.m.

4. Div'l Headquarters will close at FROHEN LE GRAND at 9.30 a.m. and open at BERNAVILLE at the same hour.

C.C.Hamilton
LIEUT-COLONEL,
A.A.&.Q.M.G.
14TH (LIGHT) DIVISION.

31-7-16.

Copies to:-
41st Inf.Bde.	O.C.Train,
42nd Inf.Bde.	Supply Column,
43rd Inf.Bde.	A.D.M.S.
11th L'pool R.	A.D.V.S.
D.A.C.	MD.A.D.O.S.
R.E.	A.P.M.
Signal Co.	Camp Commandant,
8th M.M.G.Bty.	VI Corps.

SECRET.   O.C.211.

Unit.	From.	To.	Special Instructions.
Div'l H.Qrs,	FROHEN-LE-PETIT,	BERNAVILLE.	To start from FROHEN-LE-PETIT at 9.30 am and to be across river by 10 a.m.
Section D.A.C.	Halts at BOISBERGUES.		
9th M.M.G.Bty.	FROHEN LE GRANDE,	BERNAVILLE.	Route via BEAUVOIR RIVIERE and MAIZICOURT, move independently and come under orders of 43rd Inf.Bde on arrival at their billets.
41st Inf.Bde.HQ.	OCCOCHES,	GEZAINCOURT	⎫ Group will march under
" " M.G.Co.	OCCOCHES,	GEZAINCOURT	⎬ orders of Br-Genl
" " T.M.Bty	OCCOCHES,	GEZAINCOURT	⎪ Comdg.41st Inf.Bde.
One Battn.	OCCOCHES, 9RB	LONGUEVILLETTE	⎪ To clear MEZEROLLES
One Battn.	MEZEROLLES, 2/KRR	AUTHEUX,	⎪ by 7.30 am and to be
One Battn.	BARLY, 9KRR.	GEZAINCOURT.	⎬ S.of River L'AUTHIE
One Battn.	BARLY, 8 RB.	GEZAINCOURT	⎪ by 9.30 am. The
69th Co.R.E.	BARLY,	GEZAINCOURT	⎪ OCCOCHES-DOULLENS
No.2 Co.Train,	BARLY,	GEZAINCOURT	⎪ road North of River
44th F.Amb,	BARLY,	GEZAINCOURT	⎭ L'AUTHIE is not to be used.
42nd Inf.Bde	Halt at present billets.		
Supply Column,	do.	do. BERNEVIL	
43rd Inf.Bde H.Q.	REMAISNIL,	LE MEILLARD	⎫ Group will include
M.G.Co.	REMAISNIL,	LE MEILLARD	⎪ 11th L'pool R and Mobile Vet.Section;
" " T.M.Bty.	REMAISNIL,	LE MEILLARD	⎪ will march under
One Battn.	VILLERS L'HOPITAL,	LE MEILLARD	⎪ orders of Br-Genl,
One Battn.	BONNIERES,	HEUZECOURT	⎬ Comdg.43rd Inf.Bde
One Battn.	BONNIERES,	PROUVILLE	⎪ and must not enter
One Battn.	VILLERS L'HOPITAL,	PROUVILLE,	⎪ MEZEROLLES before
11th L'pool R	(OUTREBOIS (FROHEN-LE-GRAND	BEAUMETZ,	⎪ 7.30 a.m. and must
81st Co.RE,	BONNIERES,	GRIMONT,	⎬ be South of River
No.4 Co.Train,	BONNIERES,	Mt.RENAULT Fm.	⎪ by 9.30 a.m.
43rd F.Amb,	VILLERS L'HOPITAL,	LE MEILLARD	⎪
Mob.Vet.Sectn,	FROHEN LE GRAND,	BERNAVILLE	⎭

42 Bde remain
HQ at FIENVILLIERS
9 KRR.   "
9 RB
Shropshire ⎫ CANDAS
Oxford W. BERNEVIL
62 Cy RE. ST. HILAIRE
3 Cy Train BERNEVIL
42 Ambulance ST HILAIRE

Copy.   QH 2

41st Infantry Bde.
   Billets for your Group on August 1st will be

      H.Q.   )
      Bde.M.G.Coy.   ) GEZAINCOURT
      T.M.Bty.   )

      One Battn.   LONGUEVILLETTE

      ONE Bttn.   AUTHEUX

      Two
      ~~One~~ Battns.   GEZAINCOURT.

      89th Field Coy.R.E.)
      No.2 Coy.Div.Train) GEZAINCOURT
      ~~44~~th Field Amb.   )

Orders for the move will be issued later.

                                    (sd)C.L.C.HAMILTON
9 a.m. 31/7/1916   Lt.Colonel

                                                 QH 3

43rd Inf.Bde.

   Billets for your group on August 1st will be as follows :

      H.Q.   )
      M.G.Coy.   ) LE MEILLARD.
      T.M.Battery   )

      One Battn.   LE MELLIARD

      One Battn.   HEUZECOURT

      Two Battns.   PROUVILLE

      11th Liverpools (attached) BEAUMETZ

      61st Coy.R.E.   GRIMONT

      No.4 Coy.Div.Train   Mt RENAULT FM.

      43rd Field Amb.   LE MEILLARD.

Orders for the move will follow

                                    (sd) C.L.C.HAMILTON
9 a.m. 31/7/1916   Lt.Colonel

      M.M.G. Bty.   )
      M.V.Section) to BERNAVILLE.

Appendix XLIV.

A.724.

14TH (LIGHT) DIVISION.

REINFORCEMENTS.

A Divisional Reinforcement Depot of limited accommodation has been formed at BUIRE to which all Officers and Other Ranks arriving at Railhead as reinforcements for the Division or to rejoin their units from Hospital etc etc., will be directed.

Captain Delany, 10th D.L.I. has been appointed Officer in charge and it is intended that every officer and man joining or rejoining on and after this date shall pass through his hands and their names recorded. He will arrange for all trains to be met at Railhead.

Reinforcements will be forwarded to the Transport Camps of their respective units on the day of arrival or the day following according to circumstances, rationed for the day they are handed over at Transport Camps. Rations for the following day must be obtained from 14th Div'l Train. A Guide (with bicycle if possible) will at once be detailed from each Infantry Brigade Transport Camp and 11th L'pool Regt to report to O.C. Reinforcements Depot, 42 MAIN STREET, BUIRE to conduct parties and act as Messenger between the Depot and Transport Camps.

As much notice as possible will be given by Div'l H.Qrs direct to B.T.Os and repeated to Brigades as to date reinforcements are expected. Captain Delany will also communicate direct with B.T.Os as to probable time of arrival and other matters of detail.

It is important that all rolls should be carefully checked.

Captain,
D.A.A.&.Q.M.G.
14th (Light) Division.

13/8/16.

X X X X

The following Extract from XVth Corps Standing Orders is published for information and necessary action :-

A Corps Refreshment hut has been established at MERICOURT Station. Any drafts, etc., arriving by train, can get a meal on obtaining authority from the Senior Chaplain, R.T.O, or R.S.O.

Reinforcements and detachments joining from the Base often state that iron rations have not been issued to them. This invariably turns out to be false and disciplinary action should, therefore, be taken when men join their Units without such Rations.

Reinforcements joining should be instructed in the application of the First Field Dressing and the use of the Iodine Ampoule with which each man should be provided. An inspection should be carried out to ascertain numbers not inoculated against enteric - these should be inoculated as soon as possible.

Appendix XLV

14th Divn.No. Q.829/2.

1. The Divisional Supply system will be modified from Saturday, 19th instant.

2. On that day Infantry Brigade Transport lines will be moved to the vicinity of FRICOURT. Representatives of Infantry Brigades will meet the D.A.A.&.Q.M.G. or an officer representing him at the road junction F.1.d.9.1. at 9 a.m. 19th instant, when the ground allotted will be pointed out.

3. On 19th instant the supplies for all units 41st and 43rd Infantry Brigades will be sent by rail to FRICOURT where they will be dumped in charge of Supply Officers at the old railway station.

They will be drawn by units at 2 p.m.

Such portions of these supplies as are required to be sent to the trenches on the 20th will be loaded directly into the vehicles which are to take them forward, and these vehicles will then stand loaded in the new transport camps.

The remainder of the Supplies for these Brigades will be carted in other regimental vehicles to the new transport camps and dumped there.

The same procedure will be carried out by these two Brigades daily. Supplies for other Units will be taken by lorry to the present refilling point for the present but the system of railing supplies to FRICOURT will be gradually extended to include the whole Division.

4. Transport lines will be moved to the new location during the course of the 19th. Each Infantry Brigade will call upon the Train Company to which it is affiliated for the necessary transport. Ammunition vehicles will not be used.

5. On 20th instant D.A.D.O.S. will move his store to BELLEVUE FARM. The necessary transport will be supplied to him by O.C., Div'l Train on application.

6. Mails will be drawn at the present refilling point until further orders.

C.L. Hamilton
LIEUT-COLONEL,
A.A.&.Q.M.G.
14th (Light) Division.

17th August, 1916.

Copies to :-
41st Infantry Bde.
42nd Infantry Bde.
43rd Infantry Bde.
11th L'pool R
C.R.A.,14th Divn.
C.R.E.,14th Divn.
O.C.,14th Div.Train.
A.D.M.S.,14th Divn.

A.D.V.S.,14th Divn.
14th Signal Co.R.E.
8th M.M.M.Battery.
Camp Commandant,
Salvage Coy.
A.P.M.,14th Divn.
"G"
D.A.D.O.S.
W.O. i/c Postal Services.

DADMS

O.C.55.

ADMINISTRATIVE ARRANGEMENTS,
for Move August 31st.1916.

1. Train Time Table is attached.

2. The following lorries are provided:-

<u>DIV'L H.QRS.</u> 2 Lorries to report at BELLEVUE FARM at 9 a.m. 31st.

<u>42ND INF.BDE.</u> 2 Lorries for T.M.Batteries and extra kit, to report at DERNANCOURT Church 9 a.m. 31st.

<u>43RD INF.BDE.</u> 2 Lorries for T.M.Batteries and extra kit to report at DERNANCOURT Church at 9 a.m. 31st.

<u>42ND INF.BDE.</u> 4 Lorries for carrying packs to railway to report at CARCAILLOT FARM at 10 a.m.

Staff Officers of Div'l Headquarters and Infantry Brigades will meet their lorries at the rendezvous named.

3. Billeting parties, 42nd and 43rd Infantry Brigades will go by 7.45 a.m. train from ALBERT and report to Lieutenant AKERMAN at AIRAINES.

A.A.&.Q.M.G.
14th (Light) Division.

30th August, 1916.

2 Spare Lorries at D for DADOS

O.C.58.

RAILWAY TIME TABLE 31-8-16.

PLACE.	TIME OF DEPARTURE.	UNITS.
ALBERT.	7.45 a.m.	Two Battns.42nd Infantry Brigade.
"	9.05 a.m	One Battn. 43rd Infantry Brigade. 3 Field Coys, R.E. Div'l Headquarters.
EDGEHILL.	10.40 a.m.	42nd Bde H.Qrs & Signals. 42nd T.M. Battery. One Battn. 43rd Infantry Bde. 43rd M.G. Company. 3 Field Ambulances,
	12.10 p.m.	Two Battns. 42nd Infantry Brigade. 42nd M.G. Company.
MERICOURT.	11.30 a.m.	11th Liverpools, One Battn. 43rd Infantry Brigade.
	12 noon	One Battn.43rd Infantry Brigade. 43rd Bde H.Qrs & Signals. 43rd T.M.Battery.

Troops must arrive 40 minutes before departure of trains.

It is important that all trains should leave punctually.

Lewis Gun hand-carts will be taken but no other vehicles.

Other vehicles (including bicycles) must be sent by road.

Please acknowledge.

                                                          A.&.Q.M.G.

30th August, 1916.   14th (Light) Division.

Copies to
    42nd Infantry Bde.
    43rd Infantry Bde.
    11th L'pool R (Pioneers)
    C.R.E.
    A.D.M.S.
    14th Div.Train.
    Camp Commandant,
    "G"
    A.P.M.
    Signals,
    A.D.V.S.
    D.A.D.O.S.

Appendix XLVII

SECRET.   **14TH (LIGHT) DIVISION.**   O.C.214./A.

LOCATION OF UNITS.

Unit	Location
H.Qrs, 14th (Light) Division,	BERNAVILLE.
14th Div'l Artillery,)	Not yet with Division.
No.1 Coy, 14th Div.Train)	
14th D.A.C. One Section,	BOISBERGUES.
H.Qrs, Div'l R.E.	BERNAVILLE.
61st Field Co. R.E.	GRIMONT.
62nd Field Co. R.E.	ST.HILAIRE.
89th Field Co. R.E.	GEZAINCOURT.
14th Signal Co.R.E.	BERNAVILLE.
8th M.M.G.Bty,	BERNAVILLE.
H.Qrs, 41st Infantry Bde,	GEZAINCOURT.
7th K.R.R.C.	GEZAINCOURT.
7th R.B.	GEZAINCOURT.
8th K.R.R.C.	AUTHEUX.
8th R.B.	LONGUEVILLETTE.
41st M.G.Company,	GEZAINCOURT.
41st T.M. Battery,	GEZAINCOURT.
H.Qrs, 42nd Infantry Bde,	FIENVILLERS.
5th Ox & Bucks L.I.	BERNEUIL.
5th K.S.L.I.	CANDAS.
9th K.R.R.C.	FIENVILLERS.
9th R.B.	CANDAS.
42nd M.G.Company,	FIENVILLERS.
42nd T.M. Battery,	FIENVILLERS.
H.Qrs, 43rd Infantry Bde,	LE MEILLARD.
6th Somerset L.I.	PROUVILLE.
6th D.C.L.I.	LE MEILLARD.
6th K.O.Y.L.I.	PROUVILLE.
10th Durham L.I.	HEUZECOURT.
43rd M.G.Company,	LE MEILLARD.
43rd T.M. Battery,	LE MEILLARD.
11th King's L'pool Regt (Pioneers)	BEAUMETZ.
H.Qrs, 14th Div'l Train,	BERNAVILLE.
No.2 Company,	GEZAINCOURT.
No.3 Company,	BERNEUIL.
No.4 Company,	Mt.RENAULT Fm.
42nd Field Ambulance,	ST.HILAIRE.
43rd Field Ambulance,	LE MEILLARD.
44th Field Ambulance,	GEZAINCOURT.
25th Sanitary Section,	BERNAVILLE.
26th Mobile Veterinary Section,	BERNAVILLE.
Div'l Ordnance Stores,	BERNAVILLE.

Headquarters,
  14th Division,
    3rd Aug.1916.

Appendix XLVIII

LOCATION OF UNITS.

14TH (LIGHT) DIVISION.   13th August, 1916.

Unit.	Location.	Wagon Lines.	Transport Lines
Divisional Headquarters,	BELLEVUE Fm.(E.5.c.)		BELLEVUE Fm. E.5.c.
H.Q., Div'l Artillery,	E.11.d.8.8.	)	
46th Bde R.F.A.	F.10.b.0.6.	E.11.d.	) under
47th Bde R.F.A.	X.28.b.0.2.	E.17.a.5.6.	) 33rd Division.
48th Bde R.F.A.	S.15.d.6.2.	F.8.b.	)
49th Bde R.F.A.	S.20.c.5.5.	F.7.b.	)
D.A.C.	E.16.a.		)
61st Field Co. R.E.	F.4.d.5.3.		F.7.c.
62nd Field Co. R.E.	F.4.c.9.0.		F.7.c.
89th Field Co. R.E.	F.10.a.9.8.		F.7.c.
41st Bde H.Q.	Pommier Redoubt(A.1.b.)		E.11.a.
41st Bde Area,	-		-
42nd Bde H.Q.	F.14.a.		E.10.a.
42nd Bde Area,	-		-
43rd Bde H.Q.	Pommier Redoubt(A.1.b.)		E.10.c.
43rd Bde Area,	-		-
42nd Field Ambulance,	E.5.d.0.0.		E.5.d.0.0.
43rd Field Ambulance,	F.7.d.9.9.		F.7.d.9.9.
44th Field Ambulance,	F.6.a.4.0.		F.7.d.8.8. F.7.d.8.8
Advanced Dressing Station,	F.6.a.5.0.		
Ammunition Dump,	E.18.a.9.8.		
R.E. & Salvage Dump,	F.9.a.4.7.		
Sanitary Section, 25th	BELLEVUE Fm.		BELLEVUE Fm.
H.Q.Coy of the Train,	E.10.a.		E.10.c.
No.2 Coy -do-	E.11.a.		E.11.a.
No.3 Coy -do-	E.10.a.		E.10.a.
No.4 Coy -do-	E.10.a.		E.10.a.
1st Line Trans.Echelon "A"	)		E.10.a., E.11.a.
1st Line Trans.Echelon "B"	)		
Mobile Veterinary Section,	RIBEMONT,		RIBEMONT.
Advanced Mob.Vet.Section,	E.12.c.1.3.		E.12.c.1.3.
Pioneer Battn.(11th L'pool R)	F.9.b.2.3.		F.9.b.
Water Tank Wagons attached,	E.10.b.		E.10.b.
Supply Column,	RIBEMONT,		RIBEMONT.
M.M.G.Bty, 8th	BELLEVUE Fm.(E.5.c.)		BELLEVUE Fm. (E.5.c.)

Appendix XLIX

LOCATION OF UNITS.

14TH (LIGHT) DIVISION.   19th August, 1916.

Unit.	Location.	Wagon Lines.	Transport Lines.
Divisional Headquarters,	BELLEVUE FARM, (E.5.c.)		BELLEVUE Fm. E.5.c.
H.Q., Div'l Artillery,	E.11.d.8.8.		
46th Bde R.F.A.	F.10.b.0.6.	E.11.d.	
47th Bde R.F.A.	X.28.b.0.2.	E.17.a.5.6.	under
48th Bde R.F.A.	S.15.d.6.2.	F.8.b.	33rd Division.
49th Bde R.F.A.	S.20.c.5.5.	F.7.b.	
14th D.A.C.	E.16.a.		
61st Field Co.R.E.	F.4.d.5.3.		F.7.c.
62nd Field Co.R.E.	F.4.c.9.0.		F.7.c.
89th Field Co.R.E.	F.10.a.9.8.		F.7.c.
41st Bde H.Q.	Pommier Redoubt (A.1.b.)		F.2.d.
41st Bde Area,	-		-
42nd Bde H.Q.	S.22.c.		F.2.d.
42nd Bde Area,	-		-
43rd Bde H.Q.	F.8.d.		F.2.d.
43rd Bde Area,	-		-
42nd Field Ambulance,	E.5.d.0.0.		E.5.d.0.0.
43rd Field Ambulance,	F.7.d.9.9.		F.7.d.9.9.
44th Field Ambulance,	F.6.a.4.0.		F.7.d.8.8.
Advanced Dressing Station,	F.6.a.5.0.		
Ammunition Dump,	E.18.a.8.8.		
R.E. Dump,	F.4.c.		
Salvage Dump,	F.9.a.4.7.		
Sanitary Section, 25th,	BELLEVUE Fm.		BELLEVUE Fm.
H.Q.Coy of the Train.	E.10.a.		E.10.c.
No. 2 Coy -do-	E.11.a.		E.11.a.
No. 3 Coy -do-	E.10.a.		E.10.a.
No. 4 Coy -do-	E.10.a.		E.10.a.
1st Line Trans.Echelon 'A'			F.2.d.
1st Line Trans.Echelon 'B'			
Mobile Vet.Section,	RIBEMONT,		RIBEMONT,
Advanced Mob.Vet.Sec.	E.12.c.1.3.		E.12.c.1.3.
Pioneer Battalion,(11th L'pool R)	F.9.b.2.3.		F.9.b.
Water Tank Wagons attached,	E.10.b.		E.10.b.
Supply Column,	RIBEMONT,		RIBEMONT.
M.M.G.Bty, 8th	BELLEVUE Fm.(E.5.c.)		BELLEVUE Fm.(E.5.c.)

Appendix I.

LOCATION OF UNITS.

14TH (LIGHT) DIVISION.   26th August, 1916.

Unit.	Location.	Wagon Lines.	Transport Lines.
Divisional Headquarters, H.Q., Div'l Artillery,	BELLEVUE FARM, (E.5.c.) E.11.d.8.8.		BELLEVUE Fm. E.5.c.
46th Bde R.F.A.	F.10.b.0.6.	E.11.d.	)
47th Bde R.F.A.	X.28.b.0.2.	E.17.a.5.6.	) under
48th Bde R.F.A.	S.15.d.8.2.	F.8.b.	) 33rd Division.
49th Bde R.F.A.	S.20.c.5.5.	F.7.b.	)
14th D.A.C.	E.16.a.		)
61st Field Co.R.E.	F.4.d.5.3.		F.7.c.
62nd Field Co.R.E.	F.4.c.9.0.		F.7.c.
89th Field Co.R.E.	F.10.a.9.8.		F.7.c.
41st Bde H.Q. 41st Bde Area,	Pommier Redoubt (A.1.b.) -		F.2.d. -
42nd Bde H.Q. 42nd Bde Area,	S.22.c. 7.8.d. -		F.2.d. -
43rd Bde H.Q. 43rd Bde Area,	F.8.d. S.22.c -		F.2.d. -
42nd Field Ambulance,	E.5.d.0.0.		E.5.d.0.0.
43rd Field Ambulance,	F.7.d.9.9.		F.7.d.9.9.
44th Field Ambulance,	F.6.a.4.0.		F.7.d.8.8.
Advanced Dressing Station,	F.6.a.5.0.		
Ammunition Dump,	E.18.a.8.8.		
R.E. Dump,	F.4.c.		
Salvage Dump,	F.9.a.4.7.		
Sanitary Section, 25th,	BELLEVUE Fm.		BELLEVUE Fm.
H.Q.Coy of the Train.			
No. 2 Coy -do-	E.10.a.		E.10.c.
No. 3 Coy -do-	E.11.a.		E.11.a.
No. 4 Coy -do-	E.10.a.		E.10.a.
	E.10.a.		E.10.a.
1st Line Trans.Echelon 'A') 1st Line Trans.Echelon 'B')			F.2.d.
Mobile Vet.Section, Advanced Mob.Vet.Sec.	RIBEMONT, E.12.c.1.3.		RIBEMONT, E.12.c.1.3.
Pioneer Battalion,(11th L'pool R)	F.9.b.2.3.		F.9.b.
Water Tank Wagons attached,	E.10.b.		E.10.b.
Supply Column,	RIBEMONT,		RIBEMONT.
M.M.G.Bty, 8th	BELLEVUE Fm.(E.5.c.)		BELLEVUE Fm.(E.5.c.)

14th (LIGHT) DIVISION.

==== REINFORCEMENTS. ====

Month of August, 1916.

Officers	27
Other Ranks	858
TOTAL	885

14th (Light) Division.

CASUALTIES during the month of August, 1916.

Unit.	Officers			Other Ranks.		
	K	W	M	K	W	M
41st Infantry Brigade.						
7th K.R.R.C.	3	6	-	59	236	10
8th K.R.R.C.	3	8	-	50	156	17
7th Rifle Brigade	2	6	-	75	194	11
8th Rifle Brigade	3	4	-	26	105	2
41st T.M.Batty.	-	-	-	2	7	-
41st M.G.Company	-	1	-	2	28	-
42nd Infantry Brigade.						
5th Oxf. & Bucks.	2	7	1	40	135	11
5th K.S.L.I.	6	5	1	44	180	12
9th K.R.R.C.	5	7	1	43	239	49
9th Rifle Brigade	2	4	-	22	106	4
42nd TM.Bty.	-	-	-	1	3	-
42nd M.G.Coy	-	3	-	5	24	1
43rd Infantry Brigade.						
6th Somerset L.I.	4	11	1	65	263	31
6th D.C.L.I.	7	10	-	81	304	52
6th K.O.Y.L.I.	7	3	-	36	156	12
10th Durham L.I.	-	8	-	40	264	16
43rd T. M. Bty	1	-	-	-	-	-
43rd M. G. Coy	-	2	-	-	17	-
Divl Troops						
14th Divl. Artilery	2	9	-	9	59	-
14th Divl. Engineers	1	6	-	15	35	2
11th Liverpools (P)	-	2	-	20	72	1
R.A.M.C.	-	1	-	5	14	-
Div'l Train	-	1	-	-	-	-
Div.Supply Column (Attd. Fd.Ambces).	-	-	-	-	2	-
Divl. Total	48	104	4	640	2589	230

Vol 12

Confidential.

War Diary
of
"A" & "Q" Branches
14th (Light) Division

From 1st Sept. to 30th Sept. 1916.

Volume XXIX

WAR DIARY
or
INTELLIGENCE SUMMARY.
(Erase heading not required.)

Army Form C. 2118.

Place	Date	Hour	Summary of Events and Information	Remarks and references to Appendices
	Sept 1st		Transport of 42nd and 45th Syphilitics R.E. Pioneers DIV'l Ambulances and 2 nos districts under Lt. Col Richards CO 36th Train completed to move to new area. Preparation made to transfer syphilitics to HANGEST pending supply Column — application made to change hour & body is withdrawn to go to permit this.	[init.]
	2		Permits for practice grenades drawn from CONTAY	[init.]
	3		1st Corps authorises pour permission for application for 48 hours leave in France to be forwarded for Corps sanction	[init.]
	4		[illegible signature]	[init.]

Army Form C. 2118.

WAR DIARY
or
INTELLIGENCE SUMMARY.
(Erase heading not required.)

Instructions regarding War Diaries and Intelligence Summaries are contained in F. S. Regs., Part II. and the Staff Manual respectively. Title pages will be prepared in manuscript.

Place	Date	Hour	Summary of Events and Information	Remarks and references to Appendices
	5th		Rest camp formed at AULT near LE TREPORT. under 2 hrs/s obers. One Officer at 50 men 14 FGS sent Etaples camp.	ODN.
	6th		14 officers 350 men left for AULT for 48 hours by the sea. Entraining station HONGRE-LES-SAINTS. A Lorry service was organised to convey officers men going on 48 hours leave & returning to duty.	ODN.
	7th		26 officers 700 men left for AULT. Entraining stations SENARPONT and HONGRE-LES-SAINTS. Proposal to draw supplies for relieved extence transport etc. submitted in form of handing credit nr. to stores.	ODN.
	8th	RA	Brig Gen Landy's wounded. 28 officers and 700 men left for AULT. This rest was much appreciated by the men. Lt Col Hamilton at Hong-n with list — transferred to Indian trench and home Supple	ODN.

WAR DIARY
or
INTELLIGENCE SUMMARY.

Army Form C. 2118.

Place	Date	Hour	Summary of Events and Information	Remarks and references to Appendices
	9th		41st Bde group Transport move to AILLY-SUR-SOMME.	
	10th		42nd Bde group Transport move to AILLY-SUR-SOMME 41st Bde group move to camp N. of DERNANCOURT by buses.	
	11th		43rd Bde group Transport move to AILLY-SUR-SOMME 42nd Bde group entrain at AIRAINES detrain at MERICOURT and camp N. of DERNANCOURT. Div¹ Hqrs move to BUIRE 41st Bde move to FRICOURT camp.	
	12th		43rd Bde group entrain at AIRAINES in 2 tactical trains, detrain at MERICOURT, and camp N. of DERNANCOURT 42nd Bde move to 41st Bde camp 41st Bde relieve 41st Bde in the line near DEWNIE wood. Div¹ Hqrs move to FRICOURT Chateau. Q branch remains at BUIRE.	

WAR DIARY
INTELLIGENCE SUMMARY

Army Form C. 2118.

Place	Date	Hour	Summary of Events and Information	Remarks and references to Appendices
FRICOURT	13th		A.99 Moved S. of the Mare to FRICOURT CHATEAU. We be from the ADV HQ return from wire hut.	CDN
	14th		Administrative arrangements for 15th issued. Grenade dumps completed about 1000 yds East of MONTAUBAN - formed dump for A.H.Q. supplies near Quarry S.E. corner of BERNAFAY WOOD.	Appendix I
	15th		Division carried out attack on a Brigade front 42nd Div. We pressing through H.Q. opened here but completed to later. Shell injection was rather bad. Transport road to connect forward between MONTAUBAN & POMMIERS which was to be mended. Transport rolled on forward to LONGUEVAL by hay & part of the way thence also about the entire N. front of DELVILLE WOOD. Later having the rest of the road I am a civilian at MONTAUBAN to 17th Arty and to D. Distr. recommended putting site which was just N. the front of later Later - fuel that was applied IX & hops.	

WAR DIARY or INTELLIGENCE SUMMARY

Army Form C. 2118.

Place	Date	Hour	Summary of Events and Information	Remarks and references to Appendices
	15th cont		Night held up by MG fire from MONTAUBAN road & flying over of enemy intense MG transport down. RE kept down and left bays to sites of CRUCIFIX in the wd BERNAFAY WOOD — LONGUEVAL —	
	16th		Continuation of attack carried out by 1st & 4th hyp bde, 4th Div remaining behind in r 1st & 4th at MONTAUBAN. Two up & one 3rd Bde in 1st line transport with its horses near MONTAUBAN to early hours. Report 1st Aug 6 1st & 2nd Column 1st Aust transport arrived in centre of Mametz. They moved up to & beyond LONGUEVAL — 3rd Div 3 echelon separate [?] took units at w. white MONTAUBAN — It was action of Transport in front of MONTAUBAN were more than division. Sunk when to underground line it was not by guide & apparently it was assumed to his own batteries by Division behind MONTAUBAN. After dark 21 Div left which 1st Aug 4 [?] left the transport about and N 17 D. 2 Men 4/3 were returned with 2 Aust 4/3 left [?] transport before the attack.	

1577 Wt.W.10791/1773 500,000 1/15 D. D. & L. A.D.S.S./Forms/C. 2118.

WAR DIARY
or
INTELLIGENCE SUMMARY.
(Erase heading not required.)

Army Form C. 2118.

Place	Date	Hour	Summary of Events and Information	Remarks and references to Appendices
	16th		43rd MGC Bn 2/4m left with 2/4m but 43rd attacked watch but to "FRICOURT camp" with new RECORDER (F13C) early in the night. 43rd MGC Bn 2/4m but left to fire 43rd attacked whilst a relief from PIMMIERS South. 4/1 to move from where relief from PIMMIEROS would arrived took over PIMIER MILL both.	App II
RUIRE	17th		4/1 Suffolk Bn moved to DERNANCOURT billets for a rest at FRICOURT camp (E3). 43rd Suffolk Bn 2/4m moved to camps in ALBERT AMIENS road (D18a) 2 battalions 43rd Suffolk moved to RIBEMONT. 43rd Suffolk Bn 2 Bn left with 2 from 43rd moved to FRICOURT camp. Both Bn moved to RUIRE camp. division took over administration of PIMIER MILL both. Tree casualties 13th & 14th Officers killed 131 men wounded, 38 wounded 131 men, Killed 4/12 wounded 2422 missing 1016. Railed EDGE ALL aspectively front Wood until ALBERT moving N.S. Supply arrangement for 14 K.T.A. made separately No 1 by division until Trees to remain with 14 K.T.A. a separate of supply	G.H.A

Army Form C. 2118.

WAR DIARY
or
INTELLIGENCE SUMMARY.
(Erase heading not required.)

Instructions regarding War Diaries and Intelligence Summaries are contained in F. S. Regs., Part II. and the Staff Manual respectively. Title pages will be prepared in manuscript.

Place	Date	Hour	Summary of Events and Information	Remarks and references to Appendices
BUIRES	18t		43rd Batln. moved to RIBEMONT as ordered. Headquarters & one battalion at BUIRE. 42nd Batln. location (3rd & 4th 2.5.7(CW)) returned to 43rd Bty/Batn hijacked train which is camped on ALBERT AMIENS road. Huts erected for 43rd Bty/Batn at RIBEMONT - Hutted Encampment taken over by 43rd at RIBEMONT as is 42nd Bty/Batn camp.	
	19t		Followed up teaching men in laundry of SAMOVER & cork biscuit in place at war 9 Somme men struck forward to Rd. huts. Temporary worked by Asmr. to enable 500 third race for water. Army at AMIENS.	OK
	20t		Before revised to have Lgt/Bln & dormitories R.E. by the a 22nd transport by road starts 9.15. Issued instructions movements for more	OK

1577 Wt. W10791/1773 500,000 1/15 D. D. & L.   A.D.S.S./Forms/C. 2118.

WAR DIARY
or
INTELLIGENCE SUMMARY.
(Erase heading not required.)

Army Form C. 2118.

Place	Date	Hour	Summary of Events and Information	Remarks and references to Appendices
	21st		All arrived at Rainneville RA at with the remainder of 43rd 2nd Battalion & trains & up with 2nd Battalion. Division led into temporary billeting through via LA HOUSSOYE - FRECHENCOURT - KEHENCOURT - BEAUCOURT - RUBEMPRÉ & TALMAS. dt at Rainneville by the Trans bn in reserve. Issued orders for entraining.	Appendix III
			Hutts at PIERRE NOIR held over the evening to HI Division. North of RUBEMPRÉ dismantled as required.	All.
			Capt Brown sent many reports to 3rd Army Hd. established his hdqts one rail lined to Athyencour [?] - DOULLENS for the night. Reports advanced to RE RAME generale & to Hd. formed to nearer ALBERT - AMIENS road at 7.30 hastily to extricate of 3rd Army base. 245 branch homes began arrivin about 8am - Owing to the necessity for the troops to halt & await orders to fire that at the front took them immediate traffic on the road the Brown did not set at its position to Herron to Montigny - Cachereau was not employed till 12 noon. Stores moved by Motor Lorries. Hd. division formed support group.	

Place	Date	Hour	Summary of Events and Information	Remarks and references to Appendices
	23		Lt. Hele LUCHEUX and GROUCHER 42d Supply GRAND RULLECOURT in REBRIBRICOURT 43d Hele SUS ST LEGER NERGNY and LE SOUICH. Convoy supply lt to Mr LE CHIROY. Horses, carts, wagons hired injuring orders and bikes. 43d Field Ambulance moved from Wt Suite 42.e44.t hospital TACNAS, divisible supply lt and had full admin. Few compensation cases, asked at BOUQUEMAISON — Returned fr. 24th Welsh Depot by S.E. on wing of 21st. Received travel to BOUQUEMAISON — Supply lt to the hospital will continues hospital in bikes. Re return for the men transport on 22nd & supply Co at TALMAS and train men a night of 22nd. Orders received for wing of 1st Division's transport SE of MONDAYS on 26th & future days.	App IV
	24		43d the H.S. by moved BERNEVILLE	

WAR DIARY
or
INTELLIGENCE SUMMARY.
(Erase heading not required.)

Army Form C. 2118.

Place	Date	Hour	Summary of Events and Information	Remarks and references to Appendices
	25th		41ˢᵗ Lt. Bde. moved by bus to SIMENCOURT. MERNEVILLE, WARLUS & DAINVILLE – 42ⁿᵈ Bde. by rail & 3ᵗʰ Bde. by rail. Return for 42ⁿᵈ Bde. by bus set up special by bus MERNEVILLE. 41ˢᵗ Bde. by road to WEANDED by the Advanced Survey front stations at MontJoie(?) Juberra shell MONCHIET	GHQ.
	26th		41ˢᵗ Lt. Bde. moved to more GOUY AGAINST2 LANQUETIN 41ˢᵗ Bde by road to 37ᵗʰ Bdes AdJ MAMETERIUE. 44 & J Coles & No. 2 Coy Tent & BARLY harve there. Other movements postponed to next day.	GHQ Appendix
	27th		43ʳᵈ Lt. Bde. moved by bus & rail to 9 Coles 41 & 27/5 Bde about F districts (?) Bn. 82. There been crowed may not of stored area. Dety A unit 9 concealed of Mts. 14 & BJ.	GHQ.
	28th		9th Adm moved KUARLUS.	
	29th			
	30th		3 Station reports. O/V/personnel 10000 14 Pri other ranks	GHQ.

Col Hamilton　　　　　　　　　　　　　　　　　　　*Appendix I*

SECRET.　　　　　　　　　　　　　　　　　　　　　S.Q.32/3.

ADMINISTRATIVE ARRANGEMENTS
15TH SEPTEMBER, 1916.

SUPPLY
REFILLING.　41st, 42nd & 43rd Infantry Brigade Groups will refill at FRICOURT OLD STATION as already notified, and 14th Div'l Artillery will refill at F.10.

SUPPLY
SITUATION　　Rations for 15th　　　　On man.
AFTER　　　　　"　　"　16th　　　　In Cookers & Cooks' Wagons.
REFILLING.　　"　　"　17th　　　　In Supply Section, Div. Train.

FOOD AND　　3rd Echelon 1st Line Transport, viz: Cooks wagons,
WATER SUPPLY cooks' carts and water carts will rendezvous at 4 p.m.
TO TRENCH　　on the track CARCAILLOT FARM to F.9.a. in the
LINE.　　　　following order from the front facing East and
　　　　　　　extending along the track, head of the Column to be
　　　　　at the point F.8.c.8.8. where the track crosses a
　　　　　bye-road:-

　　　　　43rd Infantry Brigade.
　　　　　42nd Infantry Brigade,
　　　　　Field Coys, R.E.
　　　　　11th Bn. L'pool Regt.
　　　　　41st Infantry Brigade.
　　　　　Field Ambulances.

　　　　　R.A. will make separate arrangements.

　　　　　The Column will remain halted until ordered to
move by a Staff Officer of Div'l Headquarters.
　　　　　Infantry Brigades, 11th Liverpools and Field
Companies will send guides to meet their 3rd Echelons
at S.23.a.6.8. on the road BERNAFAY WOOD - LONGUEVAL
at 8 p.m.
　　　　　After delivering food and water the 3rd Echelon
will return via LONGUEVAL - S.15.c. to S.22.Central
where it will bivouac.　Supply Section, Div'l Train
will deliver rations at this bivouac at 5 a.m. 16th.

WATER.　　All Water tins in possession of the troops in front
line should be full by 5 a.m. 15th.
　　　　　Water carts are with 3rd Echelon 1st Line
Transport and should be ready to start filled as
ordered in the previous paragraph.
　　　　　Water will be obtained as follows on 15th
and 16th :-

Copies to :-

41st Infantry Bde　　14th Div. Signals　　A.D.V.S.
42nd　"　　"　　　　8th M.M.G. Battery　　D.A.D.O.S.
43rd　"　　"　　　　14th Div. Train.　　　A.P.M.
11th (King's) Liverpools　A.D.M.S.
7th Divisional Artillery　Camp Commandant
14th　"　　"　　　No. 14 Div. Supply Col.
C.R.E.　　　　　　　"G"

-2-

PERIOD.	UNIT.	HORSES.	WATER CARTS.
Up to 6 p.m. 15th.	Infantry 1st Line.	BECORDEL.	BECORDEL.
	Field Coys.	FRICOURT.	FRICOURT.
	Field Ambulances,	BECORDEL.	BECORDEL.
	R.A. less D.A.C.	FRICOURT.	FRICOURT.
	D.A.C.) Train.)	VIVIER MILL.	ALBERT.
6 p.m.15th to 6 p.m. 18th.	Infantry 1st Line *	MONTAUBAN. (S.27.b.)	MONTAUBAN. (S.27.c.)
	Field Coys.	-do-	-do-
	Field Ambulances,	-do-	-do-
	R.A. less D.A.C.	X.29.b.	X.29.b.
	D.A.C.("A" Echelon)	X.29.b.	X.29.b.
	D.A.C.("B" Echelon) Train (Supply Section)	FRICOURT.	FRICOURT.
	Train (Baggage Section)	BECORDEL.	BECORDEL.

* After Midnight 15th/16th tank wagons will be available at S.23.a.6.8. for filling water carts of units in front of that point.

INFANTRY AMMUNITION. The dumps at S.22.d. and F.6.c. start filled up to 5000 Mills Grenades and 200 boxes S.A.A. each with other ammunition to correspond.

As soon as the tactical situation permits, "A" Echelon 1st Line Transport correctly loaded will be moved up by Brigades to LONGUEVAL and in the direction of FLERS to points selected by Brigades. "A" Echelon will replenish from the dump at MAMETZ (F.6.c.) until it is emptied.
D.A.C. will increase the dump at S.22.d. as soon as it is possible to take wagons there.
When the F.6.c. dump is emptied "A" Echelon will replenish from S.22.d. as may be necessary until the D.A.C. takes up a more forward position.

ARTILLERY AMMUNITION. Arrangements for supply of Artillery Ammunition will be made by G.O.C. R.A.
Ammunition will be taken by Ammunition Park to the present D.A.C. dumps until MONTAUBAN railhead becomes available on or about 17th.

TRANSPORT DIV'L H.QR UNITS. Headquarter units will be prepared to move at 4 hours notice with all transport. These include :-
Div'l H.Qrs, H.Q. R.A., H.Q. R.E., Signals, H.Q.Div.Train, Sanitary Section, Salvage Company, A.P.M.Establishment.

14th September, 1916.

LIEUT-COLONEL,
A.A.&.Q.M.G.
14TH (LIGHT) DIVISION.

App. II

S.O.32/5.

SUPPLY ARRANGEMENTS, 16TH & 17TH.

1. 3rd Echelon Infantry Transport will remain in its present location until orders are issued from Div'l H.Qrs.
   It will be prepared to move at any time after 5 p.m.
   Rendezvous today for guides from Brigades and battalions in action North of MONTAUBAN will be

   S.23.a.5.9. at 7.30 p.m.

   Units not requiring 3rd Echelon to go forward will send guides to the rendezvous to inform the 3rd Echelons of the fact, and the 3rd Echelon of those units will then go straight to bivouac.

2. Bivouac for 3rd Echelons for night 16th/17th will be notified to O.C., 3rd Echelons as early as possible and the message repeated to Brigades and Pioneer Battalion.
   C.R.E. and A.D.M.S. will notify Div.H.Qrs by 9 p.m. tonight the position of 3rd Echelons of Field Coys and Field Ambulances.

3. Supply Section of Train will deliver rations into 3rd Echelon bivouacs at 7 a.m. on 17th.

4. On Sept.17th all supplies for 14th Division including hay will be transhipped at ALBERT on to the metre guage railway and forwarded to MONTAUBAN.
   14th Supply Column will notify 14th Div.Train of the hour at which the metre guage train may be expected at MONTAUBAN, repeating the message to 14th Div.H.Qrs. The message should not be sent until the main line train has arrived at ALBERT.
   Supply Section 14th Div. Train will proceed to MONTAUBAN in accordance with the wire from 14th Supply Column and load there.
   Supplies will stand overnight on Supply Section wagons and be delivered to units in the early hours of the morning 18th.

   Clawson Joplin
   acting for LIEUT-COLONEL,
   A.A.&.Q.M.G.
   14TH (LIGHT) DIVISION.

16/9/16.
Copies to:- 41st Inf.Bde.   A.D.M.S. (ack)
(acknowledged) 42nd Inf. Bde.   Supply Column. (ack)
(acknowledged) 43rd Inf. Bde.   Div. Train. (ack)
               11th L'pool R.   14th Div.Artillery.
               41st Inf.Bde 3rd Echelon, 8th M.M.G.Battery. (received)
(acknowledged) 42nd   "   "   "
               43rd   "   "   "
               11th L'pool R "   "
(ackngd)   C.R.E.

Cancelled
per 262/12 Q

S/8/33/4.

Appendix XIII

41st Inf Bde
42nd Inf Bde
43rd Inf Bde
Camp Commandant
C.R.E.
14th Div'l Train
Salvage Company
G.

1. Troops will embuss on the ALBERT-AMIENS road at 8 a.m. tomorrow 22nd.

They will be formed up by 7.30 a.m. in the fields on the North side of the road.

43rd Inf. Bde Group from D.20.c.25 extending Eastwards.

42nd Inf. Bde Group from D.16.c.22 extending Eastwards.

Div'l Hd Qrs Group D.17.B.5.8.

41st Inf Bde Group 200 yards east of D.17.b.5.8. extending Eastwards.

At least 100 yards must be left between groups, and if groups have not room in the space assigned, the troops must be drawn up in parallel column so as to leave the space of 100 yards.

A Staff Officer from each Brigade will assist in superintending the embussing.

2. The busses will arrive at 8 a.m.

They will move off by groups at half hour intervals.

3. An interpreter is to be detailed in each group to sit on the leading bus.

4. Busses will be met at the entrance to DOULLENS by a Staff Officer Div'l HQ and directed to destinations.

5. Division HQ will close at BUIRE Camp at 12 noon and open at LE CAUROY at the same hour.

C.H. Hamilton Lt Col
AA & QMG
14 (Light) Division

21.9.16.

Appendix IV

S.Q.33/2.

ADMINISTRATIVE ARRANGEMENTS
for move 21st and 22nd Sept.

1. Supply Section of the Divl. Train will carry supplies for 21st and 22nd for the whole mounted party.

Supplies for 21st and 22nd for the dismounted party will be delivered to units by Divisional Train before 9.0. a.m. on 21st.

Supplies for 23rd will be drawn from Railhead by Supply Column on 21st. and refilled into Supply Section, Divisional Train on 22nd. at a point to be notified later and delivered to units in their new quarters the same evening.

2. One lorry per Infantry Brigade has been asked for to carry T.M.Battery equipment and extra stores of Brigade. They should report at 7.0.a.m. on 21st as follows :-

 41st Bde. Church, DERNANCOURT.
 42nd Bde. D.17.b.9.9.
 43rd Bde. Market Square, RIBEMONT.

One lorry will be detailed for extra R.E.Stores. C.R.E. will arrange to carry any extra stores of the Pioneer Battn. on this lorry. It will report at Divisional Headquarters at 7.0.a.m. on 21st.

LIEUT-COLONEL,
A.A.&Q.M.G.
14TH (LIGHT) DIVISION.

20/9/16.

Col Hamilton   Appendix IV

Q/997.

Administrative Arrangements.
Relief of 12th Div.

1. Transport lines of Brigades and Pioneer Battn. on completion of relief will be as follows :-

  41st Infantry Brigade   -   BEAUMETZ
  42nd   "   "   -   BERNEVILLE
  43rd   "   "   -   BERNEVILLE
  Pioneer Battn.   -   BERNEVILLE

Until Brigades go into the trenches, battalions will keep their transport with them in billets.

2. Refilling on 26th will be as follows :-

  42nd Infantry Brigade Group   -   immediately east of WANQUETIN on road to WARLUS at 8.0.a.m.

  41st " " "   between SOMBRIN and BARLY at 10.0.a.m.

(Supply wagons will join their units by 2.0.p.m. and stay the night with them rejoining their Company at refilling point on 27th).

  43rd Infantry Brigade Group   SUS-ST-LEGER 8.30.a.m.

Refilling on 27th will be as follows :-

  42nd Infantry Brigade Group }   East of FOSSEUX on
  41st " " "   road to WANQUETIN at 8.0.a.m.

  43rd " " "   between SOMBRIN and BARLY at 9.0.a.m.

(Supply wagons will join their units by 2.0.p.m. and stay the night with them rejoining their Company at refilling point on 28th).

Refilling on 28th for all groups will be East of FOSSEUX on the road to WANQUETIN at 8.0.a.m.

3. Mobile Veterinary Section will be at FOSSEUX from 27th inclusive.

4. Mails will be delivered at Brigade Headquarters while these are West of AVESNES. On the day of move and until 28th, mails will be delivered with supplies.

On and after 28th Postal refilling will take place at WARLUS at an hour to be notified later.

             C.L. Hamilton Lt Col
             A.A.& Q.M.G.
           14th (Light) Division.

Copies to :-
41st Inf.Bde.   11th L'pool R.   Signal Coy.   Camp Commdt.
42nd Inf.Bde.   C.R.E.   8th M.M.G.Btty.   Supply Column.
43rd Inf.Bde.   A.D.M.S.   Divl. Train.   A.D.V.S.
"G"   D.A.D.O.S.   Postal W.O.

26.9.16.

SECRET.
O.C/242/A.

14TH (LIGHT) DIVISION.

LOCATION OF UNITS.

2nd September, 1916.

UNIT.	LOCATION.
Divisional Headquarters)	
14th Signal Co. R.E.)	
25th Sanitary Section,)	BELLOY.
H.Q., R.E.)	
H.Q., 14th Div'l Train.)	

41st Infantry Brigade Group.

Headquarters,	HEUCOURT.
7th K.R.R.C.	METIGNY.
8th K.R.R.C.	HEUCOURT.
7th R.B.	WARLUS.
8th R.B.	LALEU.
41st Machine Gun Coy.	CROQUOISEN.
41st Trench Mortar Bty.	CROQUOISEN.
11th King's L'pool Regt (Pioneers) H.Q.& ½ Bn.	TAILLY.
½ Bn.	WARLUS.
62nd Field Co. R.E.	AVELESGES.
44th Field Ambulance,	L'ARBRE a MOUCHE.
No.2 Coy, A.S.C.	AVELESGES.

42nd Infantry Brigade Group.

Headquarters,	AVESNES.
5th Ox & Bucks L.I.	EPAUMESNIL.
5th K.S.L.I.	VERGIES.
9th K.R.R.C.	ST.MAULVIS.
9th R.B.	LE FAY.
42nd Machine Gun Coy.	AVESNES.
42nd Trench Mortar Bty.	AVESNES.
89th Field Co. R.E.	FRETTE-CUISSE.
42nd Field Ambulance,	ETREJUST.
No.3 Coy, A.S.C.	VERGIES.

43rd Infantry Brigade Group.

Headquarters,	HORNOY.
6th Somerset L.I.	SELINCOURT.
6th D.C.L.I.	AUMONT.
6th K.O.Y.L.I.	DROMESNIL.
10th Durham L.I.	HORNOY.
43rd Machine Gun Company,	HORNOY.
43rd Trench Mortar Bty.	HORNOY.
61st Field Co. R.E.)	
44th Field Ambulance,)	BOISRAULT.
No.4 Coy. A.S.C.)	
26th Mobile Vety Section)	
14th Div'l Supply Column,	L'ARBRE a MOUCHE.
8th Motor Machine Gun Battery,	HERICOURT.
Railhead,	HANGEST.

C. Parsons.
Captain,
D.A.A.& Q.M.G.
14th (Light) Division.

2nd Sept: 1916.

App. VII

<u>S E C R E T.</u>   <u>LOCATION OF UNITS.</u>

<u>14TH (LIGHT) DIVISION.</u>

14th Div.No.   Sept: 13th 1916.
O.C.247.A.

Unit.	Location.	Wagon Lines.	Transport Lines.
Div'l Headquarters,	F.3.b.9.1.		F.3.b.
H.Qrs, 7th Div'l Artly.	F.3.b.9.1.		F.3.b.
14th Bde R.F.A.	(F.7.c.	F.7.c.&	
	(E.11.d.	E.11.d.	
22nd Bde R.F.A.	(E.12.c & d.	E.12.c.& d	
	(F.7.c.	& F.7.c.	
35th Bde R.F.A.	E.11.b. & d.	E.11.b.& d.	
N.Z.F.A. D Group,	E.12.c. & d.		E.12.c. & d.
15th " "	F.8.a.		
D.A.C.	E.10.b.5.0.		E.10.b.
61st Field Co.R.E.	E.9.c.		E.9.c.
62nd Field Co.R.E.	F.3.b.		E.12.Central.
89th Field Co.R.E.	F.4.a.		E.12.Central.
41st Bde H.Q.)			F.13.c.
41st Bde Area.)	In the line.		F.13.c.
42nd Bde H.Qrs	F.13.c.		F.13.c.
42nd Bde Area,	F.13.c.		F.13.c.
43rd Bde H.Qrs,	E.9.c.		E.9.c.
43rd Bde Area,	E.9.c.		E.9.c.
42nd Field Ambulance,	F.13.c.		F.13.c.
43rd Field Ambulance,	E.14.b.		E.14.b.
44th Field Ambulance,	F.13.c.		F.13.c.
Advanced Dressing Station	S.28.b.7.8.		
Ammunition Dump,	E.16.b.		
R.E. Dump,	F.4.c.		
Salvage Dump,	F.9.a.4.7.		
25th Sanitary Section,	F.3.b.9.1.		F.3.b.9.1.
H.Q.Coy, Div'l Train,	E.10.c.		E.10.c.
No.2 Coy,	F.13.c.		F.13.c.
No.3 Coy,	F.13.c.		F.13.c.
No.4 Coy.	E.9.c.		E.9.c.
Mobile Vety Section,	E.15.a.		E.15.a.
Pioneer Battn.11th King's.	F.4.a.		F.4.a.
Supply Column,	HEILLY,		HEILLY.
8th M.M.G.Battery,	F.13.c.		F.13.c.
D.A.D.O.S.	E.18.a.5.6.		

App. VIII

14TH (LIGHT) DIVISION.

REINFORCEMENTS DURING MONTH OF SEPTEMBER, 1916.

Officers   102.
Other Ranks   3-801.

14TH (LIGHT) DIVISION.

SUMMARY OF ACCURATE CASUALTIES.
Second Tour on the SOMME = 13th September to 20th September.

UNIT.	Officers			Other Ranks.		
	K	W	M	K	W	M
Div'l Headquarters.	-	1	-	-	-	-
41st Brigade.						
7th Bn. K.R.R.C.	-	12	-	20	210	88
8th Bn. K.R.R.C.	-	12	-	24	194	92
7th Rifle Brigade.	1	8	-	20	200	75
8th Rifle Brigade.	7	6	-	49	263	107
41st T.M. Battery.	-	-	-	-	5	-
41st M.G. Company.	-	2	-	2	14	2
42nd Brigade.						
5th Ox & Bucks L.I.	-	7	-	13	111	33
5th K.S.L.I.	2	9	-	32	153	63
9th Bn. K.R.R.C.	2	9	-	22	143	66
9th Rifle Brigade.	5	10	-	62	156	101
42nd T.M. Battery.	1	-	-	1	5	1
42nd M.G. Company.	-	1	1	2	26	4
43rd Brigade.						
6th Somerset L.I.	3	12	2	41	203	143
6th D.C.L.I.	4	10	-	17	157	100
6th K.O.Y.L.I.	5	10	1	37	181	84
10th Durham L.I.	5	12	-	37	208	120
43rd T.M. Battery.	-	-	-	-	1	-
43rd M.G. Company.	-	3	-	8	23	10
Divl. Troops.						
Artillery.	1	11	-	11	52	-
Engineers, including Signals	-	1	-	4	27	3
Pioneer Battn. 11th L'pools.	-	2	-	14	58	1
R.A.M.C.	1	3	-	7	9	1
Div. Train.	-	-	-	-	-	-
Div'l Total,	37	141	4	423	2399	1094

(Signals - 1 OR Wounded).

Confidential.

vol 13

War Diary
of
Administrative Branch
14th (Light) Division

From 1st October to 31st October 1916.

Volume XL

WAR DIARY
or
INTELLIGENCE SUMMARY.

Army Form C. 2118.

(Erase heading not required.)

Instructions regarding War Diaries and Intelligence Summaries are contained in F. S. Regs., Part II. and the Staff Manual respectively. Title pages will be prepared in manuscript.

Place	Date	Hour	Summary of Events and Information	Remarks and references to Appendices
	1st		Nothing to report	
	2nd		14 K.B.A. Lithuanian Div. to line E. SOUPIR area and transfered to I ARMY	OFF
	3rd		14 F.B.A. transfered to GROUCHES area and later transfered to homesite to I ARMY	OFF
	4th		14 K.B.A. moved to FOSSEUX — LATTRE ST QUENTIN and HANGUETIN (HQ at FOSSEUX)	OFF
	5th		Recknd div at SAULTY & TINCQUES — 14 K.B.A. to Inf.Instruct. Depot O/C	OFF

1577 Wt. W10791/1773 500,000 1/15 D. D. & L. A.D.S.S./Forms/C. 2118.

WAR DIARY
or
INTELLIGENCE SUMMARY.

Army Form C. 2118.

Place	Date	Hour	Summary of Events and Information	Remarks and references to Appendices
	6th		14 KIA party ending of 12 LTM. draft of 7th	etc.
	7th		Wiring of STM completed	OAK
	8th		CRA 15th Div. Coopers estate of watching in come to HARLUS.	GSN
	9th		Move to Dupire	OAK
	10th		Arrived Dupire	OAK

WAR DIARY
INTELLIGENCE SUMMARY.

(Erase heading not required.)

Army Form C. 2118.

Place	Date	Hour	Summary of Events and Information	Remarks and references to Appendices
	11th		with bn.	
	12th		with bn.	
	13th		Major BURBARKER 2/O KOYLI comm Sir 14th Div and boy who has been with the Sim now taken to have up matter of ADMS look after. Cpt F GRUNDY DMC RE from 3 Coys here now command of 14 Inf Brig - Roddus camped at AUBIGNY.	CQR.
	14th			
	15th		working to asper	

WAR DIARY
INTELLIGENCE SUMMARY

Place	Date	Hour	Summary of Events and Information	Remarks and references to Appendices
	16th		return to Rouen	
	17th		Capt PEARN VIVIAN R.E. AsC DAQMG together this am with Col A H Lee hon brevet DAQMG gone to embark for England & assumes duty as DAQMG at the HQ School China Cross, Cambridge. Capt AKERMAN RFA Sd. Lt. temporary took over his duties.	Appx
	18		return to Rouen	
	19th		return to Rouen	
	20th		return to Rouen	

WAR DIARY
or
INTELLIGENCE SUMMARY.
(Erase heading not required.)

Army Form C. 2118.

Place	Date	Hour	Summary of Events and Information	Remarks and references to Appendices
	21		528 (4.5 How) battery R.F.A. arrived at SAM and moved to HAMOUSTIN preparing to proceed back any of 4th Div R.F.A. — This battery had come straight from England & I thought no horse masters.	
	22		nothing to report	
	23		nothing to report	
	24		Undue toward Friday by 15th Div to 25th as at night 26/27. A.A. RE Spicers will move out 12 R Bys.	
	25		37 Bde left relief of 41 Bgde (4) Divl. hd in to BEAUVILLE (H.Q. by Coy + 1 Hy) FIENCOURT (1 Hy) BEAUMETZ (2 Hy)	

Army Form C. 2118.

WAR DIARY
or
INTELLIGENCE SUMMARY.
(Erase heading not required.)

Place	Date	Hour	Summary of Events and Information	Remarks and references to Appendices
	26th		41st Lgt Mc moved to GRAND RULLECOURT and LOMBRIN — batt transport remained by the train. 41st & 3rd Bdes are working towards & IZEL LES HAMEAU	CRA
			36th Lgt Mc arrived 41st Lgt Mc Hd - the two new works Divs to FOSSEUX (HQ - 11ks) Coy/1 ks) WANQUETIN (2 hrs and Mc brs) lorries took up 2 Bns 36 Bde relieved to trenches FAUBOURG D'AMIENS brought from BRANQUETIN Bn Bn Hd party of [illeg] MG and hq coy took up the rmn on p 36 Hd & returned with remainder & 2 Lgts Hd. W at the post at Brick	CRA
			35th Lgt Mc Sailed HQ Lgt Mc Who tomorrow (11am, 1 kc) — Bures & LATTRES-QUENTIN (HQ by Coy and 1 kc) HAUTEVILLE (1 kc) MONTENESCOURT (1B) AGNEZ (1 kc) S Buses took up 2 Bns 35th Bde to Plan Victor Hugo ARRAS brought troops in for a ridge & LATTRE took up rmn Bn 35th Hd and brought back 2 Bns 41st to front & handed FAGNEZ - HASTE BAC processes Bdr 12 PAL by Mc & send & hny luggage.	CRA

Place	Date	Hour	Summary of Events and Information	Remarks and references to Appendices
JANUARY	27		Dr. Anthony KYLE CAUROY — 114 F.A. RE as Liaison Officer 14 KB. [illegible] of tonight.	
		4.30 p.m.	We moved to LIENCOURT [illegible] KERLENGUAT (1th.) DENIER (A. h. 6/5) SORIES ROIS (1.h.) LIGNEREUIL (1th bn 16/5) BLAVINCOURT (16/5) ANVIN (1.h.) Shire Log — 2/3 Field Ambulance moved to GIVENCHY? stations as found. Excuse form.	
		2.3 p.m.	7 Dr. moved to MANIN (MR 1 Rees) GIVENCHY (1 l6/5) BEAUFORT (1 l2 M-g 164) IZELLES HAMEAU (1 l2) [illegible] [illegible] the Nov. to LATTRE ST QUENTIN etc. Tues ALI, moved to ESTREE MANIN	OR/-
	28h		Lieut T.N. WATSON R.A.M.C. attached Highlanders moved a.s.s. as D.A.D.M.S. vice Capt. PH NN WYMAN R.F.C. Capt. HERMAN attached 8 office	ORd.

WAR DIARY
or
INTELLIGENCE SUMMARY.
(Erase heading not required.)

Army Form C. 2118.

Place	Date	Hour	Summary of Events and Information	Remarks and references to Appendices
	29⁴		Two allotted villages being thrown from Etr. Bream (MAIZIERES and MERDORGT) have been adjusted. W.I.H. back to AMBRINES (H.Q. & I/h.) MAIZIERES (I/h.) PENIN via MERDOINGT from from 40 K. Div. (I/h.) — One battery IZZEL LES HAMEN remained from N.F. by doused in BEAUFORT from them to new : PENIN.	O.h.h.
	30		No.3 H.h. moved the a.m. from RIVES to PENIN and GIVENCHY and to that by from AMBRINES & BEAUFORT.	
	30		return & report	
	31		noting to report	

C.H. Hanson Lt Col in Div
1/11/16

APPENDICES WITH OCTOBER WAR DIARY,

'A" & 'Q' Branches,

14th (Light) Division.

(I)   Casualties during month.

(II)   Reinforcements during month.

(III) Location of Units as on 1st October, 1916.

(IV)   Location of Units as on 17th October, 1916.

(V)   Table of Moves - 25th to 30th Oct, 1916.

14TH (LIGHT) DIVISION.

Appendix I

CASUALTIES DURING THE MONTH OF OCTOBER, 1916.

Unit.	Officers			Other Ranks		
	K	W	M	K	W	M
41st Infantry Bde.						
7th K.R.R.C.	-	-	-	-	24	-
8th K.R.R.C.	-	-	-	1	9	-
7th Rif. Brig.	-	1	-	2	5	-
8th Rif. Brig.	-	-	-	7	13	1
41st M.G. Coy.	-	-	-	-	1	-
41st T.M. Bty.	-	-	-	-	1	-
42nd Infantry Bde.						
5th Ox & Bucks L.I.	-	-	-	-	6	-
5th K.S.L.I.	-	-	-	-	4	-
9th K.R.R.C.	-	-	-	-	5	-
9th Rif. Brig.	-	-	-	3	6	-
42nd M.G. Coy.	-	-	-	-	-	-
42nd T.M. Bty.	-	-	-	-	-	-
43rd Infantry Bde.						
6th Somerset L.I.	-	-	-	1	4	-
6th D.C.L.I.	-	1	-	4	15	-
6th K.O.Y.L.I.	-	-	-	5	13	-
10th Durham L.I.	-	1	-	1	7	-
43rd M.G. Coy.	-	-	-	-	-	-
43rd T.M. Bty.	-	-	-	-	-	-
Div'l Troops.						
11th Bn. L'pool Regt.	-	-	-	1	1	-
14th Div'l Artillery.	-	2	-	-	-	-
14th Div'l Engineers.	-	-	-	-	1	-
R.A.M.C.	-	-	-	-	-	-
Div'l Train.	-	-	-	-	-	-
Div'l Supply Column.	-	-	-	-	-	-
Div'l Total.	-	5	-	25	115	1

Appendix II

14TH (LIGHT) DIVISION.

- * - REINFORCEMENTS - * -
Month of October, 1916.

```
Officers      101
Other Ranks  1803
             ----
Total :-     1904.
```

** ** **

S E C R E T.   O.C. 270.

14TH (LIGHT) DIVISION.

1st October, 1916.

LOCATION OF UNITS.

Unit.	Headquarters.	Transport.
Divisional Headquarters,	WARLUS,	WARLUS.
14th Signal Co. R.E.	"	"
25th Sanitary Section,	"	
14th Div'l Artillery,	Not yet rejoined.	
Headquarters R.E.	WARLUS.	WARLUS.
61st Field Co. R.E.	LE FERMONT.	LARBRET.
62nd Field Co. R.E.	AGNY.	WARLUS.
89th Field Co. R.E.	ARRAS.	WARLUS.
41st Infantry Bde H.Qrs,	BRETENCOURT.	
1 Battalion, } In	7th K.R.R.C.	MONCHIET.
1 Battalion, } defences,	8th K.R.R.C.	BEAUMETZ.
1 Battalion, }	7th R.B.	BEAUMETZ.
1 Battalion, RIVIERE.	8th R.B.	MONCHIET.
Machine Gun Company,	BRETENCOURT.	MONCHIET.
Trench Mortar Battery,	BRETENCOURT.	
42nd Infantry Bde H.Qrs,	DAINVILLE.	
1 Battalion, }	In	
1 Battalion, }	defences,	BERNEVILLE
1 Battalion, }		
1 Battalion,	DAINVILLE.	
Machine Gun Company,	DAINVILLE.	
Trench Mortar Battery,	DAINVILLE.	
43rd Infantry Bde H.Qrs,	Rue des Fours, ARRAS,	
1 Battalion, }	In	
1 Battalion, }	defences,	BERNEVILLE
1 Battalion, }		
1 Battalion,	ARRAS,	
Machine Gun Company,	ARRAS,	
Trench Mortar Battery,	ARRAS.	
11th L'pool R (Pioneers)	BERNEVILLE.	BERNEVILLE
14th Div'l Train H.Qrs,		
No. 2 Company,	BARLY.	BARLY.
No. 3 Company,		
No. 4 Company,		
42nd Field Ambulance,	GOUY.	GOUY.
43rd Field Ambulance,	WANQUETIN.	WANQUETIN.
44th Field Ambulance,	BARLY.	BARLY.
8th Motor Machine Gun Bty.	GOUY.	
No.14 Div'l Supply Column,	AVESNES.	
26th Mobile Vety Section,	FOSSEUX.	
Ordnance Store,	WARLUS.	
14th Salvage Company,	BERNEVILLE.	
Railhead,	SAULTY.	

- * - * - * -

Divisional School,	GOUY.	
Div'l Gas School,	BERNEVILLE.	

- * - * - * -

Headquarters,
  14th Division,
   1st October, 1916.

Appendix IV

S E C R E T.   O.C.305.

14TH (LIGHT) DIVISION.
LOCATION OF UNITS.

Unit.	Headquarters		Transport.
Divisional Headquarters,	WARLUS.		WARLUS.
14th Signal Co. R.E.	"		"
25th Sanitary Section,	"		"
14th Div'l Artillery H.Qrs,	"		
46th Bde R.F.A.	Rue des Capucines, ARRAS,		SIMENCOURT.
47th Bde R.F.A.	DAINVILLE.		SIMENCOURT.
48th Bde R.F.A.	BEAUMETZ.	(B/48)	SIMENCOURT.
		(A/48)	WANQUETIN.
		(D/48)	
14th D.A.C. (Nos.1,2 & 4 Secs)	FOSSEUX		FOSSEUX.
Advanced Section (No.3)	SIMENCOURT.		SIMENCOURT.
V/14 Heavy T.M.Bty,	DAINVILLE.		
Headquarters R.E.	WARLUS		WARLUS.
61st Field Co. R.E.	LE FERMONT.		LARBRET.
62nd Field Co. R.E.	AGNY		WARLUS.
89th Field Co. R.E.	ARRAS		WARLUS.
41st Infantry Bde H.Qrs.	BRETENCOURT.		
1 Battalion,	} In	7th KRRC	MONCHIET.
1 Battalion,	} defences.	8th KRRC	BEAUMETZ.
1 Battalion,	}	7th RB	BEAUMETZ.
1 Battalion,	RIVIERE.	8th RB.	MONCHIET.
Machine Gun Company.	BRETENCOURT.		MONCHIET.
Trench Mortar Battery,	BRETENCOURT,		
42nd Infantry Bde H.Qrs,	DAINVILLE.		}
1 Battalion,	} In		}
1 Battalion,	} defences		}
1 Battalion,	}		BERNEVILLE.
1 Battalion,	DAINVILLE.		}
Machine Gun Company,	DAINVILLE.		}
Trench Mortar Battery,	DAINVILLE.		}
43rd Infantry Bde H.Qrs.	Rue des Fours, ARRAS.		}
1 Battalion,	} In		}
1 Battalion,	} defences,		}
1 Battalion,	}		BERNEVILLE.
1 Battalion,	ARRAS		}
Machine Gun Company,	ARRAS.		}
Trench Mortar Battery,	ARRAS.		}
11th L'pool R (Pioneers)	BERNEVILLE.		BERNEVILLE.
14th Div'l Train H.Qrs,	}		}
No.2 Company,	} BARLY.		BARLY.
No.3 Company.	}		
No.4 Company,	}		
42nd Field Ambulance	GOUY.		GOUY.
43rd Field Ambulance,	WANQUETIN.		WANQUETIN.
44th Field Ambulance,	BARLY.		BARLY.
8th Motor Machine Gun Bty.	GOUY.		
No.14 Div'l Supply Column	AVESNES.		
26th Mobile Vety Section,	FOSSEUX.		
Ordnance Store,	WARLUS.		
14th Salvage Company.	WARLUS.		
Railhead,	AUBIGNY.		
Divisional School,	GOUY.		
Div'l Gas School,	BERNEVILLE.		

H.Qrs 14th Division,
  17th October, 1916

TABLE OF MOVES 25th to 30th Oct.

Unit.	25th/26th.	26th/27th.	27th/28th.	28th/29th.	29th/30th.	30th/31st.
41 Bde. H.Qrs.	Berneville	Grand Rullecourt.	Grand Rullecourt.			
41 M.G.C.	do.	do.	do.			
41 T.M.B.	Beaumetz	Sombrin	Sombrin			
Y.R.B.	Berneville.	Grand Rullecourt.	Grand Rullecourt.			
8 R.B.	Beaumetz	Sombrin	Sombrin			
3 K.R.R.	Simencourt	Grand Rullecourt.	Grand Rullecourt.			
8 K.R.R.	Barly	Barly	Sombrin			
44 F.R.	Gouy	Grand Rullecourt.	Grand Rullecourt.			
8 M.M.G. Bty.	Barly	Sombrin	Sombrin			
No.2. Coy Train.						
42 Infy Bde H.Qrs	Dainville	Fosseux.	Liencourt.	Liencourt.		
42 M.G.Coy.	do.	do.	do.	do.		
42 T.M.B.	do.	Gouy.	Denier & Sars-les-Bois.	Denier & Sars-les-Bois.		
5 Ox.& Bucks.L.I.	In the Line.	Wanquetin.	Lignereuil.	Lignereuil.		
5 K.S.L.I.	do.	do.	Ambrines.	Ambrines.		
9 R.B.	Dainville.	Fosseux.	Berlencourt.	Berlencourt.		
9 K.R.R.C.	In the Line.	Barly.	Ambrines.	Beaufort.		
No.3 Coy Train.	Barly	Wanquetin.	Izel-les-Hameau.	Givenchy-le-Noble		
43 F.R.	Wanquetin	Lattre-St-Quentin.	Manin	Ambrines		
43 Inf. Bde H.Qrs.	Arras.	do.	Beaufort	Beaufort.		
43 M.G.C.	do.	do.	Manin	Ambrines.		
43 T.M.B.	do.	do.	Givenchy-le-Noble.	Penin.		
6 Som.L.I.	In the Line.	Agnes-les-Duisans.	Izel-les-Hameau	Izel-les-Hameau.		
6 D.C.L.I.	do.	Hauteville.	Beaufort.	Maizieres		
10 KOYLI	do.	Montenescourt.	Manin Ambrines	Ambrines		
10 P.L.I.	Gouy.	Gouy.	Izel-les-Hameau.	Izel-les-Hameau.		
42 F.R.	Barly.	Barly.	Villers-sur-Simon	Doffine-Frame.		
No.4 Coy Train.						
14 Divl. TH.Qrs.	Warlus	Warlus.	Le Cauroy.			
H.Qrs. 14 Div Train.	Barly	Barly.	Etree-Wamin.			
25th San Sect.	Warlus.	Warlus.	Le Cauroy.			
14 Divl. Supply Col.	Avesnes-le-Comte.	Avesnes-le-Comte.	Avesnes-le-Comte.			
26th Mobile Vety Sect.	Fosseux.	Fosseux.	Lattre-St-Quentin.			
D.A.D.O.S.	Warlus.	Warlus.	Le Cauroy.			

Vol 14

Confidential

"War Diary
of
14th (Light) Division
Administrative Branch

From 1st November 1916 To 30th Novr 1916

(Volume #2)

Box 1879

1916 1st to 4th Original removed to WO 154/39

Original Removed to
W/O 154/39

Army Form C. 2118.

WAR DIARY
or
INTELLIGENCE SUMMARY.
(Erase heading not required.)

Instructions regarding War Diaries and Intelligence Summaries are contained in F. S. Regs., Part II. and the Staff Manual respectively. Title pages will be prepared in manuscript.

Place	Date	Hour	Summary of Events and Information	Remarks and references to Appendices
LE CAUROY	Nov 1st			
	2		Capt AKERMAN left R Office. Diam to his Room awaits to his D.A.Q.M.G. and left on leave pending instructions to his Battalion. As he has twice recommended to appointment as D.A.Q.M.G	OiK
	3			OiK

WAR DIARY
or
INTELLIGENCE SUMMARY.
(Erase heading not required.)

Army Form C. 2118.

Instructions regarding War Diaries and Intelligence Summaries are contained in F. S. Regs., Part II. and the Staff Manual respectively. Title pages will be prepared in manuscript.

Place	Date	Hour	Summary of Events and Information	Remarks and references to Appendices
	5th		Read Orders. Went out & the Line from the 12th Div. from an escort of 200 of the 11th Durhams for Hoppy [Doullens] Road with Div. who arrived Etrunne. Left G.H.Q. for the visit of Major WESTRUPP.	App
	6th		Officers received equipment from by 9 G. HQ. Class awarded at 8rd School. Their marquee between the returns and I sent them a vehicle for fatigue — discipline & line troops to enter cadre for school.	Appx
	7th		112 2/Lts. adjutant 8olish. E have 8is in the 8en y of GIVENCHY MANIN KEUFORT LIGNEREUIL & L BLAVINCOURT and occupy IVERGNY and BEAUDRICOURT. 41st 33 Relieve L'ITERGNY and also 42° 2/Lts, 43° 32nd from IDEL LES HAMEAU with 7 Privates will occupy the 41st Div. 144 41st MG by arrived to HANTEVILLE. Kemp and I move HQ to the evening to 2nd Battalion quarters at LIENCOURT kh. Febr. m. 6-10 by 11th D. 41° 32 Central bivouacs at GIVENCHY. We tell me Div vel 8eld Cartoon v/s tomorrow LIENCOURT 41st how & PPT HUUVIN. This will being used up by 3rd Div. at IVERGNY.	CHA.

WAR DIARY
or
INTELLIGENCE SUMMARY
(Erase heading not required.)

Army Form C. 2118

Place	Date	Hour	Summary of Events and Information	Remarks and references to Appendices
	8th		Brig received further instructions & prepare to move. Report & prepare the eight 1st 43rd Rde moved to new area HOUVIN HOUVIGNEUL MONCHEAUX MONTS TERNOIS BUNEVILLE (Piers fm Govy) Pt HOUVIN SERICOURT SIGIVILLE [illegible] (4th) 36th fm Govy) CANETTEMONT	
	9th		Railways blown up to PREVENT — to Applig to move to PREVENT.	
	10th		44th & 43rd Rdes move to L'ENCOURT & Quad Sd Ret Stri. 4th J. Indianh Cav. Bn. Rd Stas at GIVENCHY to move to Pt HOUVIN. 63rd I.I Coy and IVERGNY Lt Col V.B. BROUELL CNB Cof Ht TW R.E. apptd CRE 20 Divr. Inf. Capt. J.S. COURTAULD Adj Cft-us Dyjid Sttandtud 63rd	

Army Form C. 2118

WAR DIARY
or
INTELLIGENCE SUMMARY
(Erase heading not required.)

Place	Date	Hour	Summary of Events and Information	Remarks and references to Appendices
	11			
	12		Cpt contacted bgn w/ sgt mtr tgt to etni	
	13		etni mine (British) Russell Cpt AKERMAN BKM Lt LI appointed HQ Cpt	OAR
	14			

WAR DIARY
or
INTELLIGENCE SUMMARY

(Erase heading not required.)

Army Form C. 2118

Place	Date	Hour	Summary of Events and Information	Remarks and references to Appendices
	15th			
	16th			
	17th			
	18th			
	19th		Detachment of 11th King's despatched Pgt. to parade. working party 200 left BUNEVILLE for ARRAS in buses. Company transport lines were formed. BERNEVILLE and a P.S.L. were taken to Company lines stretched to H.Q. Company Train.	CAPN.

WAR DIARY
or
INTELLIGENCE SUMMARY.

(Erase heading not required.)

Army Form C. 2118.

Place	Date	Hour	Summary of Events and Information	Remarks and references to Appendices
	20			
	21			
	22			
	23		42 & 3 Lt.A.M.B. moved to 61.07.3.6.y RE to h/f C.E. 5th Corps. H.Q. h.g.Cy. 7th battery to 35th Bty. for work with Arm. Divn. Govt. Details in small parties being forwarded to R.E. at each new No. 3 Coy to 7th in movement. Interest his Lieut & Regt. to RAS being forward emergent — parish working party of 200 mn drawn — 200 in & RRA Rgt & 100 in 23 because his just been worked by	CDA
	24		H.Q. h.g.Cy. moved to LIENCOURT. 41st & 3rd Oct & W.26123 by car on 41st LYMA CDA 42 > 2tr changed to WARLINCOURT CDA	

1577 Wt.W.10794/1773 500,000 1/15 D.D.&L. A.D.S.S./Forms/C. 2118.

Army Form C. 2118.

WAR DIARY
or
INTELLIGENCE SUMMARY.
(Erase heading not required.)

Instructions regarding War Diaries and Intelligence Summaries are contained in F. S. Regs., Part II. and the Staff Manual respectively. Title pages will be prepared in manuscript.

Place	Date	Hour	Summary of Events and Information	Remarks and references to Appendices
	25			
	26			
	27			
	28		12 K Bgs hdqrs reoccupied the area vacated by 42? H.K.F.Bde on 23?	Apx
	29		nothing to report	Apx H
	30		Return ofممنع accumulated strength on relief by K.F. Corps.	Apx H

2/1/14

[signature] O.C. Army /14 Bn.

War Diary

SECRET.   O.C.323.

14TH (LIGHT) DIVISION.

LOCATION OF UNITS.

UNIT.	LOCATION.
14th Divisional Headquarters, 14th Signal Co. R.E. 25th Sanitary Section, D.A.D.O.S.	LE CAUROY.
Royal Artillery) Under	H.Q. WARLUS.
Royal Engineers,) 14th Divn.	H.Q. WARLUS.
11th King's L'pool Regt (Pioneers))	H.Q. BERNEVILLE.
41st Infantry Brigade H.Qrs, 41st Machine Gun Company, 41st Trench Mortar Battery,	GRAND RULLECOURT.
7th K.R.R.C.	SOMBRIN.
8th K.R.R.C.	GRAND RULLECOURT.
7th Rifle Bde.	SOMBRIN.
8th Rifle Bde,	GRAND RULLECOURT.
44th Field Ambulance,	SOMBRIN.
No. 2 Coy, Train,	SOMBRIN.
42nd Infantry Brigade H.Qrs, 42nd Machine Gun Company, 42nd Trench Mortar Battery,	LIENCOURT.
5th Ox & Bucks L.I.	DENIER.
5th K.S.L.I.	LIGNEREUIL.
9th K.R.R.C.	BERLENCOURT.
9th R.B.	MANIN and GIVENCHY-LE-NO?
43rd Field Ambulance,	GIVENCHY-LE-NOBLE.
No. 3 Coy, Train.	BEAUFORT.
43rd Infantry Brigade H.Qrs.	AMBRINES.
43rd Machine Gun Company,	BEAUFORT.
43rd Trench Mortar Battery,	AMBRINES.
6th Somerset L.I.	PENIN.
6th D.C.L.I.	IZEL-LES-HAMEAU.
6th K.O.Y.L.I.	MAIZIERES.
10th Durham L.I.	AMBRINES.
42nd Field Ambulance,	IZEL-LES-HAMEAU.
No. 4 Coy, Train,	FERME DOFFINE.
8th M.M.G. Battery,	GRAND RULLECOURT.
No. 14 Div'l Supply Column,	AVESNES-LE-COMTE.
26th Mobile Vety Section,	LATTRE ST.QUENTIN.
Salvage Company,	LE CAUROY.
14th Divisional Schools,	GRAND RULLECOURT.
Railhead,	AUBIGNY.

Headquarters,
  14th Division,
    1st November, 1916.

SECRET.   O.C.325/A.

14TH (LIGHT) DIVISION.

LOCATION TABLE.

H.Qrs, 14th Division.   )
14th Signal Co. R.E.   )   LE CAUROY.
25th Sanitary Section,   )
D.A.D.O.S.   )

14th Div. Artillery - under 12th Divn. H.Q. Warlus.
Headquarters, R.E.   LE CAUROY.
H.Qrs, 14th Div. Train,   IVERGNY.

41st Brigade Group.

H.Qrs, 41st Inf. Bde.   )
41st Trench Mortar Bty.   )   GRAND RULLECOURT.
41st Machine Gun Coy.   HAUTEVILLE.
  7th K.R.R.C.   SOMBRIN.
  8th K.R.R.C.   GRAND RULLECOURT.
  7th R.B.   SOMBRIN.
  8th R.B.   GRAND RULLECOURT.
61st Field Co. R.E.   HAUTEVILLE.
42nd Field Ambulance,   HAUTEVILLE.
No.2 Coy. Div'l Train.   SOMBRIN.

42nd Brigade Group.

H.Qrs, 42nd Inf. Bde.   )
42nd Trench Mortar Bty.   )   LIENCOURT.
42nd Machine Gun Coy.   )
  5th Ox & Bucks L.I.   DENIERS and SARS-LES-BOIS.
  5th K.S.L.I.   IVERGNY.
  9th K.R.R.C.   BERLENCOURT.
  9th R.B.   BEAUDRICOURT and OPPY.
62nd Field Co. R.E.   HONVAL - To IVERGNY
                                          Novr. 10th.
44th Field Ambulance,   IVERGNY - To LIENCOURT
                                          Novr. 10th,
No.3 Coy. Div'l Train.   LIENCOURT.

43rd Brigade Group.

H.Qrs. 43rd Inf. Bde.   )
43rd Trench Mortar Bty.   )   HOUVIN - HOUVIGNEUL
43rd Machine Gun Coy.   )
  6th Somerset L.I.   HOUVIN - HOUVIGNEUL.
  6th D.C.L.I.   MONTS-EN-TERNOIS and
                                   MONCHEAUX.
  6th K.O.Y.L.I.   SERICOURT and CANETTEMONT
                                                  (Temporary)
  10th Durham L.I.   SIBIVILLE.
89th Field Co. R.E.   MONTS-EN-TERNOIS.
43rd Field Ambulance,   PETIT HOUVIN.
No.4 Coy, Div'l Train.   SERICOURT.
11th Bn.King's L'pool Regt (Pioneers) BUNEVILLE.
26th Mobile Vety Section,   LA MONT JOIE FERME.

14th Div'l Supply Column,   Near FREVENT.
Salvage Coy.   LE CAUROY.
Divisional Schools,   GRAND RULLECOURT.
Railhead,   FREVENT.

Headquarters,
  14th Division,
    8th November, 1916.

SECRET.   O.C.330/A.

14TH (LIGHT) DIVISION.
LOCATION TABLE.

	LOCATION.	TRANSPORT.
H.Qrs, 14th Division) 14th Signal Co. R.E.) 25th Sanitary Section) D.A.D.O.S.)	LE CAUROY.	
14th Div. Artillery - under 12th Divn. H.Q.	WARLUS.	
Headquarters, R.E.	LE CAUROY.	
H.Qrs, 14th Div'l Train.	IVERGNY.	

41st Brigade Group.

H.Qrs, 41st Inf. Bde.)	GRAND RULLECOURT.	
41st Trench Mortar Bty)	HAUTEVILLE.	
41st Machine Gun Coy.	SOMBRIN.	
7th K.R.R.C.	GRAND RULLECOURT.	
8th K.R.R.C.	SOMBRIN.	
7th R.B.	GRAND RULLECOURT.	
8th R.B.	IVERGNY.	
62nd Field Co. R.E.	HAUTEVILLE.	
42nd Field Ambulance,	SOMBRIN.	
No.2 Coy, Div'l Train.		

42nd Brigade Group.

H.Qrs, 42nd Inf. Bde.) 42nd Trench Mortar Bty) 42nd Machine Gun Coy.)	GOUY	GOUY.
5th Ox & Bucks L.I.	ARRAS.	AGNEZ.
5th K.S.L.I.	DAINVILLE.	BERNEVILLE.
9th K.R.R.C.	ARRAS.	LOUEZ.
9th R.B.	BERNEVILLE.	SIMENCOURT.
61st Field Co, R.E.	ARRAS.	WARLUS.
No.3 Coy. Div'l Train.	GOUY.	GOUY.

43rd Brigade Group.

H.Qrs, 43rd Inf. Bde.) 43rd Trench Mortar Bty,) 43rd Machine Gun Coy.)	HOUVIN-HOUVIGNEUL.
6th Somerset L.I.	MONTS-EN-TERNOIS and MONCHEAUX.
6th K.O.Y.L.I.	SERICOURT
10th Durham L.I.	SIBIVILLE.
89th Field Co. R.E.	MONTS-EN-TERNOIS.
43rd Field Ambulance,	PETIT HOUVIN.
No.4 Coy, Div'l Train.	SERICOURT.(Nov.28th)
11th Bn. The King's (L'pool) Regt.	BUNEVILLE.
26th Mobile Vety Section,	LA MONT JOIE FERME.

- * - * - * -

44th Field Ambulance,	LIENCOURT.
No.14 Div'l Supply Column,	Nr. FREVENT.
Salvage Coy.	LE CAUROY.
Divisional Schools,	GRAND RULLECOURT.
Railhead,	FREVENT.

H.Qrs, 14th Division,
 24th Novr. 1916.

Confidential

Vol 15

War Diary
of
Administrative Branches
14th (Light) Division

From 1st Decr 1916 To 31st Decr, 1916

Volume 43

WAR DIARY
or
INTELLIGENCE SUMMARY.
(Erase heading not required.)

Army Form C. 2118.

Place	Date	Hour	Summary of Events and Information	Remarks and references to Appendices
LE CAUROY	Dec/1916			
	6/8		Div'l Art'y (less C/46, B/47 & A/48, and all howitzer batteries) relieved in line by 12th Div. Art'y, and marched to rest billets at ESTREE-WAMIN, BEAUDRICOURT & BERLENCOURT. C/46, B/47 & A/48 remained in the line. The howitzer batteries moved on 7th as follows: – D/46 to LA CAUCHIE (attached 30th Div), D/47 & D/48 to PAS (attached 49th Div) for practice.	1 mss.
	6		The 6th Capt Parsons, D.A.A. returned, went home sick (probably one month).	1 mss.
	8		42nd Inf. Bde relieved from fatigue work in forward area by 35th Div., & marched to billets at DENIER, SARS-LES-BOIS, GOUY-EN-TERNOIS, & MAGNICOURT.	mss
	10		About this time box respirators issued to the Division; firing engaged in protecting.	mss
	14		D/46, D/47 & D/48 rejoined their brigades in rest billets. 14th Div (Lieut Anstruther) commenced move to F, G & H Batteries, relieving 12th Div. 41st Bde to FLETE (H.Q. BRETENCOURT), 42nd to G (H.Q. DAINVILLE), & 43rd to H (H.Q. ARRAS). Move completed on 19th Dec.	mss
	16		Lt.Col. H.A. Boyce, R.F.A., joined to Mrienled R.A.Group. Lt.Col. Hamilton being sick.	
	19		Railheads – Ammunition AVESNES, Supplies SAULTY, from this date in divisional lorries. Div'l H.Q. moved to WARLUS.	

Army Form C. 2118.

WAR DIARY
or
INTELLIGENCE SUMMARY.
(Erase heading not required.)

Instructions regarding War Diaries and Intelligence Summaries are contained in F. S. Regs., Part II. and the Staff Manual respectively. Title pages will be prepared in manuscript.

Place	Date	Hour	Summary of Events and Information	Remarks and references to Appendices
WARLUS	Dec/1916			
	21		7 Officers from various formations attended R.T.O. and visited for a week. Supplies drawn from Railhead by Train Transport and sent from refilling points to Units by M.T. line transport, except in case of Div'l Art'y where supplies to Div'l Art'y Railhead were sent by lorry to refilling points & thence by Train Transport when by lorry to refilling point.	mss
	23		Div'l Art'y Railhead changed from WARLENCOURT to SAULTY, supplies still	mss
	27		Divisional Cinema opened at BERNEVILLE.	mss
	28		D/245 Bty arrived from LUCHEUX (VIII Corps area) at GOUY for instruction. Bepm lives at GOUY.	mss
	29		48' Bde R.F.A. from ETREE WAMIN & this for instruction. Waymakers at GOUY. There is a great shortage of fuel, especially coke, also of entertainers (men & women) his return reduced to 8lbs per L.D. horses).	mss
	31		Capt. F.T. NEALE S/ornithch, wounded & on this date, took to date up appointment of D.A.D.M.T. 4"Army, Replaced by Capt. T.C. TANNER 5/K.S.L.I.	mss

I.S. Bouyman
for A.A. & Q.M.G., 14th Div.

War Diary

SECRET.

14th Divn. O.C.341/1.

ADMINISTRATIVE ARRANGEMENTS
IN CONNECTION WITH 14TH DIVISION O.O.97.

TRANSPORT LINES. The Transport Lines of Infantry and Engineer Units will be as follows when the move is completed.

    41st Inf Bde.   BEAUMETZ and MONCHIET.
    42nd " "   BERNEVILLE.
    43rd " "   BERNEVILLE.
    Pioneer Battn.   BERNEVILLE.
    Royal Engineers.   WARLUS.

During the move 1st Line Transport will billet with the Unit to which it belongs until they move East of the DUISANS-DAINVILLE Railway or South of the ARRAS-DOULLENS road.

Town Majors concerned have been warned that extra transport will have to be accommodated in their villages.

EXTRA TRANSPORT. The extra transport allowed has been applied for. Lorries will not be detained overnight without permission.

SUPPLIES. Refilling Points will be as follows:-

	41st Inf Bde.	42nd Inf Bde.	43rd Inf Bde.
14th	SOMBRIN.	AMBRINES	SERICOURT.
15th	"	HAUTEVILLE.	LE CAUROY.
16th	"	HAUTEVILLE.	HAUTEVILLE.
17th	"	"	"
18th	FOSSEUX.	"	"
19th	FOSSEUX.	FOSSEUX.	FOSSEUX.

Supplies will be drawn from Railhead by the Supply Column Lorries for all Brigades beginning on 14th.
Supply wagons will remain with Units or return to Train Company billets at the discretion of O.C. Train.

TRAIN BILLETS. No. 2 Coy, Div'l Train will exchange billets with the Company 12th Div'l Train moving to SOMBRIN on the 17th instant.
Nos. 3 and 4 Coys Div'l Train will move to HAUTEVILLE until the corresponding companies 12th Div'l Train leave BARLY.
Headquarters Div'l Train will move to BARLY on 19th instant

SALVAGE Company Salvage Company will arrange to have a party in each village occupied to go round vacated billets and collect salvage. Transport will be provided as early as possible to remove salvage collected. Meanwhile it will be left in charge of Town Majors. The Salvage Company will move its Headquarters to WARLUS on 19th instant.

Mobile Vet'y Section. The Mobile Veterinary Section will move to FOSSEUX on 19th instant.

TOWN MAJORS. All Town Majors will be relieved by 12th Division by 24th instant. They will remain at their villages until they receive instructions to hand over.

AREA STORES. No Area Stores or tentage will be moved by any Unit and no stoves or shelters are to be pulled down.
Area Stores include lamps (other than equipment lamps at double scale) soyers stoves, wash basins, latrine buckets, braziers, chaffcutters etc.
Area tentage includes, tents (not included in Mobilisation Store tables), Armstrong and Nissen huts and tarpaulins.
These articles are to be handed over to the Town Majors of the villages concerned.

BATHS. All Bath and laundry arrangements of 12th Division will be taken over and run by A.D.M.S. 14th Division.

GUM BOOT STORES.
DRYING ROOMS. Gum Boot stores and drying rooms for clothes exist in all sectors and will be taken over and worked by Brigades.

CANTEENS. A Divisional Wholesale Canteen will be established at BERNEVILLE by 22nd instant.
Divisional Headquarter Canteen is at WARLUS.
Each Brigade has a Canteen.
Y.M.C.A. Establishments exist at ARRAS and DAINVILLE.
There is a Church Army hut at BERNEVILLE and a hut in course of erection at WARLUS for the use of Officers and men going and returning on courses, leave etc.

MEDICAL. 44th Field Ambulance at WARQUETIN will clear G and H. Sectors.
43rd Field Ambulance at GOUY will clear F. Sector.
Div'l Rest Station will be at BARLY.
Advanced Dressing Stations are at ARRAS at GROSVILLE.

AMMUNITION & TRENCH STORES. Copies of receipts given for Ammunition and Trench Stores will be sent by each Brigade to Divisional H.Q. within 48 hours of taking over the Sector by the Brig. General Commanding.

POSTAL. Mails will be delivered to Brigade Post Offices until the 15th inclusive.
Brigade Post Offices will be at Brigade H.Q..
On 16th, 17th and 18th there will be a Postal Refilling at HAUTEVILLE at 11 am daily.
Postal Refilling will be at WARLUS at 11 a.m. on and after 19th instant.
Mails not taken away by Units from Brigade P.O's or from Postal Refilling Point will be taken away and kept on charge by the Post Office Officials, until the following day's delivery.

Lieut. Colonel,
A.A. & Q.M.G.,
14th (Light) Division.

13/12/16.

O.C.341/1

Copies to :-

    14th Divisional Artillery
    C.R.E., 14th Division.
    41st Infantry Brigade.
    42nd   "   "
    43rd   "   "
    11th King's Liverpool Regt. (Pioneers)
    14th Divisional Signal Coy. R.E.
    14th Divisional Train.
    S.S.O., 14th Division.
    A.D.M.S., "   "
    A.D.V.S.   "   "
    A.P.M.,   "   "
    Camp Commandant.
    D.A.D.O.S., 14th Division.
    14th Divisional Salvage Coy.
    Divl. Claims Officer
    "G"
    VI Corps
    VI Corps H.A.
    12th Division.
     9th Division.
    35th Division.
    30th Division.
    D.A.D.P.S., VI Corps
    Town Major, ARRAS
    Supply Column

O.C.341/1

Copies to :-

    14th Divisional Artillery
    C.R.E., 14th Division.
    41st Infantry Brigade.
    42nd   "   "
    43rd   "   "
    11th King's Liverpool Regt. (Pioneers)
    14th Divisional Signal Coy. R.E.
    14th Divisional Train.
    S.S.O., 14th Division.
    A.D.M.S., "   "
    A.D.V.S.   "   "
    A.P.M.,   "   "
    Camp Commandant.
    D.A.D.O.S., 14th Division.
    14th Divisional Salvage Coy.
    Divl. Claims Officer
    "G"
    VI Corps
    VI Corps H.A.
    12th Division.
     9th Division.
    35th Division.
    30th Division.
    D.A.D.P.S., VI Corps
    Town Major, ARRAS

O.C.341/1

Copies to :-

    14th Divisional Artillery
    C.R.E., 14th Division.
    41st Infantry Brigade.
    42nd   "   "
    43rd   "   "
    11th King's Liverpool Regt. (Pioneers)
    14th Divisional Signal Coy. R.E.
    14th Divisional Train.
    S.S.O., 14th Division.
    A.D.M.S., "   "
    A.D.V.S.   "   "
    A.P.M.,   "   "
    Camp Commandant.
    D.A.D.O.S., 14th Division.
    14th Divisional Salvage Coy.
    Divl. Claims Officer
    "G"
    VI Corps
    VI Corps H.A.
    12th Division.
    9th Division.
    35th Division.
    30th Division.
    D.A.D.P.S., VI Corps
    Town Major, ARRAS

SECRET

OC/335/A

14th (LIGHT) DIVISION.

LOCATION TABLE

	LOCATION
H.Qrs 14th Division)	
14th Signal Coy. R.E.)	
25th Sanitary Section)	LE CAUROY.
D.A.D.O.S.)	
H.Q. 14th Div'l Artillery	LIENCOURT.
H.Q. R.E.	LE CAUROY.
46 Bde R.F.A.	ETREE WAMIN.
47 Bde R.F.A.	BEAUDRICOURT
48 Bde R.F.A.	BERLENCOURT
14 D.A.C.)	IVERGNY.
H.Q. 14th Div'l Train)	
H.Q.Coy. 14th Div'l Train	LIENCOURT

41st BRIGADE GROUP

H.Qrs. 41st Infantry Bde.)	GRAND RULLECOURT
41st Trench Mortar Bty.)	
41st Machine Gun Coy.)	LIENCOURT.
7th K.R.R.C.	SOMBRIN
8th K.R.R.C.	GRAND RULLECOURT
7th R.B.	SOMBRIN
8th R.B.	GRAND RULLECOURT
62nd Field Co. R.E.	IVERGNY
42nd Field Ambulance	HAUTEVILLE
No. 2 Coy. Div'l Train	SOMBRIN

42nd BRIGADE GROUP

H.Qrs 42nd Infantry Bde	AMBRINES
42nd Trench Mortar Bty.	SARS-LEZ-BOIS.
5th Ox & Bucks L.I.	DENIER & SARS-LEZ-BOIS
5th K.S.L.I.	GOUY-EN-TERNOIS.
9th K.R.R.C.	MAGNICOURT.
9th R.B.	AMBRINES
42nd Machine Gun Coy.)	
61st Field Coy. R.E.)	LIGNEREUIL
No. 3 Coy. Div'l Train	AMBRINES.

43rd BRIGADE GROUP

H.Qrs. 43rd Infantry Bde.)	
43rd Trench Mortar Bty.)	
43rd Machine Gun Coy)	HOUVIN-HOUVIGNEUL.
6th Somerset L.I.	
6th D.C.L.I.	MONCHEAUX
6th K.O.Y.L.I.	MONT-EN-TERNOIS & RUMEVILLE.
10th Durham L.I.	SIBIVILLE
89th Field Coy R.E.	SERICOURT
43rd Field Ambulance	PETIT HOUVIN
No.4 Coy. Div'l Train	SERICOURT.
11th Bn King's Liverpool Regt.	RUMEVILLE
26th Mobile Vety Section	LA MONT JOIE FERME.

-#-#-#-#-#-#-#-#-

44th Field Ambulance	LIENCOURT.
No. 14 Div'l Supply Column	near FREVENT.
Salvage Company	LE CAUROY
Divisional Schools,	GRAND RULLECOURT.
Railhead	FREVENT

-#-#-#-#-#-#-#-#-

Headquarters,
 14th Division,
  9th December 1916.

Duplicate War Diary

SECRET   O.C./350/A

14th (LIGHT) DIVISION
LOCATION TABLE

	Location	Transport
H.Qrs. 14th Division ⎫		
14th Signal Coy R.E. ⎬	WARLUS	
25th Sanitary Section ⎪		
D.A.D.O.S. ⎭		
H.Qrs. 14th Div'l Artillery	LIENCOURT	
H.Q. R.E.	WARLUS	WARLUS
46th Bde. R.F.A.	ETREE-WAMIN	
47th Bde. R.F.A.	BEAUDRICOURT	
48th Bde. R.F.A.	BERLENCOURT	
14th D.A.C.	IVERGNY	
H.Q. 14th Div'l Train	BARLY	
H.Q.Coy., 14th Div'l Train.	LIENCOURT	

41st BRIGADE GROUP

H.Qrs. 41st Infantry Bde.	BRETENCOURT	
41st Trench Mortar Bty.	BRETENCOURT	
41st Machine Gun Coy.	BRETENCOURT	MONCHIET
7th K.R.R.C.	BEAUMETZ	do
8th K.R.R.C.	In the line	BEAUMETZ
7th Rif. Bde.	BRETENCOURT	MONCHIET
8th Rif. Bde.	In the line	BEAUMETZ
61st Field Coy. R.E.	LE FERMONT	WARLUS
43rd Field Ambulance	GOUY	
No. 2 Coy. Div'l Train.	BARLY	

42nd BRIGADE GROUP

H.Qrs. 42nd Infantry Bde	DAINVILLE	BERNVILLE
42nd Trench Mortar Bty.	In the line	do
5th Ox. & Bucks L.I.	In the line	do
5th K.S.L.I.	AGNY	do
9th K.R.R.C.	In the line	do
9th Rif. Bde.	DAINVILLE	do
42nd Machine Gun Coy.	In the line	do
62nd Field Coy. R.E.	AGNY	WARLUS
No. 3 Coy. Div'l Train	BARLY	

43rd BRIGADE GROUP

H.Qrs. 43rd Infantry Bde	ARRAS	BERNEVILLE
43rd Trench Mortar Bty.	In the line	do
43rd Machine Gun Coy.	In the line	do
6th Somerset L.I.	ARRAS	do
6th D.C.L.I.	ARRAS	do
6th K.O.Y.L.I.	WANQUETIN	do
10th Durham L.I.	do	do
89th Field Coy. R.E.	DUISANS	WARLUS
44th Field Ambulance	WANQUETIN	
No. 4 Coy. Div'l Train	BARLY.	
11th Bn. K.L'pool.Regt.	BERNEVILLE & SIMENCOURT	
26th Mobile Vety. Section	FOSSEUX	

-*-*-*-*-*-*-*-*-*-

42nd Field Ambulance	BARLY	
No.14th Supply Column	AVESNES	
Salvage Coy.	WARLUS	
Divisional Schools	GRAND RULLECOURT	
Railhead	SAULTY	

-*-*-*-*-*-*-*-*-*-

Headquarters,
   14th Division.
     19th December 1916.

SECRET.   O.C./355/A.

14th (LIGHT) DIVISION.

LOCATION TABLE.

	Location.	Transport.
H.Qrs. 14th Division)		
14th Signal Coy. R.E.)	WARLUS.	
25th Sanitary Section)		
D.A.D.O.S.)		
H.Qrs. 14th Div'l Artillery	LIENCOURT	
H.Q., R.E.	WARLUS	WARLUS.
46th Bde. R.F.A.	ETREE-WAMIN.	
47th Bde. R.F.A.	BEAUDRICOURT.	
48th Bde. R.F.A.	BERLENCOURT.	
14th D.A.C.	IVERGNY.	
H.Q., 14th Div'l Train	BARLY.	
H.Q. Coy., 14th Div'l Train.	LIENCOURT.	

41st BRIGADE GROUP.

	Location.	Transport.
Hd.Qrs. 41st Infantry Bde.	BRETENCOURT.	
41st Trench Mortar Battery	BRETENCOURT.	
41st Machine Gun Coy.	BRETENCOURT.	MONCHIET.
7th K.R.R.C.	In the line)	
8th K.R.R.C.	BEAUMETZ)	BEAUMETZ &
7th Rif. Bde.	In the line)	MONCHIET.
8th Rif. Bde.	RIVIERE)	
61st Field Coy. R.E.	LE FERMONT	LARBRET.
43rd Field Ambulance	GOUY.	
No. 2 Coy. Div'l Train	BARLY.	

42nd BRIGADE GROUP.

	Location.	Transport.
H.Qrs. 42nd Infantry Bde.	DAINVILLE.	BERNEVILLE.
42nd Trench Mortar Battery	In the line.	- DO.-
5th Ox. & Bucks L.I.	AGNY.	- DO.-
5th K.S.L.I.	In the line.	- DO.-
9th K.R.R.C.	DAINVILLE.	- DO.-
9th Rif. Bde.	In the line.	- DO.-
42nd Machine Gun Company	In the line.	- DO.-
62nd Field Coy. R.E.	AGNY	WARLUS.
No. 3 Coy. Div'l Train.	BARLY.	

43rd BRIGADE GROUP.

	Location.	Transport.
H. Qrs. 43rd Infantry Bde.	ARRAS.	BERNEVILLE.
43rd Trench Mortar Battery	In the line.	DO.
43rd Machine Gun Company	In the line.	DO.
6th Somerset L.I.	ACHICOURT, ROEVILLE & ARRAS.	DO.
6th D.C.L.I.	ARRAS.	DO.
6th K.O.Y.L.I.	In the line.	DO.
10th Durham L.I.	In the line.	DO.
89th Field Coy. R.E.	ARRAS.	WARLUS.
44th Field Ambulance	WANQUETIN.	
No. 4 Coy. Div'l Train	BARLY.	
11th Bn. King's L'pool Regt.	BERNEVILLE & SIMENCOURT.	
26th Mobile Vety. Section	FOSSEUX.	

42nd Field Ambulance	BARLY.
No. 14th Supply Column	AVESNES.
Salvage Coy.	WARLUS
Divisional Schools	GRAND RULLECOURT.
Railhead	SAULTY.

Headquarters,
    14th Division,
        26th December, 1916.

Confidential

Vol/6

War Diary
of
14th (Light) Division
Administrative Branches

From 1st Jany 1917 to 31st Jany 1917

Volume #4

Army Form C. 2118.

WAR DIARY
or
INTELLIGENCE SUMMARY.
(Erase heading not required.)

Instructions regarding War Diaries and Intelligence Summaries are contained in F. S. Regs., Part II. and the Staff Manual respectively. Title pages will be prepared in manuscript.

Place	Date	Hour	Summary of Events and Information	Remarks and references to Appendices
	January 1917			
WARLUS	1		Following Honours awarded to Division in Gazette: 1 C.B. (Maj-Gen H.A. COUPER) 1 B.E. Col.	
	2		(Brig. Gen. SANDYS), 1 B.E. Lt. Col., 2 Bar Majors, 12 D.S.O.'s, 36 Mil. Crosses, 13 D.C.M.'s, 31 Men. Mentioned	Annd
	3		Officer of Divn. Offices in BEAUMETZ destroyed by shell-fire; records destroyed.	Annd
	4		14 Div. Supply Column moved from AVESNES to SAULTY.	Annd
	5		Two companies 1st Canadian Pioneers from AGNEZ-les-DUISANS arrived BERNEVILLE & SIMENCOURT	
	6		& a certain amount of trench-foot was reported - average 8 per diem.	Annd
	7/8		14th Div. "A.C." relieved 12th Div. "A.C." in the line (F, G & H Sectors).	
	8/9			Annd
	8		14th Div. transferred from VI to VII Corps. Area slightly readjusted, DAINVILLE being included.	
			Authority received to mount from both Thigh = 500 pm from VII Corps + 1000 from VI Corps.	Annd
			4 Cav. M.G. Sqn. (7 Off. 107 O.R. 18 horses) arrived AREAS. Transport at DAINVILLE.	
	9		Lt. Col. R.T. Bailey D.S.O. 11th Regt. appointed to command 142nd Inf. Bde.	Annd
	10		Lt. Col. R.C. MacLachlan, 8/R.B. appointed to command 112th Inf. Bde.	
			H.Q. 250 men of 20th Lanc. Fus. arrived DAINVILLE. 3 Off. 148 men of 235th A.T. Co. R.E. at SIMENCOURT.	Annd
			2 Sections 19th Kings Liverpools to MONCHIET.	Annd

Army Form C. 2118.

WAR DIARY
or
INTELLIGENCE SUMMARY.
(Erase heading not required.)

Instructions regarding War Diaries and Intelligence Summaries are contained in F. S. Regs., Part II. and the Staff Manual respectively. Title pages will be prepared in manuscript.

Place	Date	Hour	Summary of Events and Information	Remarks and references to Appendices
WARLUS.	January 1917.			
	11		Resting Battalion & 41st hrs Ride from BEAUMETZ & SIMENCOURT, moving & selecting Winter plan.	hrs
	12	4 OR. 2 SD OR. & 117th Manchester (30th Div) arrived BERNEVILLE.		hrs
		1 OR. 20 OR. & 181 Tunnelling Co arrived SIMENCOURT. Tpt 15/Cheshire SIMENCOURT & WARLUS.	
	14	30 OR. & 181 Tunnelling Co arrived BEAUMETZ. Tpt 15/Sherwood Forester BERNEVILLE & WARLUS.	
		New supply refilling point in good running order from GOUY-EN-ARTOIS. Triangle between P.30.(Ng.S.T.C. 1/40000). 43rd Hole group reported here.	hrs
	15.	42nd Hole front & new refilling point.	
		19 OR. & 90 men & horse & 181 Tunnellers arrived BEAUMETZ.	
		2 OR. 100 OR. & 4th Intendency Bn arrived SIMENCOURT.	
		Artillery preparation into Divl & Army Field MR. completed about this date. 48th Hole R.F.A. between Army 2nd & 4th Plts, & No 3 Section D.A.C. between its B.A.C. How? Battery made up to 6 guns, except 48 Hole	hrs
	16	41st Hole front & new refilling point. HQ. & HQ Co Train moved BARLY & BAVINCOURT.	
		Lt. H A LeMessurier S/or thicks replaced Capt. T. Tanner S/R.S.I. & embarked in Officers Instruction School & be relieved by 2 SP.C.	hrs
		A cease of mange reported in D/46 A.F.A.	

Army Form C. 2118.

WAR DIARY
or
INTELLIGENCE SUMMARY.
(Erase heading not required.)

Instructions regarding War Diaries and Intelligence Summaries are contained in F.S. Regs. Part II. and the Staff Manual respectively. Title pages will be prepared in manuscript.

Place	Date	Hour	Summary of Events and Information	Remarks and references to Appendices
WARLUS.	January 1917			
	17		Fall of snow, arrangements made for use of trans [sledges]. Re-adjustment of billets amongst Trmn Majors in VII Corps Area, the completed by 19th; much of the personnel for executing purposes is now being found by bn[?] coys.	1/ms
	18		S/Mt 105 O.R. Bedlam detach'd arrived Corps. Lieut Col Hamilton returned from sick to unit.	hms.
	19			
	20		Div Train moved to BAVINCOURT	12H
	21			
	22		1 Coy R.E. & 1 Coy Pioneers 30 Div available to C Scotts for work c/pink line	12H.

Army Form C. 2118.

WAR DIARY
or
INTELLIGENCE SUMMARY.
(Erase heading not required.)

Instructions regarding War Diaries and Intelligence Summaries are contained in F. S. Regs., Part II. and the Staff Manual respectively. Title pages will be prepared in manuscript.

Place	Date	Hour	Summary of Events and Information	Remarks and references to Appendices
	23			
	24			
	25			
	26		Patrols did not enter. No coal mined	O/H
	27		Patrols [illegible] yesterday morning [illegible]	
	28		TM Battery 30 [illegible] arrived at AUTHCOURT & took up position.	O/H
	29		Amongst the troops [illegible] there is no [illegible] [illegible] party from his div. Detached Canadian Party [illegible] SIMENCOURT	O/H

Place	Date	Hour	Summary of Events and Information	Remarks and references to Appendices
	30		Beginning of relief of Retiring units to rest by Bat's of 30 Bde, the covering of Battery waggons to rest being taken from 1st CRA in posns of Bivouac. Bat's of 30 Bde moving to rest being now covered by CRA 14 KD & from 6.30pm 30K Inf. 30K Bde advanced beyond KEYA on the MONCHIET on the gde REAUMEN the GOUY. 14 KD in Bivouac near BARRA to reorganise. Going to rest. Cuirs left in situ as expected attacks relieved by 30KRR. At 11p.m. Reinforced Reg't moved KERNEVILLE & DAINVILLE to move soon for HQ 30 Bde shortly about to arrive. 14st K.A. Turnpe by R.E mines at GOUY.	
			One 30 E Bde and 1 Bn Ptn 30 E Bde Pionrn mvmt to KERNEVILLE. Sept th 14 KDi arrived at GD RULLECOURT 9 Offices, 443 OR.	CMc CMc
	31		Retn of Bigds	

Ol Montrie BVC
ct Comdg 14 KDi
Jul 1 1917.

S E C R E T.   14TH (LIGHT) DIVISION.   A.A./364/A.

LOCATION TABLE.

	Location.	Transport.
Hd.Qtrs. 14th Division.		
14th Signal Coy. R.E.		
25th Sanitary Section		
D.A.D.O.S.	WARLUS.	
Hd.Qtrs. 14th Div'l Artillery		
H.Q., R.E.	WARLUS.	
46th Bde., R.F.A.	WARLUS.	
47th Bde., R.F.A.	ARRAS.	
48th Bde., R.F.A.	DAINVILLE.	
14th D.A.C. Advanced Section	BEAUMETZ.	
do. Remainder	SIMENCOURT.	
48th R.F.A., B.A.C.	FOSSEUX.	
A.48 and D.48 Wagon Lines	GOUY-EN-ARTOIS.	
Remainder	MONCHIET	
V. 14 Heavy T.M. Battery	SIMENCOURT.	
D.T.M.O.	DAINVILLE.	
	ARRAS.	

41st BRIGADE GROUP.

H.Q., 41st Infantry Bde.		
41st Trench Mortar Battery	BRETENCOURT.	
41st Machine-Gun Company	BRETENCOURT.	
7th K. R. R. C.	BRETENCOURT.	MONCHIET.
8th K. R. R. C.	RIVIERE	
7th Rif. Bde.	In the line	BEAUMETZ &
8th Rif. Bde.	SIMENCOURT	MONCHIET.
61st Fld. Coy. R.E.	In the line	
43rd Fld. Ambulance	LE FERMONT.	LARBRET.
No.2 Coy. Divisional Train	GOUY.	
	BAVINCOURT.	

42nd BRIGADE GROUP.

H.Q., 42nd Infantry Bde.		
42nd Trench Mortar Battery	DAINVILLE.	BERNEVILLE.
5th Ox. & Bucks L. I.	In the line.	do.
5th K. S. L. I.	In the line.	do.
9th K. R. R. C.	DAINVILLE.	do.
9th Rif. Bde.	In the line.	do.
42nd Machine-Gun Coy.	AGNY.	do.
62nd Fld. Coy. R.E.	In the line.	do.
No.3 Coy. Divisional Train.	AGNY.	do.
	BAVINCOURT.	

43rd BRIGADE GROUP.

H.Q., 43rd Infantry Bde.		
43rd Trench Mortar Battery	ARRAS.	BERNEVILLE.
43rd Machine-Gun Coy.	In the line.	do.
6th Somerset L.I.	In the line.	do.
6th D. C. L. I.	ARRAS, ACHICOURT & RONVILLE.	do.
6th K.O.Y.L.I.	ARRAS.	do.
10th Durham L.I.	In the line.	do.
86th Fld. Coy. R.E.	In the line.	do.
44th Fld. Ambulance	ARRAS.	do.
No.4 Coy. Divisional Train	WANQUETIN.	
11th Bn. The King's L'pool Regt.	BAVINCOURT.	
26th Mobile Vet. Section	BERNEVILLE.	

FOSSEUX.

※=※=※=※=※=※=※=

42nd Fld. Ambulance	BARLY.
14th Div'l Supply Column	SAULTY.
14th Salvage Coy.	WARLUS.
14th Divisional Schools	GRAND RULLECOURT.
Railhead	WARLINCOURT (for personnel)
do.	SAULTY (for supplies).
H.Q. Coy. Divisional Train	BAVINCOURT.

H.Q., 14th Div. 22-1-17.

Confidential

Vol 7 War Diary
of
4th (Light) Division
Administrative Branch

From 1st Feby to 28th Feby 1917

Volume 45

WAR DIARY or INTELLIGENCE SUMMARY

Army Form C. 2118.

Place	Date	Hour	Summary of Events and Information	Remarks and references to Appendices
WARLUS	July 1st		Capt BINGLEY Staff Capt RA 14 K.Div left the Division on appointment Heff Capt RA XVIII Corps. 8 K RA moved from BU Rn SIMENCOURT & GD RULLECOURT less works parties two strong to AGNEZ-lès-DUISANS and 250 strong to DAINVILLE. Pk RAR(C) moved from RIVIERE (14th Rdn) to SIMENCOURT. Adv Hr 14 K Div to RIVIERE. Rubin D. Lieut J Matthews was taken by St Di Hospital. Lt Hamilton A? T Hamilton from AGENVILLE Evng to the Division. Lt Col HARDING NEWMAN assumed the 8 K Div forward on CRA 14 K Di. PKRRC (less working parties so strong and ANERNEVILLE) moved to GD RULLECOURT. Rn = Fi RIVIERE SIMENCOURT relieved by 14 K Di.	
	2			
	3		In for SIMENCOURT to SOMBRIN – Hr for Fi to SIMENCOURT relieved by 14 K Di. Comd of F Huts moved to 14 K Di 10 a.m. – L St Vth RFA trans Hr Wr New lisst F lenten K4 E Bu. Lt Col ALL AQ FGD RULLECOURT.	

Army Form C. 2118.

WAR DIARY
or
INTELLIGENCE SUMMARY.
(Erase heading not required.)

Place	Date	Hour	Summary of Events and Information	Remarks and references to Appendices
	4		Maj Gen L. SANDYS Chg RA (9th Division) appointed as CRA XIX Corps. Lt Col HARDING NEWMAN took over duties of CRA. Pm 4/5 Bn from SIMENCOURT & SOMBRIN. Capt R F Nichols RFA attached to Q office from lately staff 42nd Div Arty.	
	5			
	6		Capt PRIDEAUX BRUNE returned to 9th KRRC as 2nd in command. 2nd Re Capt KRRC posted to Q office from Q office Capt Le Messurier Ox & Bucks L.I., Left Q office for G.	

WAR DIARY or INTELLIGENCE SUMMARY

Army Form C. 2118.

Place	Date	Hour	Summary of Events and Information	Remarks and references to Appendices
	7			
	8		Capt R.F. NATION Roy Fus. performed duties of DAQMG from 8.2.17 to 20.2.17 during absence on leave of Major I.W. WATSON A&S Highrs.	
	9		Supply train now is does late – actually arrived about 1 am 10th. Leave stopped for everyone except those entitled to travel by Mail boat.	

WAR DIARY
or
INTELLIGENCE SUMMARY.
(Erase heading not required.)

Army Form C. 2118.

Place	Date	Hour	Summary of Events and Information	Remarks and references to Appendices
	10		Supply tci nr 12 lorries 6 tr. Lieut P.A. COOKE 8th KRRC appointed acting S.T.T.O. and Q. 14th Div.	
	11		Supply tci - letr - Supply tci Sun 10th arrived about 2 p.m. - Supply tci Rigby J 2 p.m. - Major RICHARDS Wilshire joined S.K.S.L.I. in command. Capt ACKERMAN (Staff Capt 43rd L/F) took up his 6th VIII Corp on light appointment on St Q.M.G. Capt K.S.M. GLADSTONE 8th R.B. assumed duties Staff Captain 43rd Bde. Supply tci - letr - Supply tci Sun 11th arrived about 2 p.m. Reftilling 6 p.m.	
	12			
	13		Supply tci letr. The lorries in to our Gar. Capt TS BEAUMONT 18th Son Lancaster Regt arrived to take but a F.S.O. 2nd hule vice Capt G.S.R. PRIOR Gloucester Regt who departs as appointed on the Major 14th K.L.R. Tab.	

Date	Hour	Summary of Events and Information	Remarks and references to Appendices
14		Supply train now btn — arrived about 2 p.m.	
15		Supply train now btn moved about 8 p.m. began HEADE-HALDO RS arrived there at 4 pm 15 March 1974 on B.G. 2 bridge	
16		Supply train here — arrived 3 am 17th. hqrs HEADE-HALDO RS arrived here now Lt Col. 1/KO 2nd Bde. Major C.H.N. SEYMOUR 8so KRRC to command 8th KRRC	
17		Supply train here.	

Army Form C. 2118.

WAR DIARY
or
INTELLIGENCE SUMMARY.
(Erase heading not required.)

Instructions regarding War Diaries and Intelligence Summaries are contained in F. S. Regs., Part II. and the Staff Manual respectively. Title pages will be prepared in manuscript.

Place	Date	Hour	Summary of Events and Information	Remarks and references to Appendices
	18th		Major J.S. Hendry P/o 3 Bde left report KOSB I Corps. Thaw precautions came into force 7. a.m. to 21st inst	
	19th		Ashiya Major PRIDEAUX PRUNE took over command of CRA's command troops & KRRC	
	20th		Capt G.M. LEE P/o Roy. Fus. appointed Bde Major 43rd Inf Bde	
	21st		Capt F.C.C. EGERTON attached to Q Branch 14th Divn from 42nd Bde. Thaw precautions extended to 7am. 24th inst Q 671 d/ 20.2.17	
	22nd		Lt. Col. P.E. LEWIS psc RFA joined on temporary duty as A.A. & QMG	

WAR DIARY
or
INTELLIGENCE SUMMARY.

Army Form C. 2118.

Place	Date	Hour	Summary of Events and Information	Remarks and references to Appendices
	23.		Lt Col E.C.C. HAMILTON pre. DSO RFA AA & QMG evacuated sick to 20th C.C.S.	
	24.		Thaw precautions extended to 7. a.m. 26th inst. Q 722 d/ 23.2.17 Lt Col ... HIRSCH DAA & QMG 9th Divn appointed AA & QMG 14th Divn Capt H.S. ALTHAM 5th KRRC appointed DAA & QMG 9th Divn	
	25.			
	26.		Thaw precautions extended indefinitely through VII Corps area Q 225 d/26.2.17	

Army Form C. 2118.

WAR DIARY
or
INTELLIGENCE SUMMARY.
(Erase heading not required.)

Place	Date	Hour	Summary of Events and Information	Remarks and references to Appendices
	27ᵗʰ			
	28-		Major (temp & local Lieut. Col.) HIRSCH joined from leave in England on appointment as Staff Q.M.G. 14ᵗʰ Division. R./	

SECRET. O.C./372/A.

14TH (LIGHT) DIVISION.

LOCATION TABLE.

	LOCATION.	TRANSPORT.
Hd.Qtrs. 14th Division)		
14th Signal Coy. R.E.)		
25th Sanitary Section)	WARLUS.	
D.A.D.O.S.)		
Hd.Qtrs. 14th Div'l Artillery	WARLUS.	
H.Q., R.E.	WARLUS.	
46th Bde., R.F.A.	ARRAS.	
47th Bde., R.F.A.	ARRAS.	
14th D. A. C. Advanced Section	SIMENCOURT.	
do. H.Q.	FOSSEUX.	
V. 14 Heavy T.M. Battery	DAINVILLE.	
D. T. M. O.	ARRAS.	
61st Fd. Coy. R.E. 1 Coy. less 2 Secs.	ARRAS.	
do. 1 Off'r, 35 O.R.'s	WARLUS.	
do. Transport details		BERNEVILLE.
do. " less "		LABRET.
62nd Fld.Coy. R.E. 1 Section	DAINVILLE	
do. less 1 Section	AGNY.	

41st BRIGADE.

H.Q., 41st Infantry Bde.	GRAND RULLECOURT.)	
41st Trench Mortar Battery	GRAND RULLECOURT.)	
41st Machine-Gun Company	GRAND RULLECOURT.)	
7th K. R. R. C.	SOMBRIN.)	With
8th K. R. R. C.	GRAND RULLECOURT.)	Units.
7th Rif. Bde.	SOMBRIN.)	
8th Rif. Bde.	GRAND RULLECOURT.)	
43rd Fld. Ambulance	GOUY.)	
No. 2 Coy. Divisional Train	BAVINCOURT.)	

42nd BRIGADE.

H.Q., 42nd Infantry Bde.	DAINVILLE.	BERNEVILLE.
42nd Trench Mortar Battery	In the line.	do.
5th Ox. & Bucks. L.I.	AGNY.	do.
5th K. S. L. I.	In the line.	do.
9th K. R. R. C.	DAINVILLE.	do.
9th Rif. Bde.	In the line.	do.
42nd Machine-Gun Coy.	In the line.	do.
No. 3 Coy. Divisional Train.	BAVINCOURT.	

43rd BRIGADE.

H.Q., 43rd Infantry Bde.	ARRAS.	BERNEVILLE.
43rd Trench Mortar Battery	In the line.	do.
43rd Machine-Gun Coy.	In the line.	do.
6th Somerset L. I.	ARRAS.	do.
6th D. C. L. I.	ARRAS, ACHICOURT & RONVILLE.	do.
6th K. O. Y. L. I.	In the line.	do.
10th Durham L. I.	In the line.	do.
89th Fld. Coy., R.E.	ARRAS.	do.
44th Fld. Ambulance	WANQUETIN.	
No. 4 Coy. Divisional Train	BAVINCOURT.	
11th Bn. K. Liverpool Regt.	DAINVILLE & ARRAS.	do.
do. Hd.Qtrs.	DAINVILLE.	
26th Mobile Vet. Section	FOSSEUX.	

*o*o*o*o*o*o*o*o*o*o*o*o*o*o*

42nd Fld. Ambulance	BARLY.
14th Div'l Supply Column	SAULTY.
14th Salvage Coy.	WARLUS.
14th Divisional Schools	GRAND RULLECOURT.
Railhead	WARLINCOURT (for personnel)
do.	SAULTY (for supplies).
H.Q. Coy. Divisional Train	BAVINCOURT.

Hd.Qtrs., 14th Division, 4-2-17.

SECRET.

14TH (LIGHT) DIVISION.

LOCATION TABLE.

	Location.	Transport.
Hd.Qtrs., 14th Division ⎫		
14th Signal Coy., R.E. ⎪		
25th Sanitary Section ⎬	WARLUS.	
D.A.D.O.S. ⎪		
H.Q., 14th Div'l Artillery ...	WARLUS.	
H.Q., R.E.	WARLUS.	
46th Bde., R.F.A.	ARRAS.	⎫
47th Bde., R.F.A.	ARRAS.	⎬ SIMENCOURT.
H.Q., 14th D.A.C.	BARLY.	
14th D.A.C., No. 1 Section & Adv.Dump	SIMENCOURT.	
" " No. 2 Section ⎫		
" " 'B' Echelon ⎬ ...	FOSSEUX.	
V 14 Heavy T.M. Battery ⎫		
D.T.M.O.	... ...	ARRAS.

41st BRIGADE GROUP.

H.Q., 41st Infantry Brigade ...	GRAND RULLECOURT.	G.RULLECOURT.
41st Trench Mortar Battery ...	GRAND RULLECOURT.	
41st Machine Gun Company	GRAND RULLECOURT.	
7th K.R.R.C.	SOMBRIN.	SOMBRIN.
8th K.R.R.C.	GRAND RULLECOURT.	G.RULLECOURT.
7th Rif. Bde.	SOMBRIN.	SOMBRIN.
8th Rif. Bde.	GRAND RULLECOURT.	G.RULLECOURT.
61st Fld. Coy., R.E.	ARRAS.	BERNEVILLE.
43rd Fld. Ambulance	GOUY-EN-ARTOIS.	
No. 2 Coy. Divisional Train ...	DAVINCOURT.	

42nd BRIGADE GROUP.

H.Q., 42nd Infantry Brigade ...	ARRAS.	BERNEVILLE.
42nd Trench Mortar Battery ...	In the line.	do.
42nd Machine Gun Company ...	In the line.	do.
5th Oxf. & Bucks L.I.	RONVILLE.	do.
5th K.S.L.I.	ARRAS.	do.
9th K.R.R.C.	In the line.	do.
9th Rif. Bde.	DAINVILLE.	do.
62nd Fld. Coy., R.E.	ARRAS.	do.
No. 3 Coy., Divisional Train ...	DAVINCOURT.	

43rd BRIGADE GROUP.

H.Q., 43rd Infantry Bde.	ARRAS.	BERNEVILLE.
43rd Trench Mortar Battery ...	In the line.	do.
43rd Machine Gun Company ...	In the line.	do.
6th Somerset L.I.	In the line.	do.
6th D.C.L.I.	BERNEVILLE.	do.
6th K.O.Y.L.I.	DAINVILLE.	do.
10th Durham L.I.	ARRAS.	do.
89th Fld. Coy., R.E.	ARRAS.	do.
44th F.A.	~~BARLY~~ ARRAS	
No. 4 Coy. Divisional Train ...	DAVINCOURT.	
11th Bn. K. L'pool R.	ARRAS.	BERNEVILLE.

*o*o*o*o*o*o*o*o*

26th Mobile Veterinary Section ...	FOSSEUX.	
42nd F.A.	BARLY.	
14th Divisional Supply Column ...	SAULTY.	
14th Salvage Coy.	WARLUS.	
14th Divisional School	GRAND RULLECOURT.	
Railhead	WARLINCOURT (for personnel).	
do.	SAULTY (for supplies).	
H.Q. Coy. Divisional Train ...	DAVINCOURT.	

Hd.Qtrs., 14th Division. 8-2-17.

SECRET.

14th (LIGHT) DIVISION.

LOCATION TABLE.

	Location.	Transport.
Hd. Qtrs., 14th Division)		
14th Signal Coy., R.E.)		
25th Sanitary Section) ...	WARLUS.	
D.A.D.O.S.)		
H.Q., 14th Div'l Artillery ...	WARLUS.	
H.Q., R.E.	WARLUS.	
46th Bde., R.F.A. ...	ARRAS.	) Q.3.d.ref.1/40000
47th Bde., R.F.A. ...	ARRAS.	)
H.Q., 14th D.A.C. ...	BARLY.	
14th D.A.C. No. 1 Section & Adv. Dump	SIMENCOURT	
" " No. 2 Section))		
" " 'B' Echelon) ...	FOSSEUX.	
V 14 Heavy T.M. Battery)		
D.T.M.C.) ...	ARRAS.	

41st. BRIGADE GROUP.

H.Q., 41st Infantry Brigade ...	GRAND RULLECOURT.	G. RULLECOURT.
41st Trench Mortar Battery ...	GRAND RULLECOURT.	
41st Machine Gun Company ...	GRAND RULLECOURT.	
7th K.R.R.C.	SOMBRIN.	SOMBRIN.
8th K.R.R.C.	GRAND RULLECOURT.	G. RULLECOURT.
7th Rifle Bde.	SOMBRIN.	SOMBRIN.
8th Rifle Bde.	GRAND RULLECOURT.	G. RULLECOURT.
61st Fld. Co., R.E. ...	ARRAS.	BERNEVILLE.
43rd Field Ambulance ...		SCHOOL BERNEVILLE.
No. 2 Coy. Divisional Train ...	BAVINCOURT.	

42nd BRIGADE GROUP.

H.Q., 42nd Infantry Brigade ...	ARRAS.	BERNEVILLE.
42nd Trench Mortar Battery ...	In the line.	do.
42nd Machine Gun Company ...	In the line.	do.
5th Oxf. & Bucks. L.I. ...	DAINVILLE	do.
5th K.S.L.I.	RONVILLE.	do.
9th K.R.R.C.	ARRAS.	do.
9th Rifle Bde.	In the line.	do.
62nd Fld. Coy., R.E. ...	ARRAS.	do.
No. 3 Coy., Divisional Train ...	BAVINCOURT.	

43rd BRIGADE GROUP.

H.Q., 43rd Infantry Brigade ...	ARRAS.	BERNEVILLE.
43rd Trench Mortar Battery ...	In the line.	do.
43rd Machine Gun Company ...	In the line.	do.
6th Somerset L.I. ...	DAINVILLE.	do.
6th D.C.L.I.	In the line.	do.
6th K.O.Y.L.I. ...	ARRAS	do.
10th Durham L.I. ...	ARRAS.	do.
89th Fld. Coy., R.E. ...	ARRAS.	do.
44th Field Ambulance ...	ARRAS.	
No. 4 Coy. Divisional Train ...	BAVINCOURT.	
11th Bn. K. L'pool Regt. ...	ARRAS.	BERNEVILLE.

****

26th Mobile Veterinary Section	FOSSEUX.	
42nd Field Ambulance ...	BARLY.	
14th Divisional Supply Column ...	SAULTY	
14th Salvage Coy. ...	WARLUS.	
14th Divisional School ...	GRAND RULLECOURT.	
Railhead	WARLINCOURT (for personnel)	
do.	SAULTY (for supplies)	
H.Q. Coy. Divisional Train ...	BAVINCOURT	

ATTACHED.

179th Tunnelling Coy. ...	ARRAS.
181st " " ...	BEAUMETZ.
4th Entrenching Battalion ...	GOUY-EN-ARTOIS.
5th " " ...	GOUY-EN-ARTOIS.

28/2/17.

Vol 18

Confidential

War Diary
of
Administrative Branch
4th (Light) Division

From 1st March to 31st March 1917

Volume 46

Army Form C. 2118.

WAR DIARY
or
INTELLIGENCE SUMMARY.
(Erase heading not required.)

Instructions regarding War Diaries and Intelligence Summaries are contained in F. S. Regs., Part II. and the Staff Manual respectively. Title pages will be prepared in manuscript.

Place	Date	Hour	Summary of Events and Information	Remarks and references to Appendices
WARLUS	1917 March 1st		Thaw precautions withdrawn in III Army area from 2/3/17 except for roads closed to traffic. 46 H.D. horses & Train down with influenza.	R.
"	2nd			R.
	3rd		Major C.H.S. PAGE Middlesex Regt assumed duties as Bde Major 43rd Bde. Capt. J.C. COOKE assumed duties of Staff Capt. 41st Bde. 97 horses of Train with influenza	R.
	4th		106 horses of Train, influenza	R.

1577 Wt. W10791/1773 500,000 1/15 D. D. & L. A.D.S.S./Forms/C. 2118.

Army Form C. 2118.

WAR DIARY
or
INTELLIGENCE SUMMARY.
(Erase heading not required.)

Instructions regarding War Diaries and Intelligence Summaries are contained in F. S. Regs., Part II. and the Staff Manual respectively. Title pages will be prepared in manuscript.

Place	Date	Hour	Summary of Events and Information	Remarks and references to Appendices
	5			
	6		Refilling point of 42nd Bde Group moved to Q.19.d.3.2. 140 horses of Train sick in Fluenza	E.
	7			
	8		Refilling point of 43rd Bde Group moved to Q.19 a 5.2.	E
	9		156 horses of Train sick in Fluenza	E.

Army Form C. 2118.

WAR DIARY
or
INTELLIGENCE SUMMARY.
(Erase heading not required.)

Instructions regarding War Diaries and Intelligence Summaries are contained in F. S. Regs., Part II. and the Staff Manual respectively. Title pages will be prepared in manuscript.

Place	Date	Hour	Summary of Events and Information	Remarks and references to Appendices
	10		Divisional Ammunition dump started at RONVILLE, with 600 boxes of S.A.A.	E.
	11		Horse alspinning St.S' Amm" Dump set on fire by German shell. The S.A.A. boxes were got clear of the fire. Hot weather precautions ordered in VII Corps.	E.
	12			E.
	13		166 horses of Train with in/Auenga and 16 for light duty.	E.
	14		Dumps selected in GOUY for D.A.D.O.S. Salvage and Surplus kits.	E.

Army Form C. 2118.

WAR DIARY
or
INTELLIGENCE SUMMARY.
(Erase heading not required.)

Instructions regarding War Diaries and Intelligence Summaries are contained in F.S. Regs., Part II. and the Staff Manual respectively. Title pages will be prepared in manuscript.

Place	Date	Hour	Summary of Events and Information	Remarks and references to Appendices
	15		Capt EGERTON left to join 1/5th Gloucester Regt on completion of attachment.	E.
	16		Detonating party commenced work at Div'l Grenade dump North of CITADELLE ARRAS.	E.
	17		Detonating of Stokes ammunition began at billet 37 RONVILLE.	E.
	18		Capt NATION left to join 2nd Batt'n Roy. Fus. on completion of attachment.	E.
	19		2nd Cpl HIRSCH standing Evacuated sick to C.C.S.	E.
	20			

WAR DIARY
or
INTELLIGENCE SUMMARY.
(Erase heading not required.)

Army Form C. 2118.

Place	Date	Hour	Summary of Events and Information	Remarks and references to Appendices
	21			
	22		232 Bde FA & TMC moved into BERNEVILLE. Village very crowded. Had to put up men in baths.	E.
	23		Capt H.B. Moore M.C. Staff Capt 42nd I Bde appointed S.T.A.A. & QMG 14th Div. vice Lt Col HIRSCH evacuated sick. Remaining HdQrs & 2 Sects 14 DAC moved into SIMENCOURT	E.
	24		Lt Col P.E. LEWIS RA appointed A.A. & QMG 14th Divn authority A.G./Appointments/65 dated 23/3/17	E.
	25		Lieut M.T. COSSAR relieved from Town Major MONCHIET to rejoin 7th R.B.	E.
	26			
	27			
	28		8,000 Rations dumped in Div: Ration dump, The Arsenal Arras.	E.

Army Form C. 2118.

WAR DIARY
or
INTELLIGENCE SUMMARY.
(Erase heading not required.)

Place	Date	Hour	Summary of Events and Information	Remarks and references to Appendices
	29		41st 42nd & 43rd Brigades began to draw ammunition for Brigade dumps from Divisional Dump.	E.
	30			
	31		Lieut N.T. COSSAR appointed to assist Div. Grenade Officer in charge of Div. Ammn: Dump. Cinema closed. To be opened as Surplus kit Store tomorrow	E. E.

E. Nuin Lt.Col.
A.A. & Q.M.G.
14th High. Div.

S E C R E T. 14th (Light) DIVISION. O.C./406/A.

LOCATION TABLE.

	Location.	Transport.
Hd. Qrs. 14th Division)		
14th Signal Co. R.E.)	WARLUS	
25th Sanitary Section)		
D.A.D.O.S.)		
H.Q., 14th Div'l Artillery ...	WARLUS	
H.Q., R.E.	WARLUS	
46th Bde. R.F.A.	ARRAS	
47th Bde. R.F.A.	ARRAS	
H.Q., 14th D.A.C.	BARLY	
14th D.A.C. No.1 Sec. & Adv. Dump ...	SIMENCOURT *all in 22/2/17*	
" " No.2 Sec.		
" " 'B' Echelon	~~FOSSEUX~~	
D.T.M.O.)		
V 14th Heavy T.M. Battery) ...	ARRAS	

41st BRIGADE GROUP.

H.Q., 41st Inf. Brigade	GOUY	
41st T.M. Battery ...	GOUY *SOMBRIN*	*SOMBRIN*
41st M.G. Company ...	~~GRAND RULLECOURT~~	G. RULLECOURT
7th K.R.R.C.	SIMENCOURT	BERNEVILLE
8th K.R.R.C.	FOSSEUX	"
7th R.B.	GOUY	"
8th R.B.	DAINVILLE	"
61st Field Coy., R.E. ...	ARRAS	"
43rd Field Ambulance ...	SCHOOL BERNEVILLE	
No. 2 Coy., Divisional Train ...	BAVINCOURT	

42nd BRIGADE GROUP.

H.Q., 42nd Brigade	ARRAS	BERNEVILLE
42nd T.M. Battery ...	In the Line.	
42nd M.G. Company ...	In the Line	BERNEVILLE
5th Oxf. & Bucks. L.I. ...	SOMBRIN	SOMBRIN
5th K.S.L.I.	In the Line	BERNEVILLE
9th K.R.R.C.	SOMBRIN	SOMBRIN
9th R.B.	RONVILLE	BERNEVILLE
62nd Field Coy., R.E. ...	ARRAS	BERNEVILLE
No. 3 Co., Divisional Train ...	BAVINCOURT	

43rd BRIGADE GROUP.

H.Q., 43rd Inf. Brigade ...	ARRAS	BERNEVILLE
43rd T.M. Battery ...	In the Line	
43rd M.G. Company ...	In the Line	BERNEVILLE
6th Somerset L.I. ...	In the Line	"
6th D.C.L.I.	ARRAS	"
6th K.O.Y.L.I. ...	GRAND RULLECOURT	G. RULLECOURT
10th Durham L.I. ...	GRAND RULLECOURT	"
89th Field Co., R.E. ...	ARRAS	BERNEVILLE
44th Field Ambulance ...	ARRAS	
No. 4 Coy., Divisional Train ...	BAVINCOURT	
11th Bn. K. Liverpool Regt. ...	ARRAS	BERNEVILLE

26th Mobile Vet'y Section. ...	FOSSEUX	
42nd Field Ambulance. ...	BARLY	
14th Div'l Supply Column ...	SAULTY	
14th Salvage Coy. ...	WARLUS	
14th Div'l School ...	GRAND RULLECOURT	
Railhead	WARLINCOURT (personnel)	
"	SAULTY (supplies)	
H.Q., 14th Divisional Train ...	BAVINCOURT	
Div'l Claims Officer. ...	WANQUETIN	

ATTACHED.

179th Tunnelling Coy. R.E. ...	ARRAS.	
"P" Coy. Special R.E. ...	ACHICOURT.	

18-3-17.

Confidential

War Diary   Administrative Branch
       14th Light Division.
April 1st to April 30th 1917.

Army Form C. 2118.

WAR DIARY
or
INTELLIGENCE SUMMARY.
(Erase heading not required.)

Instructions regarding War Diaries and Intelligence Summaries are contained in F. S. Regs., Part II. and the Staff Manual respectively. Title pages will be prepared in manuscript.

Place	Date	Hour	Summary of Events and Information	Remarks and references to Appendices
WARLUS	1917 April 1st		Div! Train moved to GOUY near new railhead. M.X sent to SIMENCOURT. Surplus kit Store opened at Cinema Theatre BERNEVILLE for all units of 14 division. Under charge of Town Major BERNEVILLE & a guard. Water tank & pump completed at spring in moat of CITADELLE for filling petrol tins for carrying up water. 2,000 petrol tins received from Corps.	E
	2nd		Conference at Corp's H.Q: at which AA & QMG & O-division attended to discuss question connected with Operations.	E
	3rd		AA & QMG and DAA & QMG went round Sir! Amm" dumps, Ration dumps, Tank store & arranged details for stacking, filling petrol tins.	E
	4th		Brigade ammunition dumps completed. Preliminary bombardment begun.	E
	5th		Selected sites at G. 26.c. for west of CITADELLE ARRAS for advanced wagon lines of 47th and 232nd Bdes R.F.A.	E
	6th		Personnel withdrawn from battalion under S.S. 135 LE SOUICH and BREVILLERS. Total about 83 Officers 1442 O.R. Attached for rations to Corps Reinforcement depot BOUQUE MAISON.	E

Army Form C. 2118.

WAR DIARY
or
INTELLIGENCE SUMMARY.
(Erase heading not required.)

Instructions regarding War Diaries and Intelligence Summaries are contained in F. S. Regs., Part II. and the Staff Manual respectively. Title pages will be prepared in manuscript.

Place	Date	Hour	Summary of Events and Information	Remarks and references to Appendices
	7		Arrangements made with Town Major BERNEVILLE and SIMENCOURT for billeting of troops of 17th Div: coming in. Completed drawing and iss: of 3 days iron + oat rations for Z+1, Z+2, o Z+3 days.	E.
	8		Refilling for infantry at 5.30 a.m. Last day of normal supply. Pack animals went up to forward transport lines in moat of CITADELLE. Div: Train drew 1 days supply & remain loaded. DADOS stores went back to GOUY.	E
	9		Attack on enemy's lines along whole front of Third Army. 14th Div: formed first objective by 11. a.m. 43rd Bde pack animals moved forward from CITADELLE to BEAURAINS. 600 prisoners passed through Div: Cage. Total estimated infantry casualties up to 10.12 p.m. 57 officers 1350 O.R. Arrangements for sending up ration + water by pack animals worked well. Party of 40 men under Div Burial officer opened new Cemetery on TELEGRAPH HILL also new Cemetery in RONVILLE G 34. a 6.8. for dead from Adv: Dressing Station. German prisoners utilized to carry wounded back to A.D.S.	E.

WAR DIARY
or
INTELLIGENCE SUMMARY.
(Erase heading not required.)

Army Form C. 2118.

Place	Date	Hour	Summary of Events and Information	Remarks and references to Appendices
	10th		41st Inf Bde went forward to attack WANCOURT. Pack animals sent forward to RONVILLE. Rations & water sent up by pack to each brigade.	
	11th		42nd & 43rd Inf Bdes relieved by 149th & 151st of 50th Divn and sent to WANQUETIN and GOUVES areas respectively. Rum & hot tea arranged for them on arrival. Lorries to carry blankets & packs from pack store.	
	12th		Relief of 41st Inf Bde begun. 2 batts withdrawn to ARRAS. 42nd & 43rd to HABARCQ and MANIN areas. Burying party provided by 50th Divn. Cemetery on Telegraph HILL contains 120 dead of 14th Divn.	
	13th		7th KRRC taken to MONCHET on buses. 8th RB & 8th KRRC into ARRAS. Transport arrangements for move to back area see App A.	App A.
	14th		3 batts 41st Bde to MONCHET. Remainder of Divn to GRAND RULLECOURT area less Divl Hdqrs remaining at WARLUS. Supply direct to units by Divl Train. BSC lorries employed on transport of blankets & packs.	

Army Form C. 2118.

WAR DIARY
or
INTELLIGENCE SUMMARY.
(Erase heading not required.)

Place	Date	Hour	Summary of Events and Information	Remarks and references to Appendices
	15		Accurate casualties for period April 9–12 completed as follows:— Killed Off 26 OR 280. Wounded Off 63 OR 1199. Missing Off 1 OR 228. Total Off 90 OR 1707. Estimated casualties were Off 82 OR 2018.	
	16		42nd I.B. supplied by D.S.C. to refilling point near LIENCOURT. Remainder of division supplied by Div Train. No 1 Co Train moved to BERNEVILLE for supply of 14th DA attached to 50th Div. Personnel left behind at LE SOUICH under SS 135 rejoined their units together with available reinforcements from the Depôt batts at BOURQUEMAISON. Practice ammunition drawn from No 7 dump SIMENCOURT & issued to Bstn by 3 DAC wagons.	E.
	17		Burial party completed burying the dead in action 9–12. 19 Officers and 304 other ranks buried in the Cemeteries at M.4.b.2.5. M.12.b.33. N.1.a.6.1. and N.15.a.5.5. Lieut CLIFTON appointed Off k Butter + Lanncher.	E.
	18		AA.QMG went round Brigades with G.O.C. and discussed working and possible improvements on the transport + supply arrangements during operations.	E.

WAR DIARY
or
INTELLIGENCE SUMMARY.
(Erase heading not required.)

Army Form C. 2118.

Place	Date	Hour	Summary of Events and Information	Remarks and references to Appendices
	19		Formation of a Divisional Company ordered under Command of Lieut C. RYAN 6 Som. L.I. to contain all men on Divisional employ, who are temporarily unfit. All men to be inspected weekly & fit men returned at once to their units.	Z.
	20		Went round Brigade with G.O.C.	
	21		Rail head for N.T. Div. changed to ARRAS. Arrangements made for N.T. Co. Train to go to RONVILLE and draw direct from rail head.	Z.
	22		Went to VI Corps H.Q.rs to discuss location & hutting of Div. H.Q.rs in forward area. Brigade ordered to move forward to the BARLY - STULTY - POMMIER area	
	23		Brigade moved to new area. Div'l Train cleared pack train & dumped.	
BAILLEUL-MONT	24		Div. H.Q.rs WARLUS to BAILLEULMONT. Form additional lorries required for the move. Billetting accommodation but found.	
	25		42nd Bde moved up into line in the HARP to relieve a Bde of 50th Div. Left their blankets dumped in billets vacated.	

WAR DIARY
or
INTELLIGENCE SUMMARY.
(Erase heading not required.)

Army Form C. 2118.

Place	Date	Hour	Summary of Events and Information	Remarks and references to Appendices
ARRAS	26		Div H.Q[rs] moved from BAILLEULMONT, G.O.C. & branch Signals + CRE to dugouts on East slope of TELEGRAPH Hill, Q Branch + remainder of H.Q[rs] to ARRAS. 41" Role into line. Salvage Co moved into ACHICOURT.	R
	27		Selected site for Salvage camp + forward dump alongside of Decauville railway at N.13 central 1000 x N of Neuville Vitasse. Burial parts + staff moved into ACHICOURT.	R
	28		Pitched 20 tents at N.13 central for Chaplain, burial staff + party and Salvage Co. Then marched in from ACHICOURT.	R
	29		Baths started at ACHICOURT for the division. Salvage Co began salving + formed dump at N.13 central on the Decauville railway.	R
	30.		Selected new site for Div. H.Q. west of WANCOURT at N.13 d. Applied to VII Corps for 20 NISSEN huts + 40 tents.	R

E. Division.

Supply & Transport arrangements in connection
move of the Division to back area.

1. The Supply Wagons of the Divisional Train will deliver supplies to all units of the Division tomorrow at their new billets. Divisional H.Q. does not move till April 15th.

2. Nos. 3 and 4 Companies of the Divisional Train will billet tomorrow (14th) after delivery in LIENCOURT and SUS St. LEGER, respectively.

3. On 15th Nos. 3 and 4 Companies will draw from Refilling Point GOUY. No. 4 Company will deliver to Units of 43rd Brigade Group, but No. 3 Company will dump rations for 42nd Brigade Group at a point on the LE CAUROY - LIENCOURT Road near LIENCOURT for all Units of the Group not actually in LIENCOURT, where First Line Transport must pick up.

On 15th the 41st Brigade Group and No. 2 Company of the Train move to GRAND RULLECOURT and SOMBRIN. The Supply Company billeting at SOMBRIN.

The Company will draw from Refilling Point GOUY and deliver to Units on 15th and 16th.

4. The Divisional Supply Column will deliver to Refilling Points as under:-

17th & onwards	41st Bde. Group	on Road SOMBRIN - GRAND RULLECOURT Central.
16th & onwards	42nd Bde. Group (With Div. H.Q.)	on Road LE CAUROY - LIENCOURT near LIENCOURT.
16th & onwards	43rd Bde. Group	on Road WARLUZEL - SUS St.LEGER Central near Cross Roads.

Refilling will be at 9-30 a.m.

5. Four lorries of the 14th Sub. Park will report at fuel dump GOUY tomorrow, April 14th, at or before noon, to distribute fuel in the various villages in proportion to numbers as arranged by S.S.O.

From these coal dumps Brigades will arrange for a sufficient proportion of the coal to be allotted to baths.

6. Lorries from Supply Column in following proportion will be detailed to help the move of troops, as they become available before or after clearing pack train of supplies:-
   Brigade H.Q.   2   Battalion   2
   M.G.C.   1   Field Coy.   1

The time at which these lorries will be available for transport depends on the time at which the Pack Train comes in and will be settled by the O.C. Divisional Supply Column. As they may be sent early in the morning Units will be ready to load them at any hour from 6 a.m. onwards. Lorries will on no account be delayed.

7. On 14th the Divisional Supply Column will dump supplies at GOUY for Divisional Train to pick up on the 15th.

On 15th the Divisional Supply Column will stand loaded to deliver to Refilling Points on the 16th, except for the lorries serving the 41st Brigade Group which will dump at GOUY on 15th in order to be free for supplying transport to the 41st Brigade Group for their move on the 15th.

8. Baggage Wagons will be returned to Units.

9. Railhead will be changed from GOUY to SAULTY probably on the 16th.

10. From 15th instant Divisional H.Q., Signal Coy., Mobile Vet'y Section, D.A.D.O.S. and A.P.M. will refill with 42nd Brigade Group and 11th Bn. King's Liverpool Rgt. with 41st Brigade Group.

E. Lewis L. Col.
A.A. & Q.M.G.,
14th (Light) Division.

13/4/1917.

S E C R E T.

14TH (LIGHT) DIVISION.

O.C./118/A.

LOCATION TABLE.

	Location.	Transport.
Hd.Qtrs. ('G' Staff) (C.R.A.) (C.R.E.) ('Q' Staff)	N.7.d.2.5.	
Div'l Artillery, 'Q' Staff	No.1 BOULEVARD VAUBAN.	
14th Signal Coy. R.E.	No.1 RUE L'ABBE HALLOUIN.	
A.D.M.S.	DITTO.	
A.D.V.S.	No.12 BOULEVARD CARNOT.	
A.P.M.	DITTO	
D.A.D.O.S.	DITTO.	
Hd.Qtrs., Div'l Train	No.53 RUE L'ABBE HALLOUIN.	
Camp Commandant	No.2 BOULEVARD VAUBAN.	
	No.1 RUE L'ABBE HALLOUIN.	

-----:0:-----

Hd.Qtrs., 41st Infantry Brigade   N.7.d.4.3.
41st Machine Gun Company)
41st Trench Mortar Battery)
7th K.R.R.C.)
8th K.R.R.C.) ... In support.   RONVILLE.
7th R.B.)
8th R.B.)

-----:0:-----

Hd.Qtrs., 42nd Infantry Brigade   N.15.d.5.2
42nd Machine Gun Company)
42nd Trench Mortar Battery)
5th Oxf. & Bucks. L.I.)
5th K.S.L.I.) ... In the line.   RONVILLE.
9th K.R.R.C.)
9th R.B.)

-----:0:-----

Hd.Qtrs., 43rd Infantry Brigade   N.7.a.3.8
43rd Machine Gun Company)
43rd Trench Mortar Battery)
6th Somerset L.I.)
6th D.C.L.I.) ... In reserve.   RONVILLE.
6th K.O.Y.L.I.)
10th Durham L.I.)

-----:0:-----

11th Bn. K. Liverpool Regt. ... 15 RUE EMILE LANGLET.

-----:0:-----

61st Field Coy. R.E.		
62nd " " "	N.20.b.6.8.)	
89th " " "	N.15.b.3.3)	BEAURAINS.
	N.7.a.2.0)	

-----:0:-----

42nd Field Ambulance ... NEUVILLE VITASSE.
43rd " " ... CONVENT ST.SACRAMENT
44th " " ... MERCATEL

-----:0:-----

No.1 Coy. Divisional Train)
No.2 " " ") ACHICOURT
No.3 " " ") (G.34.c.central)
No.4 " " ") ACHICOURT
                        (G.33.c.central)

-----:0:-----

26th Mobile Veterinary Section   BERNEVILLE.
14th Div'l Supply Column ... SAULTY.
Div'l Salvage Company ... ACHICOURT.
Div'l Burials Officer ... DO.
Div'l Claims Officer ... WANQUETIN.
Div'l Depot Battn. ... BOUQUEMAISON.
Railhead (Supplies) ... ARRAS.
  Do. (Personnel) ... DO.
Supply Refilling Points :-
   Div'l Troops Group ... ACHICOURT - BEAURAINS Road.
   Infantry Brigades ... Road from G.34.b.3.3 to
                                G.34.c.1.4.

27-4-17.

SECRET. O.C./121/A.

14th (LIGHT) DIVISION.
29th Apr. 1917.

LOCATION TABLE.

	Location.	Transport.
Advanced Hd.Qtrs. ('G' Staff / C.R.A. / C.R.E.)	N.7.d.2.5.	
Hd.Qtrs., 'Q' Staff	No.1 BOULEVARD VAUBAN.	
Div'l Artillery, 'Q' Staff ...	No.22 BOULEVARD CARNOT.	
14th Signal Coy., R.E. ...	No.1 RUE L'ABBÉ HALLUIN.	
A.D.M.S.	No.12 BOULEVARD CARNOT.	
A.D.V.S.	DITTO.	
A.P.M.	DITTO.	
D.A.D.O.S.	No.53 RUE L'ABBÉ HALLUIN.	
Hd.Qtrs., Div'l Train ...	No.2 BOULEVARD VAUBAN.	
Camp Commandant	No.1 RUE L'ABBÉ HALLUIN.	

-----:o:-----

Hd.Qtrs., 41st Infantry Brigade   N.22.d.5.7.
41st Machine Gun Company   )
41st Trench Mortar Battery   )   In the line.
7th K.R.R.C.   )
8th K.R.R.C.   )   } RONVILLE.
7th R.B.   ) ... ...   In support.
8th R.B.   )

-----:o:-----

Hd.Qtrs., 42nd Infantry Brigade   N.15.d.5.2.
42nd Machine Gun Company   )
42nd Trench Mortar Battery   )   In the line.
5th Oxf. & Bucks. L.I.   )
5th K.S.L.I.   )   ... In support.   } RONVILLE.
9th K.R.R.C.   ... ...   In the line.
9th R.B.   ... ...   In support.

-----:o:-----

Hd.Qtrs., 43rd Infantry Brigade   Factory, G.35.a.0.7.
43rd Machine Gun Company   )
43rd Trench Mortar Battery   )
6th Somerset L.I.   )
6th D.C.L.I.   )   In reserve.   } RONVILLE.
6th K.O.Y.L.I.   )
10th Durham L.I.   )

-----:o:-----

11th Bn. K. Liverpool Regt.   ~~15~~ RUE EMILE LANGLET.   N 12.B, 45.85.

-----:o:-----

61st Field Coy., R.E. ...	N.15.b.3.3.)	
62nd " " " ...	N.20.b.6.8.)	BEAURAINS.
89th " " " ...	N.7.a.2.0.)	

-----:o:-----

42nd Field Ambulance	NEUVILLE VITASSE.
43rd " "	CONVENT ST. SACRAMENT.
44th " "	MERCATEL.

-----:o:-----

No.1 Coy. Divisional Train)	ACHICOURT.
No.2 " " ")	(G.34.c.central)
No.3 " " ")	ACHICOURT.
No.4 " " ")	(G.33.c.central)

-----:o:-----

26th Mobile Veterinary Section	BERNEVILLE.
14th Div'l Supply Column ...	SAULTY.
Senior Chaplain)	
O.C. Divisional Coy.)	
Div'l Salvage Coy.) ...	N.13.central.
Div'l Burials Officer)	
Div'l Claims Officer	WANQUETIN.
Div'l Depot Battn.	~~BOUQUEMAISON~~ BREVILLERS
Div'l Details Camp	MONCHIET.

CONTINUED.

```
Railhead (Supplies)      ...    ...    ...    ARRAS.
   Do.   (Personnel)     ...    ...    ...    DO.
Supply Refilling Points :-
     Div'l Troops Group   ...    ...    ACHICOURT - BEAURAINS Road.
     Infantry Brigades    ...    ...    Road from G.34.b.3.3 to
                                                    G.34.c.1.4.
```

CONFIDENTIAL.

WAR DIARY

OF

14th (Light) D I V I S I O N (Administrative Branches)

for

1st May, 1917 To 31st May, 1917.

Volume 47

--------oOo--------

Army Form C. 2118.

WAR DIARY
or
INTELLIGENCE SUMMARY
(Erase heading not required.)

Instructions regarding War Diaries and Intelligence Summaries are contained in F. S. Regs., Part II. and the Staff Manual respectively. Title Pages will be prepared in manuscript.

Place	Date	Hour	Summary of Events and Information	Remarks and references to Appendices
ARRAS	May 1		Third Army decided that issue of iron ration to troops engaged in operations is unnecessary. Our application for 10,000 iron rations for consumption 2nd Army in Hænfrie refused.	
	2		Conference at Corps Hd Qrs on question of lorries for use of divisions. Eventually decided that while Pack Train is being cleared by BN? Train each division should have still use of 10 lorries from its D.S.C., of which 2 go to C.R.E. Rest & 2xBOS lorries not included in the 10.	
	3		Attack at dawn by 41st & 42nd Bdes. The objective was reached but Bdes. had to return later to original lines. Rations could not be got up to 2 battalions & they ate their emergency ration.	
	4		A good number of German shell were falling into valley west of WANCOURT near our advanced transport lines. Had all the transport moved back to west of TELEGRAPH HILL.	
	5		Estimated casualties for action of 3rd = W.O. 41st Bde 19 Off 730 OR 42nd Bde 16 Off 720 OR	
	6.7.		Burial parties not able to do any work on account of hostile shelling.	

Army Form C. 2118.

WAR DIARY
or
INTELLIGENCE SUMMARY
(Erase heading not required.)

Place	Date	Hour	Summary of Events and Information	Remarks and references to Appendices
	7		Railway just S.W. of ARRAS station frozen by shell fire. Repaired by French railway troops before the evening, but ARRAS railhead blocked all day.	E.
	8		8 transport animals killed by a shell in ROIVILLE. Arrangements made with VII Corps for an enlargement of 14 Div: Area to the South to include NEUVILLE VITASSE. Div: H.Q: Area to hut now occupied by 18th Div H.Q. when new H.Q°: has been erected for them further South.	E.
	9		Arrangement made for opening a Div. Canteen at NEUVILLE VITASSE on the 11th. New baths being erected on Telegraph Hill.	E.
	10		Administrative arrangements for new area see Q 306/2 attached owing to hostile shelling site of Reserve Bde camp changed from M 12 b 2.9. to M 10 d 0.5 just west of BEAURAINS. Site for Div: H°Q°: selected at M. 23 a 6.6.	E. APP I. E.
	11			E.
	12		Arranged with VII Corps for baths on Telegraph Hill to be moved to Beaurains.	E.

Army Form C. 2118.

WAR DIARY or INTELLIGENCE SUMMARY

(Erase heading not required.)

Place	Date	Hour	Summary of Events and Information	Remarks and references to Appendices
ARRAS	13		Corps Q Conference held at BOISLEUX au MONT, attended by A.A. & Q.M.G.'s of Division, when the following points were discussed. 1. Bringing Camps west of MERCATEL - BEAURAINS road out of howitzer range. 2. Distribution of available huts and tents to division to form standing camps for Bns. in reserve. 3. Precaution against fire in ammunition dumps.	E.
"	14		Selected new site for battery wagon line & "Ammn." dumps into C.R.A. Moved Div'l. S.A.A. dump from Ronville to Beaurains. Regimental transport lines moved but of Ronville to the Beaurains - Tilloy Road. Spent all day in revising recommendation for immediate removal.	E. E.
"	15.		Started pitching new Div. H.Q. Camp at M 23 a 6.6.	E.
"	16		D.A.C. moved into Camp West of A.B.N.Y. from Simencourt.	E.
"	17		Div. H.Q. moved into new Camp, consisting of 6 Nissen huts 8 Armstrong huts 15 tents C.S.L 2 Marquees & various shelters. No 3 Men consisting of about 10 officers went into billets at AGNY as there is no room for them in the Camp.	E.
M 23 a 6.6. 1500x N of MERCATEL	18		Maj. ASHBY the new S.C.F C2E vice TELFER, arrived.	E.

Army Form C. 2118.

WAR DIARY
or
INTELLIGENCE SUMMARY
(Erase heading not required.)

Instructions regarding War Diaries and Intelligence Summaries are contained in F. S. Regs., Part II. and the Staff Manual respectively. Title Pages will be prepared in manuscript.

Place	Date	Hour	Summary of Events and Information	Remarks and references to Appendices
Camp on Beaurains–Mercatel Road	19.		Improvements made to Ammunition Refilling Point. Wire Put round it. Notices against smoking & fire. Sandbag traverses. Tins of water & sand.	E.
"	20.		Reconnoitred site for moving forward the "Rest Brigade" Camp if the Germans go back.	E.
"	21.		One Officer and 103 other ranks arrived for Divisional employment company. Went into billets in AGNY.	E.
"	22.		Went round transport lines with G.O.C. Decided to allot 10 tents C&L to each Brigade. The new VII Corps huts arrived for Rest Brigade Camp. Made of corrugated iron on wooden frames to hold 40 men. They seem more suited for winter than for hot weather.	E.
"	23.		Went with Gen Couper & VII Corps to discuss question about immediate honours & rewards. Corps agree that there is in truth to numbers so long as standard is maintained.	E.
"	24.		7 Remount Chargers arrived. Rather small & light but otherwise a fairly level lot. The rest went to B.G.C. 43rd I.B. Salvage dump; exploded near AGNY, owing to an tom-a detonated grenade getting into the Salved Grenades. One man killed.	E.

WAR DIARY
or
INTELLIGENCE SUMMARY

Army Form C. 2118.

Place	Date	Hour	Summary of Events and Information	Remarks and references to Appendices
Camp on Beaurains - Mercatel road.	25		GOC inspected Out Train Camp, and the Stanchin Camp for Rest Brigade.	E.
	26		Went to Abbeville to inspect the Divisional Laundry there. 3 rotary washers + 1 centrifugal drying machine run by steam from the engine of the Cotton Mill in which the machines are erected. The output is at present limited by the drying room to about 10,000 pieces a week.	E.
	27		Issued new Salvage scheme for clearing up divisional area now that the front has become stationary. See Appendix 2.	See App 2. E.
	28		Div HQrs shelled by long range German gun. One man wounded. Issued Sanitary instruction based on experience of what is found in various stages of trench warfare.	E.
	29			See App 3
	30		Very heavy thunderstorm in afternoon. Loushying camps flooded.	E.
	31		Selected site for new Rest Brigade Camp on slopes NE of La Cauchie Maigre. VII Corps asked to extend the Fickeure pipe line to this site.	

F. Duncan
A+CRE ?

App. 1.

Q. 308/2.

ADMINISTRATIVE ARRANGEMENTS IN CONNECTION WITH O.O. 122 of 10th MAY.

1. **AMMUNITION DUMPS.**

    Divisional Dump :-

    All Stokes Ammunition   M.5.c.6.0.   (BROWN)
    Grenades, S.A.A. & Flares   N.19.b.8.9.   (NEUVILLE VITASSE)

    Front Brigade Dumps :-

    N.23.a.2.5.   (WANCOURT)
    N.23.d.3.0.   (CEMENT)
    N.29.a.9.5.   (HENINEL)
    O.25.c.Central   (SWAN)

    Support Brigade Dump :-

    N.15.a.2.8.   (GAUNTS)

    Reserve Brigade Dump :-

    M.12.b.1.9.   (Reserve Brigade)

2. **BRIGADE TRANSPORT LINES.**

    Front Brigade :-

    M.12.b.2.8.   (Present lines of 43rd Bde.)

    Support Brigade :-

    M. 5. d.

    Reserve Brigade :-

    M.12.b.2.9.   (Reserve Brigade Camp)

3. **BATHS.**

    A new bath will be opened, probably on May 13th, on TELEGRAPH HILL, at N.7.a.0.2.

    There are also Baths at AGNY and NEUVILLE VITASSE.

    The following will be the allotment :-

    TELEGRAPH HILL.   Whole time.

    Whole of Infantry Brigade in Reserve.
    11th King's Liverpool Rgt.
    All Infantry Transport Details of three Brigades and 11th King's.
    3 Field Companies R.E.

    Detailed allotment to be made by Headquarters of Brigade in Reserve.

    AGNY.

    Royal Artillery.
    Divisional Train.

    Detailed allotment to be made by Officer i/c Baths & Laundries on application from Units.

    (CONTINUED)

NEUVILLE VITASSE.

Infantry Brigade in Support.
Divisional Headquarters.
44th & 42nd Field Ambulances.
Salvage Company.

Detailed allotment to be made by Officer i/c Baths & Laundries on application from Units.

4. D.A.D.O.S. Dump is at M.17.c.Central on the BEAURAINS - MERCATEL Road.

5. The following are the Water Points in the Divisional Area :-

Map reference	Remarks.
For men and Horses.	
M. 5. d. 8. 6.	450 horses per hour.
M.12. a. 9. 7.	450　"　　"　　"
N.15. a. 3. 8.	900　"　　"　　"
M.24. b. 8. 8.	2,000　"　　"　　"
For horses only.	
M. 8. a. 9. 6.	320 Horses per hour.
M. 3. d. 5. 2.	
M. 9. b. 9. 6.	350　"　　"　　"
M.10. d. 1. 2.	
M.16. d. 8. 6.	
M.17. c. 6. 4.	1,500　"　　"　　"
M.24. d. 8. 8.	

R. Lewis.

LIEUT. COLONEL,
A.A. & Q.M.G.
14th (LIGHT) DIVISION.

10/5/1917.

1	2	3	4	5	6
Food Storage.	-	In clean sandbags.	Clean sandbags or, where possible, tins and boxes.	As in Column 4.	(1) Cupboards. (2) Safes, i.e., boxes with canvas or muslin front piece weighted at the bottom. See Fig.3.
Kitchens.	-	-	-	-	Firm flooring – bricks or filled tins. Good table. This is always available if forming one side of wooden carrier crates attachable to cookers. Windows of kitchen fly-proof.

1.	2.	3.	4.	5.	6.
Disposal of liquid refuse.	—	—	Sump holes in saps labelled "Liquid refuse".	(1) Deep hole with cover or Wired round. or (2) Specially constructed grease trap.	Specially constructed grease trap. Tin box filled with straw. Perforations in bottom opening on channel filled with brick rubble or burnt tins leading to pit 4 feet deep covered with wooden cover. See Fig. 2.
Ablution.	—	—	Bench made from trench board etc. in a sap. Gutter drain leading into deep sump pit at distant end of sap.	Bench, gutter and sump pit. Sump pit covered in if possible.	Specially constructed table with central groove leading by gutter or pipe into tin (full of hay, etc.) with perforations. Thence through sump pits in series. Sump pits to be covered in. Firm flooring of burnt tins filled with earth or brick flooring where possible.
Disposal of Manure.	—	—	Collected and buried daily. Each addition to burial pit covered with earth.	—	Dump daily on limed ground and cover completely with whole of previous day's manure. As an extra precaution spray surface with 5% cresol. The stack of manure should be thoroughly battered and compressed.

1	2	3	4	5	6
Collection of dry refuse, prior to disposal.	Sanitary men collect by hand priodically.	Sandbags pegged to wall of trench and labelled "Dry Refuse".	As in Col.3.	Sandbags pegged to posts etc., and labelled.	Bags or boxes or tins specially labelled. Each Cooker or Cookhouse must have special receptacle with lid in its <u>immediate</u> proximity, labelled "Dry Refuse".
Disposal of dry refuse.	Buried in shell holes.	Buried in deep holes which are filled in when ¾ full.	As in Col.3.	As in Col.3.	Burnt in incinerator. Burnt tins are then stacked and kept. Remainder of incinerated residue buried in large deep pit with wooden or other cover or wired round to prevent access for other purposes.
Collection of liquid refuse.	—	—	To be carried direct to sump holes.	In non-leaky receptacles and in case of cookers, one receptacle next each cooker.	As in Col. 5.

ITEM 1	While digging in after an attack. 2	Primitive Trench System. 3	Consolidated trench System. 4	Temporary encampment in forward area. 5	Standing Camp or Billets. 6
LATRINES.	Single deep trench latrines in saps dug through parados. Filled in when ½ full and fresh ones dug. (See Figure 1)	As in Col. 2, but covered by portable wood platform with hinged lid in centre. Platform made by Bn. Pioneers to supplement issue by San'y Section.	(1) Box latrines (at the ends of shaped saps) containing buckets, or placed over deep pits. N.B. Biscuit tins are not satisfactory receptacles. Or (2) Cresol drums fitted with lidded seats. Seats made from biscuit boxes. All seats to be scrubbed daily with sandbag & diluted cresol.	As in Col. 4. Screen or shelter where possible. Supply of latrine paper in a receptacle covered from rain.	(1) As in Col. 5. with screen or shelter Or (2) Fly-proof seating (with several lidded apertures) over a long deep pit, with screen and shelter.
Disposal of faeces	Earth thrown over daily, and trench filled in when ½ full.	As in Column 2.	Burial in specially dug holes as far as possible from the trenches, those holes to have earth thrown over every night and to be filled in when ¾ full.	As in Column 4.	As in Column 4, or by closed incinerator when possible.

1.	2.	3.	4.	5.	6.
Urinals	Round hole 2 ft wide x 3 ft deep in floor of sap.	As in Column 2.	(1) On porous ground cresol drum, biscuit tin or other receptacle with perforated base placed over hole 2 ft. deep. Receptacles fitted with baffle plates. (2) On impervious ground cresol drum or strong receptacle fitted with baffle plate and wire handle. Emptied periodically into pit dug for urine only.	Cresol drum with baffle plate. N.B. Biscuit tins unsatisfactory as containers of urine and if used should be regarded as a temporary expedient. Where ground is porous biscuit tins with perforated base placed over hole 2 ft. deep will answer.	As in Column 5. Top of urinal 2" 3" from ground by means of wood or brick stand. The whole to be placed on solid flooring of brick &c. or empty burnt tins.(from incinerator) filled with earth and placed bottom upwards.
Night Urinals.	As for day.	As for day.	As for day.	Receptacles painted white close to sleeping accommodation.	Receptacles painted white or stands whitewashed close to billets.
Disposal of Urine.		—	Poured periodically into deep hole behind trench.	Poured into (1) Deep hole or (2) Special soakage pit, either of which are wired round to prevent access for other purposes. Soakage pit is a large hole 3' x 3' x 4' (deep) filled with brick rubble or punctured burnt tins up to the top and labelled "Urine only".	As in Column 5. Special soakage pit whenever possible.

Sanitary arrangements.

Fig. 1. Plan of latrines in sap.

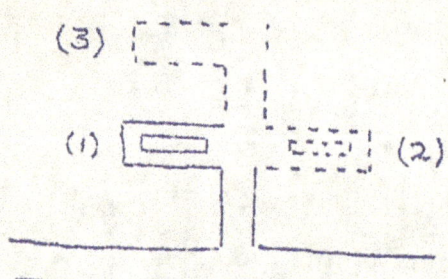

Fig. 2. GREASE TRAP

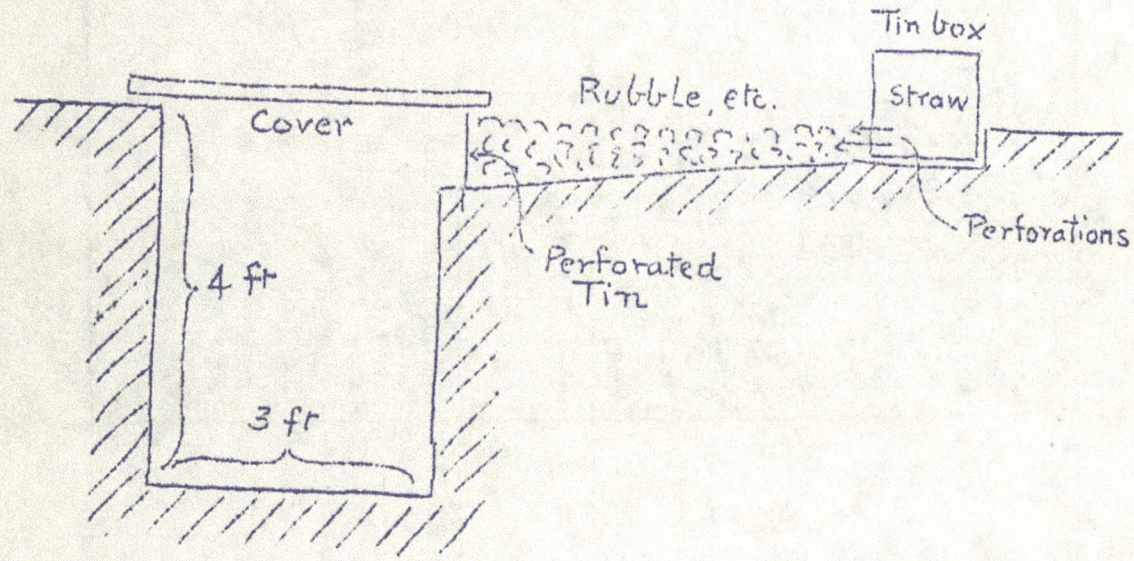

Fig 3. Fly proof safe for food made from a box with weighted curtain in front. Front edges of box cut on a curve to ensure curtain lying close

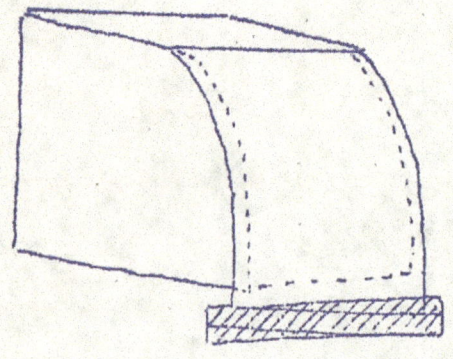

App III.

Q.44/16.

SANITATION.

1. With the advent of hot weather the importance of good sanitary arrangements cannot be over estimated and the attached table is circulated to assist Commanding Officers of Units in making the best sanitary arrangements which circumstances will allow.

2. The main principle underlying all sanitation is to prevent flies from having access to any refuse or to any food.
   The appliances described in the table are all designed for this purpose.
   These appliances will be shortly on view at Divisional Headquarters and are such as can be made by units from materials readily available. Batteries and Battalions should see that they have a stock of the simple portable appliances made beforehand and kept in their wagon or transport lines for use if required in the front line. Brigades should apply to O.C. Train Company attached for biscuit boxes required, and send Brigade Pioneers to assist units in adapting them.

3. When latrines are not available or when men are obliged to make use of shell holes, trenches, etc., it is of great importance that earth is thrown over the excreta on the spot by the man before he leaves it.
   It should be impressed on all ranks that if excreta are left uncovered, the health and even the lives of their comrades are thereby endangered.

4. Units should take steps for their own safety from disease to ensure that the areas they occupy are clean by sending their Sanitary men to search the area systematically by day if possible for uncovered excreta and food refuse and to cover them immediately with earth.
   The sanitary men should report to their C.O. if much excreta is found uncovered in order that he may in that case again impress on his men the importance of para. 3 above.

5. The sanitary arrangements for the personnel belonging to and attached to the Headquarters of units are apt to be overlooked. Units should detail at least one sanitary man for unit Headquarters, whose duty would be to look after H.Q. sanitation only.

6. Commanding Officers must remember that the responsibility for the sanitation of their units rests with them. The Medical Officer of a unit acts in an advisory capacity only. The Sanitary Section is now an area unit and does not undertake Sanitary work for units to the same extent as it did when the Sanitary Section was part of the Division.

7. Sufficient copies of these instructions are issued for distribution of a copy to every Battery and Company Commander.

E. Lewis Lt.Col.
A.A. & Q.M.G.,

29/5/1917.   14th (Light) Division.

App. 2.

Q.34/33.

SALVAGE.

1. The following system will be adopted for cleaning up the Divisional Area and collecting salvage.

2. Salvage Areas are allotted to Brigades etc. as shewn on the attached map, and Brigades etc. will be responsible for clearing the area allotted to them except for the actual sites of Camps allotted to Army and Corps troops or to other units of the Division, which will be kept clean by the units occupying them.

3. All stuff which is useless for salvage, such as dead animals, broken tins, refuse etc. will be disposed of by burning or burying.
   Refuse must not be thrown into old trenches, where it will only breed flies, unless it is immediately covered over with earth.

4. All articles fit for salvage will be dumped at the Salvage Dumps shown by circles on the map.
   These Dumps will be marked, under Divisional arrangements, with notice boards bearing the Divisional sign and the words "Salvage Dump."

5. Arrangements will be made by the 14th Divisional Salvage Company to clear these Dumps periodically - at least twice a week - to sort the stuff at the main Salvage Dump and to dispose of it according to instructions.

6. The Salvage Dumps will be formed in two distinct portions :

   (a) Ammunition of all sorts including -
       S.A.A.
       Gun ammunition, complete rounds, empty cartridge cases and exploded shells. The latter are wanted for the sake of the copper driving band.
       Trench Mortar ammunition.
       Flares and Very Lights.
       N.B.- Grenades and "dud" shell will NOT be collected into Salvage Dumps. They will be dealt with as in paras. 7 and 8.

   (b) All other salvage, such as clothing, equipment, ordnance and R.E. Stores.

7. Bombs of all sorts will be left untouched where they lie, and the areas where bombs are to be found will be notified to O.C. Salvage Company.
   O.C. Salvage Company, on finding or receiving notification of any bombs will send a party of the trained bomb collectors to salve them. The bomb collecting parties will -

   (a) remove the detonator at the spot where the bomb is found,
   (b) bury the detonators at a depth of at least 5 feet,
   (c) dump the bombs at the special bomb dump for despatch to railhead, under arrangements made by Divisional Hd.Qrs.

(CONTINUED.)

8. "Dud" shell will not be touched or removed by units.

Brigade etc. responsible for an area will make a sketch of its area on a scale of 1/10,000 (i.e., twice as large as attached map) and mark on it with a red dot the position of each "dud" shell.

These sketches will be sent in to Divisional Hd.Qrs. on Sunday, June 2nd and on every subsequent Sunday shewing the position of all "dud" shell located up to date.

Arrangements will then be made by Divisional Hd.Qrs. for their destruction or disposal.

Each "dud" shell located will be marked by planting a stake or screw picket close to it with a bit of white cloth attached.

9. In order to carry out this system it is suggested that Brigades etc. should subdivide their areas and allot subdivisions to units.

All parties of men sent out for work or training should bring back with them all the salvage they can carry and deposit it at the nearest dump.

Salvage parties should be organised daily from men not actually required for other work or men on light duty.

The collection of refuse and burying of dead animals should be done by defaulters, as far as possible.

10. Brigades etc. may make sub-dumps for the convenience of units, but these sub-dumps must be cleared daily and the salvage deposited at the dumps marked on the map so that they can be cleared by the Salvage Company.

If Brigades etc. find that the position of any of the Salvage Dumps marked on the map is not convenient, they should select an alternative site near a road and notify its position to Divisional Hd.Qrs. one day before taking it into use.

11. The foregoing system is not applicable to the Brigade in line. In that case, all salvage which can be collected will be either:

(a) Sent back at night in the returning transport and dumped at N19.b.8.8, where it will be cleared by the Salvage Company every morning, or

(b) Collected in dumps in positions where the Salvage Company can come up to bring it back. The location of these dumps will be notified to the Salvage Company.

Grenades and "dud" shell in the area of the Brigade in line will not be dealt with at present.

12. Brigades, on relief, will hand over copies of their "dud" shell sketches and their scheme for organizing their area for salvage.

13. Brigades etc. will call for assistance from the Div'l Salvage Company to deal with any large accumulations of salvage found in their area which could more conveniently be carried direct to the main salvage Dump.

14. Additional copies of these instructions, but not of the map, can be obtained on application to Div'l Hd.Qrs., "Q" Office.

R. Lewis Lt.Col.
A.A. & Q.M.G.,
14TH (LIGHT) DIVISION.

27/5/17.

S E C R E T.
O.C/129.

14th (LIGHT) DIVISION.

6th May, 1917.

LOCATION TABLE.

TRANSPORT.

Advanced Hd.Qtrs. ('G' Staff / C.R.A. / C.R.E.)	N.7.d.2.5.
Hd.Qtrs. 'Q' Staff	No. 1, BOULEVARD VAUBAN.
Div'l Artillery 'Q' Staff ...	No. 22 BOULEVARD CARNOT.
14th Signal Coy., R.E. ...	No. 1 RUE L'ABBÉ HALLUIN.
A.D.M.S.) A.D.V.S.) ... ... A.P.M.)	No. 12 BOULEVARD CARNOT.
D.A.D.O.S.	No.53 RUE L'ABBÉ HALLUIN.
Hd.Qtrs. Divisional Train ...	No. 2 BOULEVARD VAUBAN.
Camp Commandant	No. 1 RUE L'ABBÉ HALLUIN

Hd.Qtrs. 41st Infantry Bde.	N.7.d.4.0.	
41st Machine Gun Company		
41st Trench Mortar Battery		
7th K.R.R.C.	In reserve.	RONVILLE.
8th K.R.R.C.		
7th R.B.		
8th R.B.		

Hd.Qtrs. 42nd Infantry Bde.	Factory, G.35.a.0.7.	
42nd Machine Gun Company		
42nd Trench Mortar Battery		
5th Oxf. & Bucks. L.I.	In reserve.	RONVILLE.
5th K.S.L.I.		
9th K.R.R.C.		
9th R.B.		

Hd.Qtrs. 43rd Infantry Bde.	N.21.a.8.6.	
43rd Machine Gun Company		
43rd Trench Mortar Battery		
6th Somerset L.I.		
6th D.C.L.I.	In the line.	M.12.b.
6th K.O.Y.L.I.		
10th Durham L.I.		

11th Bn. K. Liverpool Regt.	M.12.b.45.85.

61st Field Coy. R.E. ...	N.15.b.3.3.)	
62nd " " "	N.20.b.6.8.)	BEAURAINS.
89th " " "	N.7.a.2.0.)	
42nd Field Ambulance ...	NEUVILLE VITASSE.	
43rd " "	CONVENT ST. SACRAMENT.	
44th " "	MERCATEL.	
No. 1 Coy., Divisional Train)	ACHICOURT	
No. 2 " " ")	(G.34.c.central)	
No. 3 " " ")	ACHICOURT	
No. 4 " " ")	(G.33.c.central)	

26th Mobile Vet'y Section ...	BERNEVILLE.
14th Div'l Supply Column ...	BEAUMETZ.
Senior Chaplain) O.C. Divisional Coy.) Div'l Salvage Coy.) Div'l Burials Officer)	N.13.central.
Div'l Claims Officer ...	DAINVILLE.
Div'l Depot Battalion ...	BREVILLERS.
Div'l Details Camp ...	MONCHIET.
Railhead (Supplies)) Do. (Personnel))	ARRAS.
Supply Refilling Points :-	
Div'l Troops Group ...	ACHICOURT - BEAURAINS Road.
Infantry Brigades ...	Road from G.34.b.3.3 to G.34.c.1.4.

SECRET.   14th (LIGHT) DIVISION.   O.C./157.
                           L O C A T I O N   T A B L E.   13th May, 1917.
                                                              TRANSPORT.

Advanced Hd.Qtrs. { 'G' Staff }   N.7.d.2.5.
                  { C. R.A.   }
                  { C. R.E.   }   No. 1 BOULEVARD VAUBAN.
Hd.Qtrs. 'Q' Staff   ...   ... No. 1 RUE L'ABBE HALLUIN.
14th Signal Coy. R.E.
A.D.M.S. }
A.D.V.S. }   ...   ... No. 12 BOULEVARD CARNOT.
A.P.M.   }
D.A.D.O.S.   ...   . M.17.c.Central.
                                         M.9.b.4.9.
Hd.Qtrs. Div. Train   ...   ... No. 1 RUE L'ABBE HALLUIN.
Camp Commandant   ...   ... N.7.d.4.0.

Hd.Qtrs. 41st Infantry Bde.
41st Machine Gun Coy.
41st Trench Mortar Bty. }
7th K.R.R.C.   }   ...   Support area.   RONVILLE.
8th K.R.R.C.   }
7th R.B.   }
8th R.B.   }

                                    Factory, G.35.a.0.7.
Hd.Qtrs. 42nd Infantry Bde.
42nd Machine Gun Coy.
42nd Trench Mortar Bty. }
5th Ox. & Bucks. L.I.   }   ...   Reserve area.   RONVILLE.
5th K.S.L.I.   }
9th K.R.R.C.   }
9th R.B.   }

                                    N.21.a.8.6.
Hd.Qtrs. 43rd Infantry Bde.
43rd Machine Gun Coy.
43rd Trench Mortar Bty. }
6th Somerset L.I.   }   ...   In the line.   M.12.b.
6th D.C.L.I.   }
6th K.O.Y.L.I.   }
10th Durham L.I.   }

11th Bn. K. Liverpool Regt.   M.12.b.45.85.

61st Field Coy. R.E.   ...   N.15.b.3.3. }
62nd Field Coy. R.E.   ...   N.20.b.6.8. }   BEAURAINS.
89th Field Coy. R.E.   ...   N.7.a.2.0. }
42nd Field Ambulance   ...   NEUVILLE VITASSE.
43rd   "   "   ...   CONVENT ST.SACRAMENT.
44th   "   "   ...   MERCATEL.
No. 1 Coy., Div. Train   ...   M.3.b.9.0.
No. 2 "   "   "   ...   M.3.d.8.6.
No. 3 "   "   "   ...   M.9.b.4.9.
No. 4 "   "   "   ...   M.8.b.7.9.

26th Mobile Vet'y Section   BERNEVILLE.
14th Div. Supply Column   ...   BEAUMETZ.
Senior Chaplain   }
O.C. Div. Coy.   }   ...   N.13.central.
Div. Salvage Coy.   }
Div. Burials Officer   ...   N.13.central.
Div. Claims Officer   ...   DAINVILLE.
Div. Depot Battalion   ...   BREVILLERS.
Railhead   ...   ...   ARRAS.
Supply Refilling Point   ...   M.3.b.
Hd.Qtrs. 14th D.A.C.   ...   SIMENCOURT.
Adv. Sec 14th D.A.C.   ...   M.17.b.7.4.
1st Lab. Coy. Seaforths   ...   No. 11 RUE JEU de PAUME.
VII Corps Cyclists   ...   10 RUE VICTOR HUGO.
1st Troop, VII Corps Cavalry   M.12.d.6.9.
Details, 3rd Bn. W.India Regt. }   { DAINVILLE Dump,
                          R.E. }   {   FAUBOURG D'AMIENS.

Secret.

Vol 21

War Diary
of
14th (Light) Division
Administrative Branches
1st June 1917 to 30th June 1917
Volume 48

Copies to :-

        C. R. A.
        C. R. E.
        41st Infantry Bde.
        42nd Infantry Bde.
        43rd Infantry Bde.
        11th Bn. King's Liverpool Regt.
        14th Div'l Signal Coy.
        A. D. M. S.
        14th Div'l Train.
        D.A.D.V.S.
        D.A.D.O.S.
        Senior Chaplain C. of E.
            "   "Non-C. of E.
        A. P. M.
        Camp Commandant.
        'G'.
==

WAR DIARY
or
INTELLIGENCE SUMMARY

Army Form C. 2118.

Place	Date	Hour	Summary of Events and Information	Remarks and references to Appendices
Div! HQ. Camp at M 23 a 6.6. 1500 x N of MERCATEL	June 1-3		Normal routine work.	E.
	4		Relief of Bdes. 42nd Bde went into Rest Brigade Camp which is not to be moved to a new site. Started preparation for its destruction of "dud" shell. Destroyed 7 by gun cotton, including 2 9". The explosion caused a radius of at least 50° and it was decided to try exploding them in a trench so as to localize the effects. Got location sketches from units of the "dud" shell in the divisional area.	E.
	5.6		More destruction of "dud" shell. Found best result by exploding nest of 10-12 shell in pit at bottom of shell hole.	
	7		Issued instructions for handing over to 58th and 18th Divisions. See App 1.	App 1 E
	8		Reconnoitred new rest area. Issued administrative orders see App 2	App 2 E
	9		Railhead in new area changed to ROSEL. Issued new administrative orders for supply see App 3. Scheme for destroying dud shell sent in to Corps see App 4.	App 3 E App 4 E

Army Form C. 2118.

WAR DIARY
or
INTELLIGENCE SUMMARY
(Erase heading not required.)

Instructions regarding War Diaries and Intelligence Summaries are contained in F. S. Regs., Part II. and the Staff Manual respectively. Title Pages will be prepared in manuscript.

Place	Date	Hour	Summary of Events and Information	Remarks and references to Appendices
MARIEUX	10		Div. H.Q. moved to Marieux. D.S.C. came under divisional orders. Lorries used for transport of kit and also for the Inpt men of Salvage Co, Div Co, Div Employment Co, Traffic Control and Div H.Q.	
"	11		Selected site for Div. Horse Show on June 20th. Preliminary arrangements made. 42nd Bn Gp arrived in new area billeted in BEAUQUESNE PUCHEVILLERS RAINCHEVAL	
"	12		VII Corps ordered us to clean out of Div Kit Store at LARBRET for Berneville and proceeded to allot huts at LARBRET for storing kit.	
"	13		41st Inf Bde Group arrived in Rest area & billeted in LOUVENCOURT and BERTRANCOURT.	
"	14		43rd Inf Bn Group arrived in Rest area Billeted in AUTHIE, SAILGER -LES-AUTHIE, BUS-EN-ARTOIS	
"	15/16/17/18		Normal routine work: Committee meeting for Bn Horseshows held on 15th and 18th	
"	19		Divl artillery returned by 50th Div HQ & proceeded to HENDECOURT-LES-RANSART to refit	

Army Form C. 2118.

WAR DIARY
or
INTELLIGENCE SUMMARY

(Erase heading not required.)

Instructions regarding War Diaries and Intelligence Summaries are contained in F.S. Regs., Part II. and the Staff Manual respectively. Title Pages will be prepared in manuscript.

Place	Date	Hour	Summary of Events and Information	Remarks and references to Appendices
MERIEUX	20.		Normal Routine	
	21.			
	22.		Forecast move to 1X Corps in MERRIS area received. Div° Arty on JULY 4th to Div (less A/S) on July 11th	
	23.		Normal routine	
	24.		Orders received to move on 11th July Anchorat Regt + 3 M.G.Coys by rail on 28th inst to 1X Corps	
	25.		Normal routine	
	26.		Divisional Horse Show all day. List of prize winners attached see App 5.	App 5.
	27.		Orders issued for move by rail tomorrow of 11th Kings Liv Regt and 3 Field Coys R.E. see App 6.	App 6.
	28.			
	29.		Normal routine.	
	30.			

B. Lumisden
AAnQMG

App 1.

SECRET.

Q/345.

HANDING OVER.

Copy : No. 24

Administrative Orders in connection with 14th Division

O.O. No. 128 of 5/6/17.

1. General. Administrative arrangements continue under the control of 14th Division until 6. a.m. on 10th June 1917 when the Northern half of the Divisional Area including BEAURAINS, TELEGRAPH HILL and WANCOURT, but excluding the RESERVE BRIGADE CAMP, will be handed over to the 56th Division, and the Southern portion including AGNY and NEUVILLE VITASSE will be handed over to the 18th Division.

The Reserve Brigade Camp will be handed over to the 56th Division when vacated by the 43rd Infantry Brigade on the 12th June.

2. Ammunition Dumps.

2/Lieut. A.E.HOPSON, acting Divisional Bombing Officer will hand over to a representative of 56th Divisional S.A.A. and Grenade Dumps at M.5.c.5.1 (Brown Dump) and M.12.d.1.4 (Battery Dump) and will obtain receipts.

Brigade Dumps will be handed over by Brigades to the relieving Brigades.

3. Police.

A.P.M., 14th Division will get into touch with A.P.M's 56th and 18th Divisions and will arrange to hand over control posts etc. to those Divisions on 10th June.

4. Baths.

The Officer-in-Charge Baths and Laundries will hand over the baths at AGNY and NEUVILLE VITASSE to the 18th Division and the bath at the Rest Brigade Camp to the 56th Division. Stocks of coal will be handed over but clothing will not.

5. Canteens.

The Divisional Canteens at M.3.b.5.3. (wholesale) and N.19.b.8.8. (retail) will be closed on 8th June and will reopen in the Rest Area under instructions to be issued later.

All empty beer barrels will be returned by units to the Divisional Canteen at M.3.b.5.3. on or before June 8th.

6. Water Supply.

The following Water Points will be handed over :-

To 56th Division.

M.4.b.6.6. Horse Troughs & Water Cart Point	1 N.C.O.	4 men.
M.5.d.8.6. Water Cart Point)	1 "	3 "
M.12.a.9.7. Horse Trough & Water Cart Point)	1 "	2 "
M.9.b.9.6. Horse Troughs both sides of Road	1 "	2 "
M.3.d.9.3. " " " " " "	1 "	2 "
N.15.a.8.2. " " " " " "	None. Rarely used owing to shelling	

To 18th Divsion.

M.24.b.8.8. Horse Troughs & Water Cart Point.	2 N.C.O's	5 men
M.8.a.9.6. Horse Troughs	1 "	2 "
M.17.c.7.4. Horse Troughs both sides of Road	1 "	7 "

A map of the pipe lines in the area (VII Corps Q.2) has been handed over to 18th Division.

7. Sanitation.

Every C.O. will render a certificate through Brigades, etc. to Divisional Headquarters that the trenches, bivouacs, Transport Lines, etc., vacated by his unit were left in a thoroughly clean and tidy state. Special attention will be devoted to this point and it is hoped that no complaints will be received later on from incoming Divisions.

8. Huts.

All huts will be left standing and will be handed over as follows :-

To 56th Division.

	Nissen.	VII Corps.	Armstrong.
Rest Bde Camp.	14	7	-

To 18th Division.

Divisional Headquarters	6	-	8

9. Tents.

The following tents will be left standing and handed over as follows :-

To 56th Division.

	Marquees.	Tents C.S.L.
Rest Brigade Camp.	-	208

To 18th Division.

Divisional Headquarters	2	15

The following tents C.S.L. will be struck on June 9th and handed in complete to D.A.D.O.S. on that day, for return to A.D.O.S., VII Corps :-

41st Brigade Transport	5
42nd " "	5
43rd " "	5
11th King's Liverpool Regt.	8
Div'l R.E.	9
Salvage Company	1
	33

The 40 Tents C.S.L. issued to 14th Div'l Artillery will remain on charge of units to which they were allotted and will be taken on charge by the 18th Division.

The 75 Tents C.S.L. and 30 Trench Shelters on charge of 14th Div'l Artillery in "C" Camp at K.6.c.7.4 will remain standing and be taken over by 18th Division.

10. Area Stores.

No Area Stores - e.g., Latrines, Ablution Benches, Sheds, Corrugated Iron, Trench Shelters etc. - will be removed, but will be handed over to incoming units.

11. Picks and Shovels.

Infantry Brigades will ensure that Battalion and Brigade reserves of tools laid down in Mobilization Store Tables are complete. A sufficient number of Picks and Shovels to complete the reserves will be collected from the forward area before handing over.

12. Cemeteries.

The following cemeteries will pass to the control of the incoming Divisions :-

To 56th Division :
    M.12.b.5.5.
    N.24.c.3.9.

To 18th Division :
    M.24.d.6.2.
    N.29.a.9.4.

6/6/17.

R. Lewis Lt.W.
A.A. & Q.M.G.,
14TH (LIGHT) DIVISION.

COPIES to :

1. 'G'.
2. C. R.A.
3. C. R.E.
4. 41st Infantry Bde.
5. 42nd Infantry Bde.
6. 43rd Infantry Bde.
7. 11th Bn. K. L'pool R.
8. 14th Div'l Train.
9. A.D.M.S.
10. D.A.D.O.S.
11. A.D.V.S.
12. A.P.M.
13. Camp Commandant.
14. 14th Salvage Company.
15. O. i/c Baths & Laundr's
16. VII Corps "Q".
17. VI Corps "Q".
18. 56th Division.
19. 18th Division.
20 - 25. 14th Div. "Q" Office & file.

SECRET.   Q.345/1.

ADMINISTRATIVE ARRANGEMENTS FOR THE NEW AREA.

1. The following is the allotment of villages to Groups :-

GROUP.	VILLAGE.	DISTRIBUTION (a)
Div. Hd.Qtrs.	MARIEUX.	Div'l Hd.Qtrs., C. R.A., C. R.E., D.A.D.O.S.
	VAUCHELLES (Less Chateau).	Div'l Company, Salvage Co., Div'l Empl. Company, A.P.M. personnel.
41st Inf. Bde.	LOUVENCOURT (Less accommodation for Div'l Train).	Brigade Hd.Qtrs., 1 Battalion, M.G. Coy., T.M. Bty., Field Coy.
	BERTRANCOURT.	3 Battalions.
	VAUCHELLES CHATEAU.	Field Ambulance.
42nd Inf. Bde.	BEAUQUESNE.	Brigade H.Q., 1 Battalion, M.G. Coy., T.M. Bty.
	RAINCHEVAL.	1 Battalion, Field Ambce.
	PUCHEVILLERS.	2 Battalions, Field Coy.
43rd Inf. Bde.	AUTHIE.	Brigade H.Q., M.G. Coy., T.M. Bty., Field Coy.
	ST. LEGER LES AUTHIE.	Pioneer Battn., 26th Mob. Vet'y Section.
	BUS LES ARTOIS.	4 Battalions, Field Ambce. (in hospital).
Div'l Train.	LOUVENCOURT.	Hd.Qtrs., and 3 Companies.

(a) This distribution is given as a guide to Brigades and can be altered if desired for the units in their Group.

2. Brigades will send a billeting Officer and one man from each unit a day ahead of their arrival in the new Area, to select the billets etc. and to guide units in.
  There are Town Majors at :
   BUS LES ARTOIS,   for AUTHIE and ST. LEGER LES AUTHIE.
   BERTRANCOURT.
   LOUVENCOURT,   for VAUCHELLES.
   MARIEUX,   for BEAUQUESNE and RAINCHEVAL.

3. Tables of billets and huts in each village are attached to the copies addressed to Infantry Brigades.
  These tables are correct as regards huts but should be reduced by about 30 % as regards billets.

CONTINUED.

4. The location of Baths and their allotment to Groups are as follows :-

Div'l Hd.Qtrs.	VAUCHELLES (Shared by V Corps School)
41st Inf. Bde.Group.	LOUVENCOURT.
	BERTRANCOURT.
42nd Inf. Bde.Group.	BEAUQUESNE.
	RAINCHEVAL.
43rd Inf. Bde.Group.	AUTHIE.
	BUS LES ARTOIS.

    Brigades can draw Coal on arrival from the Div. Train at LOUVENCOURT. Clean clothes will be supplied under Divisional arrangements.
    Brigades will furnish men to run their Baths and will make their own allotments to their Group.

5. Moves of Units not shewn in Table "C" of 14th Division O.O. 128 of 5/6/17 :-

UNIT.	DATE.	FROM	TO
Div'l Train Hd.Qtrs.	10th June.	AGNY	LOUVENCOURT.
Nos.2,3,4 Companies (With Bde. Div'l Train. (Group.		AGNY	LOUVENCOURT.
26th Mob. Vet. Sec.(With 43rd (Bde.Group.		AGNY	ST.LEGER LES AUTHIE.
Div'l Employmt.Coy. and personnel ...	10th June.	AGNY	VAUCHELLES.(a)
Div'l Salvage Coy. and Div'l Company	10th "	N.13	VAUCHELLES. (b)
D.A.D.O.S. ...	10th "	M.17.c.	MARIEUX.

    (a) 7 lorries to carry this personnel and their kits will be at the cross-roads, AGNY, at 8.0 A.M. on June 10th.
    (b) 9 lorries will be at NEUVILLE VITASSE, N.19.b.8.9, at 8 A.M. on June 10th.

6. RAILHEAD. Railhead will be as follows :-

DATE.	DIV. H.Q.	41st I. B.	42nd I. B.	43rd I. B.
June 10.	ARRAS.	ARRAS.	ARRAS.	ARRAS.
" 11.	VAUCHELLES.	"	VAUCHELLES.	"
" 12.	"	"	"	"
" 13.	"	VAUCHELLES.	"	"
" 14.	"	"	"	"
" 15.	"	"	"	VAUCHELLES.
" 16.	"	"	"	"

7. REFILLING POINTS.

DATE.	DIV. H.Q.	41st I. B.	42nd I. B.	43rd I. B.
June 9.	M.17.c.	M.17.c.	M.17.c.	M.17.c.
" 10.	BEAUMETZ.	"	BEAUMETZ.	"
" 11.	LOUVENCOURT.	"	SAULTY.	"
" 12.	"	BEAUMETZ.	RAINCHEVAL.	"
" 13.	"	SAULTY.	"	"
" 14.	"	LOUVENCOURT.	"	BEAUMETZ.
" 15.	"	"	"	SAULTY.
" 16.	"	"	"	BUS.
" 17.	"	"	"	"

8. CANTEENS.

    There is an E.F. Canteen, wholesale and retail, at RAINCHEVAL.
    A Div'l Canteen, wholesale and retail, will be opened at LOUVENCOURT on June 12th.

CONTINUED.

9.   As there is a large amount of ground under cultivation in the new Area, the attention of all units is drawn to G.R.O.'s 1377 and 1941.

Officers or men, whether on foot or horseback, are forbidden to go across tilled fields.

It should be a point of honour with all ranks to prevent all damage to the crops which are of great importance to the French nation.

R. Lewis Lt.W.
A. A. & Q.M.G.,
14TH (LIGHT) DIVISION.

8/6/1917.

COPIES to :

1. "G".
2. C. R.A.
3. C. R.E.
4. 41st Infantry Bde.
5. 42nd Infantry Bde.
6. 43rd Infantry Bde.
7. 14th Signal Coy.
8. 11th Bn. K. L'pool R.
9. 14th Div'l Train.
10. S. S. O.
11. 14th Div'l Supply Column.
12. A.D.M.S.
13. A.D.V.S.
14. D.A.D.O.S.
15. A.P.M.
16. Camp Commandant.
17. Div'l Employment Coy.
18. Div'l Company.
19. 14th Salvage Coy.
20. Q. BEAUVAL.
21. Town Major, BUS LES ARTOIS.
22.   "   "   BERTRANCOURT.
23.   "   "   LOUVENCOURT.
24.   "   "   MARIEUX.
25 - 30. "Q", File and Diary.

Q.345/3.

Secret

SUPPLY ARRANGEMENTS FOR REST AREA.

1. Reference this Office Q.345/1 of 8/6/17 :
   The Rail-head at VAUCHELLES is cancelled and ROSEL substituted.
   ROSEL is 5 miles South of DOULLENS on the DOULLENS - AMIENS road.
   The dates on which ROSEL becomes Rail-head for the various Groups are the same as those given for VAUCHELLES.

2. Consequent on this change, the Companies of the Div'l Train will billet with their Brigade Groups as follows :-

Div'l Train Hd.Qtrs.	LOUVENCOURT.
No. 2 Company	LOUVENCOURT.
No. 3 "	PUCHEVILLERS.
No. 4 "	BUS LES ARTOIS.

3. Refilling Points, on arrival at the Rest Area, will be as follows :-

Div'l Hd.Qtrs.	LOUVENCOURT (a).
41st Infantry Bde.	LOUVENCOURT (a).
42nd Infantry Bde.	PUCHEVILLERS (b).
43rd Infantry Bde.	BUS LES ARTOIS (a).

   (a) Supplies delivered to units by Supply Section of the Div'l Train.
   (b) Supplies will be drawn from Refilling Point by 1st line transport of units.

   Time of refilling, 8.30 A.M.

4. Supplies will be drawn by the D.S.C. and Div'l Train, respectively, from Rail-heads as follows :-

	Div.H.Q.	41st I.B.	42nd I.B.	43rd I.B.
June 10.	ARRAS (a)	ARRAS (b)	ARRAS (a)	ARRAS (b)
" 11.	ROSEL (a)	ARRAS (a)	ROSEL (a)	"
" 12.	"	"	ROSE (b)	"
" 13.	"	ROSEL (a)	"	"
" 14.	"	"	"	ARRAS (a)
" 15.	"	"	"	ROSEL (a)

   (a) Drawn by D.S.C.
   (b) " " Div'l Train.

5. The 14th Div'l Supply Column will move complete to BEAUQUESNE on or before June 15th. Sufficient lorries will be sent ahead to BEAUQUESNE to draw supplies from ROSEL for Div'l Hd.Qtrs. and 2 Brigades as they arrive and to provide 10 lorries for the Division.

R. Lewis Lt.W.
A.A. & Q.M.G.,
14TH (LIGHT) DIVISION.

COPIES to :
Recipients of Q.345/1 dated 8/6/17.

App 4

SCHEME FOR DESTROYING "DUD" SHELL.

1. Divisional Area divided into "salvage areas" and each salvage area allotted to a Unit. Each Unit locates the dud shell in its salvage area, marks them with a picket and piece of white cloth, and sends in a sketch to Divisional Headquarters of its salvage area showing the location of each dud shell by a red dot.

2. Party as follows:-

    Artillery. 1 Officer in charge with Field glasses, whistle and note-
                1 N.C.O.)   book.
                5 men.)Mounted with red flags.
                1 N.C.O.)
                5 men.)Dismounted, with picks, shovels & sandbags.

    Engineers. 1 Officer to superintend laying of charges.
                1 N.C.O.) Dismounted with exploder guncotton slabs primers
                3 men.) detonators and 300 yards of double   line cable.
    R.A.M.C.   1 Orderly.

3. Artillery party start work to
    i.   Collect shell into groups of about 10 at a shell hole.
    ii. Prepare shell hole with pit as in attached diagram.
    iii. Place shell in pit.
         The Field Gun shell are carried by hand, the 5.9" and 6" in a stretcher. Shell larger than 6" detonated in situ if this is possible. If not they must be buried 7 ft deep.

4. Engineer party (with R.A.M.C. orderly) start work 3 hours later to
    i. Place charges.
    ii. Lay out cable from shell pits to   trench or dug out selected for exploding party.

5. When all is ready for detonation Artillery Officer sends out the mounted men to
    i. Warn units within 500 yards that the explosion will take place in 5 minutes on a blast of the whistle.
    ii. Keep individuals or vehicles from approaching the spot and clear away parties within 500 yards.

6. When the Artillery Officer sees with his glasses that the red flags have gone to units and that the latter are warned and that the ground is clear he blows one long blast on the whistle. As soon as he sees that any men within 500 yards have taken cover the Artillery Officer tells the Engineer Officer to explode the charge.

7. When the charge has exploded the Red flags come in and wait for orders when next charge is ready. The craters are examined to see that no unexploded shell remain. If they do they are placed with the next lot to be exploded or are given a second charge.

8. Several "nests" of shell can be exploded simultaneously. It is better not to explode more than 12 shell together unless the ground is quite clear of troops.

9. The Artillery Officer notes the shell destroyed each day and enters them on a schedule giving map reference, nature of shell, charge used and remarks as to method and results.

PIT
for exploding nest of "dud" shell.

Sectional Elevation

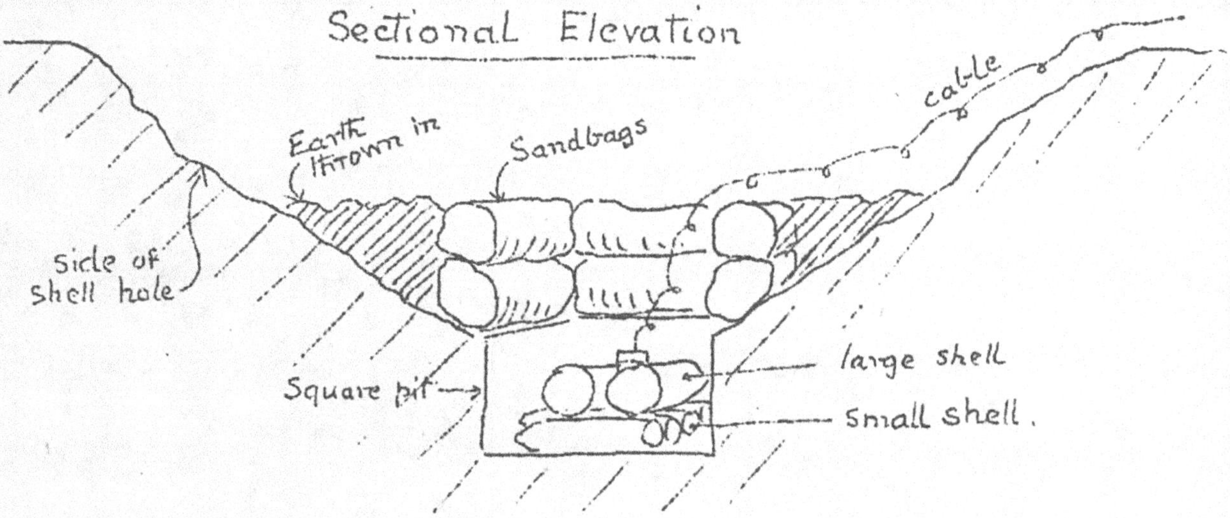

Plan of Pit

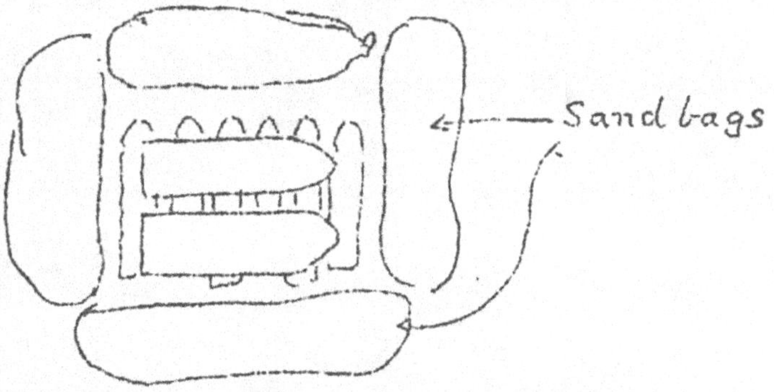

Square pit at bottom of shell hole. Sandbags round top of pit with earth filled in behind. Field Gun shell on floor of pit. 5.9" and 6" shell on top. Charge 2 slabs of guncotton, one between two of the big shells and one across the top of the shell and the first slab.

Section of charge

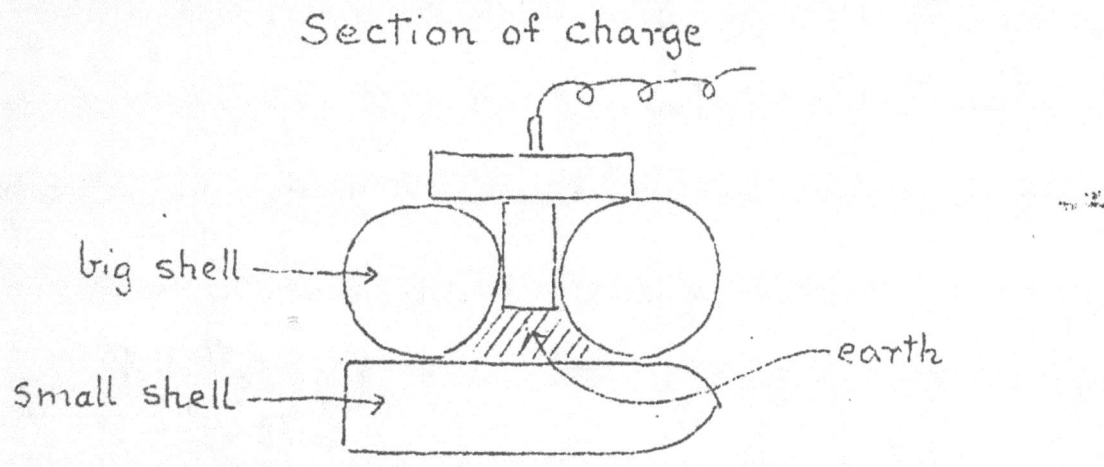

14th (LIGHT) DIVISION.

SCHEDULE OF "DUD" SHELL DESTROYED.

NATURE of SHELL	MAP REFERENCE	CHARGE USED.	REMARKS.

DATE.................

....
OFFICER i/c PARTY.

App 5

DIVISIONAL HORSE SHOW
held
JUNE 26th 1917.

LIST OF PRIZE WINNERS.

---oOo---

EVENT 1. WRESTLING.

    1. ....No.3 Coy. 14th Divisional Train.
    2. ....11th Bn. King's Liverpool Regt.

EVENT 2. TURNOUT G.S. WAGGON OR FIELD AMBULANCE.

    1. ....No.3 Coy. 14th Divisional Train.
    2. ....No.2 Coy. 14th Divisional Train.
    3. ....43rd Field Ambulance.

EVENT 3. TURNOUT - COOKER.

    1. ....9th Bn. Rifle Brigade.
    2. ....8th Bn. Rifle Brigade.
    3. ....10th Bn. Durham Light Infantry.

EVENT 4. GROOMS COMPETITION.

    1. ....Lt. Col. G.A.P. Rennie's groom.
    2. ....Lt. Col. F.A.U. Pickering's groom.
    3. ....Major Mead Waldo's groom.

EVENT 5. PACK PONIES TURNOUT.

    1. ....43rd Machine Gun Coy.
    2. ....10th Durham Light Infantry.
    3. ....9th Rifle Brigade.

EVENT 6. TURNOUT G.S. LIMBERED WAGGON.

    1. ....9th Rifle Brigade.
    2. ....43rd Machine Gun Coy.
    3. ....6th Somerset Light Infantry.

EVENT 7. HARNESSING COMPETITION.

    1. ....No. 2. Coy. 14th Divisional Train.
    2. ....9th Rifle Brigade.
    3. ....6th Somerset Light Infantry.

EVENT 8. RELAY RACE.

    1. ....6th Somerset Light Infantry.
    2. ....14th Divisional Signals.

EVENT 9. MULE HURDLE RACE.

    1. ....42nd Machine Gun Coy.
    2. ....9th Rifle Brigade.

EVENT 10. OFFICERS JUMPING.

    (a) Dismounted Units ......Major F.M. Micholls, 6th Bn. K.O.Y.L.I.

    (b) All Units ....Major A.L. Brown, A.P.M.

App. 6

SECRET.   Q.364.

C. R.E.
11th Bn. K. L'pool R.
14th Div'l Train.
S.S.O.
14th Div'l Supply Column.
"G".
IX Corps "Q".

Reference para. 1 (a) of 14th Division S.G.3151 dated 24/6/17 :

Arrangements for the move of 3 Field Co.'s and 11th Bn. K.L'pool R. on June 28th are as follows :-

1. **TRAIN ARRANGEMENTS.**

ENTRAIN AT	TIME OF DEPARTURE.	COMPOSITION OF TRAIN. COACHES. COVERS. FLATS.			UNIT.
S A U L T Y	11.15	1	30	17	11th King's less personnel of 1 Co.
DO.	15.15	1	26	21	89th Fld. Co. R.E. Half 61st F.Co.RE with half transp. Half Coy.11th King's
DO.	19.15	1	26	21	62nd Fld.Co. R.E. Half 61st Fd.C.RE with half Transpt. Half Co.11th King's

Units will entrain 3 hours before time of departure.
The senior officer with each train will be in Command of the whole of the personnel on that train from the beginning of entraining until detraining is completed.

2. **SUPPLY.**

Rations for 3 Field Co.'s R.E. and 11th K. L'pool R. for consumption on 29th and 30th are being drawn on 27th instant.
Rations for 29th will be issued to the above units to-day and will be carried by them on the 28th
Rations for 30th will be carried to destination on Supply Lorries, dumped on arrival under charge of advance parties.
Rations for July 1st will be drawn at destination by Supply Lorries on June 29th.

3. **ADVANCE PARTIES.**

The following advance parties will move on the Supply Lorries on June 28th :-

        For 3 Field Co.'s ... 1 Officer, 3 O.R.
        " 11th King's ... 1 " 4 "

This personnel will go to BEAUQUESNE this evening (27th), will report to the Town Major for billets and will leave BEAUQUESNE by lorries, starting at 7.0 A.M. on 28th instant from Hd.Qtrs. Div'l Supply Column.

4. **REPORT ON ARRIVAL.**

Units and advance parties will report on arrival to Commandant Area II LOCRE for further instructions.

R. Lewis Lulu
A.A. & Q.M.G.,
14th (Light) Division.

27/6/17.

Secret

Vol 22

War Diary
of
13th (Light) Division
Administrative Branch
July 1st 1917 to 31st July 1917
Volume 49

WAR DIARY or INTELLIGENCE SUMMARY

Army Form C. 2118.

(Erase heading not required.)

Place	Date	Hour	Summary of Events and Information	Remarks and references to Appendices
MARIEUX	July 1		42nd hy Bde Sports and 14th Div Signal Co Sports.	
	2		Went to see IX Corps and got information about new area and accommodation round St JANS CAPEL.	
	3-5		Normal routine.	
	6		Went to VII Corps & make preliminary arrangements about the move by rail.	
	7		Arranged with DADRT & Albert the preliminary allotment of units to trains.	
	8		Completed arrangement with DADRT V. & orders for move by rail see App 1.	App 1.
	9		Issued detailed orders for move of division by rail see App 1.	App 2.
	10		Issued admin'v instrns arrangements for new area.	
	11		Move by railway commenced. Trains punctual in starting. Arrived about an hour late. Lorries took unit men to station after dumping supplies. S.C. Went up by Noed Enqty picking up Div Depot Batt (staff duty) en route.	

Army Form C. 2118.

WAR DIARY
or
INTELLIGENCE SUMMARY

(Erase heading not required.)

Instructions regarding War Diaries and Intelligence Summaries are contained in F. S. Regs., Part II. and the Staff Manual respectively. Title Pages will be prepared in manuscript.

Place	Date	Hour	Summary of Events and Information	Remarks and references to Appendices
S Jeans Capel	12		Gens Couper Dudgeon & Wood attended inspection by H.M. at Third Army HQ at Albert & came on to the new area by car. Lent train left Doullens about 6 p.m.	
	13		Detrain went of lent train completed about 2 a.m.	
	14.		Normal routine	
	17.		Went to II Army Workshops to see water carts. Demonstration of Yukon pack. Seems satisfactory. D.S.C. drew one day's preserved rations for dumping as a Reserve.	
	18-20		Normal routine	
	21		Conference at IX Corps HdQ on future movement of division and new areas to be allotted.	
	22.		Normal routine	
	23		Reconnoitred the area about WYTSCHAETE.	
	24.		Normal routine	

Army Form C. 2118.

WAR DIARY
or
INTELLIGENCE SUMMARY

(Erase heading not required.)

Place	Date	Hour	Summary of Events and Information	Remarks and references to Appendices
S' Jans Capel	25 26 27		normal routine	
	28 29		Issued instruction for formation of Div' Employment Co.	Appx III
	30 31		normal routine.	

E. Duningham

War Diary.

App. 1.

SECRET.   O.C/50/2.

ADMINISTRATIVE ORDERS FOR THE MOVE.

1. Reference 14th Division D.O. No.129 dated 8/7/17, the entraining stations, times of departure and units in each train are shown in the attached schedules. The train journey takes about 6 hours.

2. <u>All trains</u> consist of

1 coach	to hold	30 Officers
30 covered trucks	" " each	40 men or 6 H.D. horses or 8 L.D. "
17 flat trucks	" " each	4 axles.

   2 Brake vans in which no personnel or stores may be carried.

3. <u>Baggage</u> may be carried in the covered trucks so long as the the space required for personnel is not restricted. The largest amount of spare truck accommodation is in the last train from each station, and any surplus personnel or baggage should be carried in these trains.

4. <u>Loading Parties</u> of two officers and 100 men will be detailed by each Brigade for duty at their entraining station. They will report to the R.T.O. four hours before the first train is due to leave each station. They will entrain with the last train from each station and should therefore be detailed from a unit travelling by that train. Brigades will arrange to ration them.

5. <u>Unloading Parties</u> of two officers and 100 men will be detailed by each Brigade for duty at their detraining station from the units travelling by the first train at each station. They will report to the R.T.O. at the detraining station immediately on arrival.

6. <u>Entraining Officers.</u> At each entraining station the Brigade Transport Officer, or other suitable officer detailed by the Brigade, will act as entraining officer. His duties are to organize the entrainment of the transport in consultation with the R.T.O.
   Names to be reported to this office on July 10th.

7. <u>Detraining Officers.</u> At each detraining station an officer will be detailed by the Brigade to organize the detrainment. He will proceed by the first train from each entraining station. Names to be reported to this office on July 10th.

8. <u>Staff Officers for Entraining.</u> The D.A.Q.M.G. and G.S.O.II will be at the R.T.O's office DOULLENS during the entrainment. O.C.14th Signal Company will detail three motor cycle orderlies for duty under the D.A.Q.M.G. They will proceed in the last train from DOULLENS.

9. <u>Staff Officers for Detraining.</u> The D.A.A.G. and G.S.O.III will be at the R.T.O's office, BAILLEUL during the detrainment. Three motor cycle orderlies, detailed by O.C.14th Signal Company, will proceed by the first train from DOULLENS NORTH and will report to the D.A.A.G. on arrival at BAILLEUL.

CONTINUED.

10. **Entraining.** Infantry Battalions. The transport will arrive at the entraining station three hours and the personnel one and a half hours before the departure of the train.

Other units will arrive complete three hours before the departure of the train.

Troops will halt outside the station yard until permission has been obtained from the R.T.O. to enter. For this purpose, each unit on arrival will send an officer and orderly to report to the R.T.O.

A complete marching out state, showing the numbers of men, horses, G.S., Limbered G.S., and two wheeled wagons and bicycles, will be sent down with the transport of each unit and given to the R.T.O. at the beginning of each entrainment.

The entrainment of all units must be completed half an hour before the time of departure of the train, when it will be moved from the loading siding.

11. **Wagons.** Supply and baggage wagons will accompany their own units in every case. Ropes for lashing vehicles to trucks will be provided by the Railway. Supply wagons will entrain loaded.

12. **Horses.** Breast Ropes for horses' trucks are not provided by the Railway. The Brigade Transport Officer will arrange to draw from the R.E. Headquarter Transport lines at H.30.c.8.6. on the MARIEUX - RAINCHEVAL Road, sufficient rope for all the horses entraining at his station.

Harness will be taken off and packed neatly in sets in the centre of each truck so that it can be quickly put on when the destination is reached.

All horses must be provided with head collars and head ropes for the journey.

Arrangements must be made to water all horses immediately before entrainment.

13. **Water carts** must entrain full, and water bottles must also be full.

14. **Police.** The A.P.M. will detail three M.M.P. to be on duty at each entraining station throughout the entrainment. These M.M.P. will proceed by the last train from each station.

Three M.M.P. will proceed by the first train at each station and will be on duty at the detraining station during detrainment.

Each unit on arrival at the detraining station will post picquets as required by the detraining officer to prevent men leaving the station premises.

15. **Billeting Parties** from each unit will proceed by the first train of their group and will report on arrival to the Commandant of the Areas as under:-

Group.	Area.	Commandant.
41st Brigade.	15	Lt.Col.FORBES, KOKEREELE Farm R.22.b.6.9.
42nd Brigade.	13	Lt. WEST, Billet 22, St.JANS CAPEL
43rd Brigade.	14	Capt. DOUGLAS, M.20.d.5.5.

Brigade H.Q. Billeting parties will proceed by motor ambulance (see para.16) on the morning of July 11th and report to the Area Commandant.

CONTINUED.

-3-

16. **Medical.**

A.D.M.S. will detail three motor ambulances to report to Brigade Headquarters at 8.0 A.M. on July 11th to take Brigade H.Q. billeting parties to the new Area. These motor ambulances will proceed to the detraining stations at 6.0 A.M. on July 12th and remain there until detraining is completed under orders of the D.A.A.G.

A.D.M.S. will also arrange for one motor ambulance to be at CANDAS Station and one at DOULLENS Station during the period of entrainment, under the orders of the D.A.Q.M.G.

17. **Motor Vehicles.**

All motor vehicles will go to the new Area by road on July 11th unless detailed for work in this area on that day, in which case they will go on July 12th.
Route: ST. POL, BRUAY, MERVILLE, NEUF BERQUIN, VIEUX BERQUIN, BAILLEUL.
No restrictions as to time.
D.S.C. will move in one column, under orders of O.C.14th D.S.C., to S.3.Central (Sheet 28).
Motor ambulances in a separate column under orders from A.D.M.

18. **Latrines.**

If a unit halts outside the station and has to wait before entering the station to entrain, latrines must be dug immediately. When the unit moves into the station, these latrines will be filled in and all loose paper, rubbish etc. collected and buried in them.

19. **Supply.**

Railhead, on and before July 11th   ...   ROSEL
  "   on and after July 12th   ...   HAEGEDOORNE.

Refilling Points :-

GROUP.		JULY 11th.	JULY 13th AND AFTER.
41st Infantry Bde.		BEAUVAL.G.28.c.0.5.	Road S.E. of BERTHEN.
42nd " "		1st...PUCHEVILLERS.	HAEGEDOORNE.
" " "		2nd...CANDAS.	
43rd " "		GEZAINCOURT.Billet 57.	MONT NOIR.

There will be a double refilling on July 11th, as shown in the attached Supply Schedule.

All units will entrain with :
  Iron ration on the man.
  Rations for 12th on the man or on cooker.
  Rations for 13th on Supply Wagons.

Supply wagons and teams will be included in the Marching out State of each unit (para.10).
Supply wagons will rejoin their Companies of the Train on July 12th after delivering rations for consumption on 13th.

In the case of the Salvage Company, Div'l Employment Coy. and Div'l Company, the rations for consumption on July 12th and 13th will be delivered by Div'l Train on July 11th at 2.0 P.M. at CANDAS Station, to a representative to be detailed by O.C. Salvage Coy. On arrival of the units, the rations for the 12th will be distributed to the men, and those for the 13th will remain on the wagon and be entrained with the unit. O.C. Salvage will include this G.S. Wagon, 2 horses and 1 driver in his Marching out State (para.10).

19. (Contd.)
In the case of Div'l Hd.Qtrs., Signals and A.P.M., the rations for 13th will be sent after 2nd refilling on July 11th direct to DOULLENS Station in Supply Wagons and the A.P.M.'s Limber, and will there wait for their units to entrain.

Div'l Train will be billeted in the new Area at K.11.a.5.0, half-way between St.Jans CAPEL and METEREN.

D.S.C. will be at S.3.central, half-way between BAILLEUL and LOCRE.

SUPPLY SCHEDULE.

41st and 43rd Bde. Groups.

DATE.	RATIONS FOR CONSUMPTION ON			
	11th.	12th.	13th.	14th.
9th.	D.S.C. draw.			
10th.	Train refills and delivers.	D.S.C. draw and dump at R.P.		
11th.		Train refill and deliver.	D.S.C. draw and dump at R.P. Train refill and entrain loaded with units.	
12th			Supply Wagons with units.	D.S.C. draw.
13th.				Train refill.

42nd Bde. Group.

	11th.	12th.	13th.	14th.
9th.	Train draw.			
10th.	1st line refill.	Train draw.		
11th.		1st line refill.	D.S.C. draw and dump at R.P. CANDAS. Train refill and entrain loaded with units	
12th.			Supply Wagons with units.	D.S.C. draw.
13th.				Train refill.

ENTRAINING STATION, DOULLENS (SOUTH).

TRAIN NO.	DATE.	TIME OF DEPARTURE.	SERIAL NO.	UNIT.
3	11th	20.19	1410	41st Brigade Head Quarters.
			1411a	1 Coy., 1 Cooker & Team, 7th K.R.R.C.
			1412a	" " " 8th K.R.R.C.
			1415	41st Brigade Signal Section.
			1416	41st Machine Gun Company
			1417	41st Trench Mortar Battery.
6	12th.	0.19	1411	7th K.R.R.C., less 1 Company.
9	12th	4.19	1412	8th K.R.R.C., less 1 Company.
12	12th	8.19	1413	7th R.B., less 1 Company.
15	12th	12.19	1414	8th R.B., less 1 Company.
18	12th	16.19	1413a	1 Company, 1 Cooker & Team, 7th R.B.
			1414a	" " " 8th R.B.
			1488	44th Field Ambulance.

DETRAINING STATION - GODEWAERSVELDE.

Picquets. During the journey picquets will be provided of 8 troops for each end of the train to prevent troops leaving. They will be told off beforehand and entrained in trucks near the end of each train.

24. The Senior Officer travelling by each train will be in command of the train and will be responsible for discipline during the journey.

P.E. Lewis Lt.Col.
A.A. & Q.M.G,
14th (Light) Division.

9/7/17.

Copies to:-

VII Corps............... 1	Camp Commandant............. 1
IX Corps................ 1	D.A.D.O.S................... 1
R.T.O. CANDAS.......... 1	D.A.D.V.S................... 2
" DOULLENS........ 1	A.P.M....................... 1
" GODEWAERSVELDE 1	Salvage Coy.................. 1
" BAILLEUL........ 1	Div'l Coy................... 1
41st Infantry Bde...... 8	215th Employment Coy......... 1
42nd " " ... 8	French Mission.............. 1
43rd " " ... 8	A.A.& Q.M.G................. 1
B.T.O.41st Inf.Bde..... 1	D.A.A.G..................... 1
B.T.O.42nd " " ... 1	D.A.Q.M.G................... 1
B.T.O.43rd " " ... 1	G.S.O. II.................... 1
Div'l Train............ 5	G.S.O. III.................. 2
S.S.O.................. 1	G, ... 2
D.S.C.................. 1	Diary....................... 2
A.D.M.S................ 4	File........................ 1
14th Signal Coy........ 1	

ENTRAINING STATION - DOULLENS (NORTH).

Train No.	Date.	Time of Departure.	Serial No.	UNIT.
1.	11th	18.19	1430	43rd Infantry Bde H.Q.
			1431a	1 Coy, 1 Cooker & team 6th D.C.L.I.
			1435	43rd Bde Sig. Sect.
			1436	43rd M.G.Coy.
			1437	43rd T.M.Bty.
			1478	No. 4. Coy. Div'l Train.
4	11th	22.19	1401	Div'l Hd. Qrs.
			1405	Hd.Qrs.& No.1 Sect. Signals.
			1496	Hd.Qrs. Div. Depot Battln.
7	12th	2.19	1431	6th Bn. D.C.L.I. less 1 Coy.
10	12 th	6.19	1432	6th Bn. K.O.Y.L.I.
13	12th	10.04	1433	6th Som. L.I. less 1 Coy.
16	12th	14.19	1434	10th Durham L.I. less 1 Coy.
19	12th	18.19	1433a	1 Coy, 1 Cooker & team 6th Som.L.I.
			1434a	" " " 10th Dur.L.I.
			1486	42nd Field Ambulance.
			1490	26th Mob. Vet. Sect.

DETRAINING STATION - BAILLEUL (MAIN)

ENTRAINING STATION - CANDAS.

Train No.	Date.	Time of Departure.	Serial No.	UNIT.
2	11th	18.51	1420 1421a 1425 1426 1427 1477	42nd Infantry Bde H.Q. 1 Coy, 1 Cooker & team 5th Ox.&Buck 42nd Bde. Sig.Sect. 42nd M.G.Coy. 42nd T.M.Bty. No.3 Coy.Div'l Train.
5	11th	22.51	1407 1489 - 1475 1495 1476	Salvage Coy. 215 Div'l Emp. Coy. Div.l Coy. Hd. Qrs. Div'l Train. A.D.Cable Section. No.2. Coy. Div'l Train.
8	12th	2.51	1421	5th Ox. & Bucks L.I.less 1 Coy.
11	12th	6.51	1422	5th K.S.L.I.
14	12th	10.51	1423	9th K.R.R.C. less 1 Coy.
17	12th	14.51	1424	9th R.B. less 1 Coy.
20	12th	18.51	1423a 1424a 1487	1 Coy, 1 Cooker & team 9th K.R.R.C. " " " 9th R.B. 43rd Field Ambulance.

DETRAINING STATION - BAILLEUL (WEST).

SECRET.   O.C./50/2.

ADMINISTRATIVE ORDERS FOR THE MOVE.
* * * * * * * * * * * * * * * * *

With reference to the Train Schedules issued with O.C./50/2 of 9/7/17, the following amendments are made with a view to easing the accommodation in some of the trains.

The Schedules will be amended accordingly.

ENTRAINING STATION, DOULLENS (SOUTH).
TRAIN NO.

3. For "1 Coy., 1 Cooker and Team, 7th K.R.R.C.,"
    Substitute "2 Platoons, 7th K.R.R.C."

    For "1 Coy., 1 Cooker and Team, 8th K.R.R.C.,"
    Substitute "2 Platoons, 8th K.R.R.C."

6. For "less 1 Company,"
    Substitute "less 2 Platoons."

9. For "less 1 Company,"
    Substitute "less 2 Platoons."

ENTRAINING STATION, CANDAS.
TRAIN NO.

2. Delete "No. 3 Coy. Div'l Train."

5. Add ("No. 3 Coy. Div'l Train."
        ("26th Mobile Vet'y Section."

ENTRAINING STATION, DOULLENS (NORTH).
TRAIN NO.

1. After "43rd Infantry Bde. Hd.Qtrs.,"
    Insert "less Brigade Pioneer Coy."

    Delete "43rd T.M. Bty."

4. After "Div'l Hd.Qtrs.,"
    Insert "less Traffic Control men."

    After "Hd.Qtrs. Div'l Depot Battn.,"
    Insert "transport only."

7. Add "Traffic control men."

10. Add "Brigade Pioneer Coy."

13. Add "43rd T.M. Bty."

19. Delete "26th Mobile Vet'y Section."

A.A. & Q.M.G.,

9/7/17.   14th (Light) Division.

App II
O.C/50/7.

ADMINISTRATIVE ARRANGEMENTS IN THE NEW AREA.

1. The location of units is given in the table below. Further details will be given to advanced parties by Area Commandants

Unit.	Hd.Qrs to be at:
Divisional H.Q.	St. JANS CAPEL.
AREA 13.	
42nd Bde.	S.7.b.6.4.
"A" Battn.	S.1.d.7..6.
"B" "	S.8.a.8.3.
"C" "	S.8.a.6.3.
"D" "	S.2.a.8.8.
43rd Fld Amb.	S.9.a.6.9.
42nd M.G.Coy.	M.32.d.9.1.
42nd T.M.Bty.	S.2.a.4.0.
AREA 14.	
43rd Bde.	M.20.d.5.5.
"A" Battn.	M.20.a.0.6.
"B" "	R.24.a.05.
"C" "	M.20.d.6.6.
"D" "	M.13.d.6.1.
42nd Fld Amb.	M.15.c.1.0.
43rd M.G.Coy.	M.14.b.1.5.
43rd T.M.Bty.	M.20.a.0.6.
AREA 15.	
41st Bde.	R.16.d.6.5.
"A" Battn.	R.22.a.4.4.
"B" "	R.22.b.7.8.
"C" "	R.18.a.7.7.
"D" "	R.17.b.5.3.
44th Fld Amb.	R.17.b.5.2.
41st M.G.Coy.	R.22.b.7.5.
41st T.M.Bty.	R.22.b.6.9.
Div'l Train.	X.11.a.5.0.
Div'l Supply Column.	S.3.Central.
Div'l Depot Battn.	M.21.b.4.3.

2. Supply Railhead is HAEGEDOORNE. On and after July 14th the Pack Train will be cleared by the Divisional Train.
   First Line transport will draw supplies from refilling point daily on and after July 14th.
   Time of refilling to be notified later.
   Refilling points will be:
   (i) M.32.c.5.9. between St. JANS CAPEL and Cx de POPERINGHE.
   (ii) S.2.b.0.6. Just east of MEULE HOUCK.
   The allotment of Groups to refilling points will be notified later.

3. The Field Ambulances will each deal with the sick of their own Brigade Group. In addition, the 43rd Field Ambulance at HAEGE-DOORNE will deal with the sick of Div'l Head Quarters, Div'l Train, and Div'l Supply Column, and the 42nd Field Ambulance will deal with the Div'l Depot Battalion.

CONTINUED.

-2-

4. **BATHS.** The Divisional Baths & Laundry are at St. JANS CAPEL, South end of village.
The Baths will deal with about 80 men an hour and will be open daily from 8.0 a.m. to 6.0 p.m. continuously.
They will be open on and after . July 13.
Allotment will be as follows:-

    July 13th. ------------Divisional Headquarters.
    " 14th.)
    " 15th.)
    " 16th.} ... ... 41st Infantry Brigade.
    " 17th.)

Clean clothes and coal will be supplied under Divisional arrangements.

5.   D.A.D.O.S. Store will be in St.JANS CAPEL, Billet 83.

6.   The I.O.M. IX Corps and the IX Corps Ordnance Workshops are at M.28.d,6.9. on the BAILLEUL-LOCRE Road.
There is a medium Ordnance Workshop in Rue de la Gare, BAILLEUL.
Second Army Ordnance Mobile Workshops (heavy) are at HAZEBROUCK.
The IX Corps R.E.Park is at ZEVECOTEN C.36.c.1.1. and at BAILLEUL Station.
IX Corps Horse dip for Mange, St.JANS CAPEL S.1.d.1.8.
IX Corps Salvage dump, HAEGEDOORNE Siding S.9.a.4.4.

7. **POSTAL.** The ordinary and special delivery of mails will cease after the mail delivered to F.P.O.'s to-morrow, 11th instant.
Postal arrangements in the new Area will be notified on arrival.

8. **LEAVE TRAINS.** Depart CANDAS EXCHANGE 21.00 daily to catch boat sailing on the following day.
Depart HAZEBROUCK 3.53 daily to catch boat sailing on the same day.
All "Move" trains should arrive at HAZEBROUCK 5 hours after time of departure from Entraining Station. Units whose "Move" trains do not arrive at HAZEBROUCK in time to catch the 3.53 should send personnel sailing on 13th instant by the train from CANDAS on 12th. All "Move" trains stop at HAZEBROUCK for 15 minutes, so that units whose "Move" trains catch the connection at HAZEBROUCK can put off their men for leave there with instructions to report to the R.T.O.
All men proceeding on leave must be in possession of rations for day of arrival in England.
Arrangements for transport of leave parties to HAZEBROUCK from units' new locations from 14th instant, will be issued after arrival in the new Area.

                                                                   A.A. & Q.M.G.,
10/7/17.   14th (Light) Division.

A.A. & Q.M.G.   File   A.342/24. App II

In continuation of this Office No. A.342/14 dated 18/6/17 :-

1. The Divisional Employment Company will now be formed in accordance with the instructions outlined in the above letter. All extra-regimental employments within the Division will in future be carried out by men on the establishment of the D.E.C. or by men who are authorised to be attached to it : the same will eventually be the case with all men extra-regimentally employed outside the Division ; but as Corps and Area Employment Companies have not yet been formed it will still be necessary to call on Units to provide men for employment at Corps Schools, with Area Commandants, for extra traffic control or for any employments for which the Division is called upon to provide men.

For this purpose convalescent men will be employed and arrangements will be made for a Convalescent Company to be formed on the same lines as the present Divisional Company. These arrangements will be notified separately.

2. Without special authority from the Corps Commander no men beyond the numbers laid down are to be withdrawn from their units except in the case of tactical working parties. This will reduce the numbers of men shown as absent from their Battalions in the Fighting Strength Return, which will in future only show men absent from their Units for the following purposes :-

    (i) Attending Courses.
    (ii) Sick in Divisional Area.
   (iii) Leave.
    (iv) Employed outside the Division.

A new pro forma for Strength Returns is shown in "Appendix I" and will be taken into use for the Strength Return for the week ending August 4th, 1917.

3. The attached "Appendix II" shows the employments found by :

X. Men at present with D.E.C.

Y. Men to be transferred to D.E.C., having been examined by a Medical Board and classified "B.1" or some lower category.

Z. Men attached to D.E.C., showing
    (i) Class "A" men attached to D.E.C., under para. 4 of this Office A.342/14 dated 18/6/17.
   (ii) Class "A" men attached to D.E.C., under para. 5 of this Office A.342/14 dated 18/6/17.

4. 2nd Lieut. E.H. JONES, Officer Commanding D.E.C., will arrange with O/C Units concerned to supply the numbers of men shown in Column X as early as possible. These men will relieve the men at present employed on the duties shown opposite each figure in Column X and the men relieved will be returned to their Units by 31st July, 1917.

5. The attached "Appendix III" gives a nominal roll of all men in column Y who have been classified "B.1" or some lower category by a Medical Board and who will be transferred to the Labour Corps and taken on to the establishment of the D.E.C. under arrangements to be made by O.C. D.E.C. with O.C. Units concerned. These men may be struck off the establishment of their Battalions as soon as their transfer is completed.

6. The attached "Appendix IV" gives a nominal roll of all men shown in Column Z (i) : these men will be attached to the D.E.C. and may be struck off the establishment of their Battalions, with effect from 1st August, 1917.

(CONTINUED)

7. The attached "Appendix V" gives a nominal roll of all men shown in Column Z (ii) : these men will be attached to the D.E.C. until such time as they are relieved by suitable Class "B.1" men, when they will rejoin their Units. They may be struck off the strength of their Battalions, with effect from 1st August, 1917, and reinforcements demanded in their place.

8. The existing arrangements made by D.A.D.O.S. with Battalions for the employment of certain shoemakers, tailors and saddlers will hold good. The fatigue men at present employed by D.A.D.O.S. and C.R.E. and the Guard attached to the A.P.M. will be returned to their Battalions as soon as they can be replaced by temporarily unfit men from the Convalescent Company. A nominal roll of men at present attached is given in "Appendix VI".

9. A certain proportion of the men who will be returned to their Units as a result of these instructions will be men who have been attached to the Divisional Company for a considerable time and are not fitted for front line work with their Battalions : any such men who cannot be usefully employed within their Battalions should be disposed of in accordance with the instructions issued under this Office No. A/206 dated 26/2/17.

10. No allowance has been made in the establishment of the D.E.C. for men employed at the Divisional Depot. These men will remain detached from their Battalions at present and will be shown in Column B of the new Strength Return pro forma.

11. A certificate will be rendered by the following Officers to reach this Office by 1st August, 1917, to the effect that no men of this Division are being employed by them in excess of the numbers shown in "Appendix II" except as allowed by para. 8 and shown in "Appendix VI" :-

    D.A.D.O.S.   O.C. Baths & Laundries.
    C. R.E.   Camp Commandant.
    O.C. Div. Train.   Divisional Supply Column.
    O.C. Salvage Coy.

12. The attached "Appendix VII" gives the posting of N.C.O.s to fill the establishment of the D.E.C.

13. The attached "Appendix VIII" shows the distribution of loaders for all Units in the Division.

    NOTE. - The last sentence of para. 2 refers only to Infantry Brigades and 11th Bn. King's Liverpool Regt. (Pioneers)

R. Lewis Lt.W?
A. A. & Q.M.G.,
14th (Light) Division.

28/7/17.

App'x

FIGHTING STRENGTH - ....INFANTRY BRIGADE.

Made up to 8.0 A.M. FRIDAY, ...191 .

A	B	C		D	E	F	Z	Z(i)
Available number of rifles.	On Courses or at Schools.	Detached for Duties other than 'B'.		At F'ld Amb. including D.R.S.	Short Leave and Absentees.	Total Strength as reported to Second Army.	In Div'l Depot Bn. included in Col. 'F'.	Untrained in Div'l Depot Bn.
		C.1 Within the Corps other than 'D.1'	C.2 Outside the Corps.					
Offs. O.R.	Offs. O.R.	Offs. O.R.	Offs. O.R.	Offs. O.R.	Offs. O.R.	Offs. O.R.	Offs. O.R.	Offs. O.R.
Brigade H.Q.								
...Bn.								
...Bn.								
...Bn.								
...Bn.								
M.G. Coy.								
T.M. Bty.								

..........191 .

Brigadier-General,

Commanding ..... Infantry Brigade.

APPENDIX II.

Employment.	X	Y	Z (i)	Z (ii)	TOTAL.
INFANTRY BRIGADES.					
41st Infantry Bde.					
(a) Clerks			2	1	3
(b) Cooks		1	2		3
(c) Mess Sergt.				1	1
(d) Asst. Q.M.S.			1		1
(e) Train Loaders	7	5			12
	7	6	5	2	20
42nd Infantry Bde.					
(a) Clerks		1	1		2
(b) Cooks		2			2
(c) Orderlies			2		2
(d) Canteen		1			1
(e) Train Loaders	9	3			12
	9	7	3		19
43rd Infantry Bde.					
(a) Clerks		3			3
(b) Cooks		2			2
(c) Storeman			1		1
(d) Orderlies		2			2
(e) Train Loaders	7	5			12
	7	12	1		20
	23	25	9	2	59

Employment.	X	Y	"1"	"2"	TOTAL.
DIVISIONAL TROOPS.					
Canteen, Div'l		2	1		3
Train Loaders	38				38
Entertainments (Cinema)		2	2		4
Salvage Coy.	26	20	4		50
Baths and Laundries	6	15	1		22
D.A.D.O.S.					
(a) Clerks		3			3
(b) Storeman		1			1
(c) Cook		1			1
		5			5
Supply Column Loaders	2	7			9
Burials Clerk				1	1
Railhead Disb'g Off'r				1	1
Div'l Bomb Store			1		1
	72	51	9	2	134

APPENDIX II.
(Continued)

Employment.			"1"	"2"	TOTAL.
DIVISIONAL HD.QTRS.					
Cooks		2	3		5
Train Loaders	1				1
Clerks	1	2	3		6
Orderlies	4	2			6
Sanitary	1	2			3
Guard		5			5
Mess Waiters		5	1		6
Transport		2	1		3
	7	20	8		35
EMPLOYMENT COMPANY.					
C.Q.M.S.	1				1
Clerk	1				1
Batman	1				1
Reserve	12				12
Band		4		26	30
	15	4		26	45
T O T A L.	117	100	26	30	273

APPENDIX III.   Column "Y".

INFANTRY BRIGADES.

41st Infantry Brigade.

6122	Rifleman	G. Treblo	7th R.B.
R.10919	"	F. Ash	7th K.R.R.C.
8331	"	J. Ship	8th R.B.
33636	"	A. G. Lyons	8th K.R.R.C.
22166	"	W. J. Pilcher	8th K.R.R.C.
B/3312	"	W. Yates	7th R.B.

42nd Infantry Brigade.

30407	Rifleman	W. J. Sear	9th R.B.
17829	Private	H. Campion	5th K.S.L.I.
16706	"	A. Derbyshire	5th K.S.L.I.
18596	A/Cpl.	W. C. Lutz	9th R.B.
B.2564	Rifleman	C. Cordwell	9th R.B.
R/1803	"	R. Magowan	9th R.B.
12412	Private	E. Neild	5th Oxf. & Bucks.L.I.

43rd Infantry Brigade.

11626	Private	L. Willmott	6th D.C.L.I.
15274	"	J. Nield	"
12297	"	C. A. Blake	"
20836	"	C. E. Adams	"
21459	"	C. Rogers	10th Durham L.I.
12033	"	A. L. Playor	6th Somerset L.I.
10747	"	J. W. Vaughan	6th D.C.L.I.
25905	"	A. Turnpenny	6th K.O.Y.L.I.
27232	"	H. Day	6th Somerset L.I.
1714	"	C. Kent	"
11363	"	E. G. Perrin	6th D.C.L.I.
202746	"	W. Bailey	"

DIVISIONAL TROOPS.

Canteen.

9750	Private	H. Cross	6th D.C.L.I.
R.2899	Rifleman	W. Samways	8th K.R.R.C.

Cinema.

20797	Private	A. B. Smith	5th K.S.L.I.
33180	"	H. Mitchell	6th K.O.Y.L.I.

Salvage Company.

21710	Rifleman	W. Brown	7th R.B.
31903	Private	B. Webb	6th Somerset L.I.
21948	Rifleman	A. Haydon	9th K.R.R.C.
54470	Private	J. Nightingale	6th D.C.L.I.
27288	"	A. Gilbert	6th Somerset L.I.
17096	Corpl.	G. Salmon	11th K. L"pool R.
20733	Co.Q.M.Sgt.	F. Mawston	10th Durham L.I.
Z/787	Rfn	G. Millin	7th R.B.
R/5442	Rfn.	J. Humphreys	7th K.R.R.C.
32892	Rfn.	W. Hart	9th K.R.R.C.

CONTINUED

Salvage Co. (Cont.)

		Pte.		
34296		W. Rose	6th K.O.Y.L.I.
7947		J. Tanner	5th Ox & Bucks L.I.
8399	Rfn.	A. Bowman	9th K.R.R.C.
41135	Pte.	C. Chambers	6th K.O.Y.L.I.
27306	Pte.	B. Potter	6th Somerset L.I.
13947	Pte.	J.E. Green	5th Ox & Bucks L.I.
23764	Rfn.	G. Walker	7th R. B.
11939	Pte.	W. Winstanley	10th Durham L.I.
19741	Pte.	E. Wilson	6th D.C.L.I.
17834	Pte.	E. Symes	6th Somerset L.I.
15133	Pte.	H. Slaughter	6th D.L.I.

Baths & Laundries

2903	Rfn.	G.E. Tothill	7th K.R.R.C.
6870	Rfn.	W. Wood	8th K.R.R.C.
36716	Pte.	E. Wolstenholme	11th King's L'pools
26569	Rfn.	H.T. Woolen	8th R. B.
33538	Rfn.	L. Robards	9th K.R.R.C.
6109	Rfn.	W. Richer	8th R. B.
26732	Pte.	J. Ovens	5th K.S.L.I.
9823	Pte.	F. Mathews	10th Durham L.I.
20884	Pte.	A.G. Last	5th K.S.L.I.
16602	Pte.	G.H. Giles	5th K.S.L.I.
8503	Pte.	E. Gardner	5th K.S.L.I.
24460	Pte.	G. Eason	5th Ox & Bucks L.I.
17195	Pte.	F. Dowell	6th Somerset L.I.
18111	Rfn.	H. Clarke	7th K.R.R.C.
S.10876	Rfn.	C. Carter	8th R. B.

D.A.D.O.S.

S.26119	Rfn.	H. Northover	9th R.B.
S.10292	Rfn.	J. Weldon	9th R.B.
S.11945	Rfn.	L. Parrett	9th R.B.
10563	Rfn.	A. Howells	9th K.R.R.C.
38394	Pte.	W.H. Kynaston	11th K.L'pool R.

Supply Column Loaders.

28479	Rfn.	A. Barnes	8th R.B.
14782	Rfn.	E. Hassell	8th R.B.
6110	Rfn.	A. Crowther	8th R.B.
26211	Rfn.	J. Barly	8th R.B.
13897	Rfn.	W. Ellis	8th R.B.
13675	Rfn.	H.T. Cross	8th R.B.
26288	Rfn.	W.H. Gowlett	8th R.B.

DIVISIONAL HEADQUARTERS

8855	Rfn	J. Ridley	9th R.B.
19083	Pte.	H. Nuttycombe	6th Somerset L.I.
10821	Rfn	J. Cotter	8th K.R.R.C.
11114	Sgt.	E. Turner	5th K.S.L.I.
26289	Pte.	F. Mallard	5th Ox & Bucks L.I.
32094	Pte.	B. Sowerby	10th Durham L.I.
5095	Pte.	G. Ponting	6th D.C.L.I.
10707	Pte.	J. Sherman	6th Somerset L.I.
195	Rfn.	H. Johnson	8th R.B.
12949	Pte.	J. Schofield	6th K.O.Y.L.I.
20911	Pte.	W. Gibb	10th Durham L.I.
2784	Rfn.	E. Cochrane	8th R.B.

CONTINUED.

DIVISIONAL HEADQUARTERS (Contd.)

19466	Private W. Shear	5th Ox. & Bucks.L.I.
18833	" F. Pittick	"
29437	Rifleman J. H. Claydon	7th K.R.R.C.
10644	Private J. Rawlings	6th D.C.L.I.
10087	Rifleman W. Pearce	7th K.R.R.C.
28624	Private G. Stafford	6th D.C.L.I.
11891	" H. Hobbs	6th D.C.L.I.
19762	" J. Woollcott	6th D.C.L.I.

EMPLOYMENT COMPANY.

Band.

7929	Sergeant C. Owen	6th Somerset L.I.
3554	Rifleman H. Jordan	7th R.B.
12468	" H. Thomas	8th K.R.R.C.
B. 2784	" W. J. Lank	8th R.B.

APPENDIX IV.

Men classified "A" and allowed to be attached to the D.E.C.

INFANTRY BRIGADES.

41st Infantry Brigade.

2366	Rifleman	C. Owen	8th R.B.
R.2203	"	G. Wadman	7th K.R.R.C.
B.203667	"	S. J. Bruton	7th R.B.
9860	"	S. R. Kinsey	8th R.B.

42nd Infantry Brigade.

R.26532	Rifleman	W. Coates	9th K.R.R.C.
~~30407~~	~~"~~	~~W. J. Sear~~	~~9th R.B.~~
3383	"	C. Hill	9th R.B.
9308	"	R. Withington	5th K.S.L.I.

43rd Infantry Brigade.

20404 Lce.-Cpl. M. R. Robson — 10th Durham L.I.

DIVISIONAL TROOPS.

Canteen.

R.15656 Lce.-Cpl. H. J. Smart — 8th K.R.R.C.

Cinema.

20748 Sergeant E. Sykes — 10th Durham L.I.
40062 Sapper C. Quinse — R.E.

Salvage Company. *4/10304 L/C L Rogers 7RB*

~~15133 Private T. Slaughter — 10th Durham L.I.~~
18691 " A. Lewis — 5th K.S.L.I.
S/8486 Rifleman C. G. Wade — 9th R.B.

Baths & Laundries.

31606 Corpl. T. Culley — 6th D.C.L.I.

Divisional Bomb Store.

14473 Sergeant O. W. Taylor — 6th D.C.L.I.

DIVISIONAL HEADQUARTERS.

50337	Private	E. Chalker	R.A.M.C.
3777	Rifleman	A. G. Bradley	7th K.R.R.C.
18007	Corpl.	C. A. Bean	8th R.B.
12031	Sergeant	S. N. Wear	6th D.C.L.I.
23883	Lce.Cpl.	A. H. Parsons	5th Ox. & Bucks.L.I.
A.699	Rifleman	G. M. Coker	7th K.R.R.C.
26191	Private	H. Mable	5th K.S.L.I.
52933	Driver	J. Tilbury	B/47th Brigade R.F.A.

APPENDIX V.

S/5866	A/Sergeant D. Parmiter	7th R.B.
749	Sergeant J. Green	7th R.B.
9017	" J. W. Suthill	10th Durham L.I.
43298	" J. E. Wildo	10th Durham L.I.
11455	Corpl. W. J. Bartlett	6th D.C.L.I.
18557	Private W. C. Roberts	"
18556	" F. Grenham	"
10377	" F. Hamid	"
5797	" W. Delacey	"
11014	" R. Rolfe	"
5115	" S. A. Davies	"
28114	" F. Durston	"
5109	" S. Lister	"
5113	" A. Shaw	"
5107	" F. W. Startin	"
5112	" H. Wilson	"
~~4230~~	~~Rifleman S. Hills~~	~~9th R.B.~~
20183	Private F. Soarlo	5th K.S.L.I.
7593	" J. Goodall	"
17027	" A. Davies	"
7953	Corpl. S. Smith	"
~~1839~~	~~Rifleman E. Wickett~~	~~7th K.R.R.C.~~
4771	A/Corpl. S. Harrison	7th R.B.
10486	Rifleman F. Martin	"
8312	" J. Jordon	8th R.B.
5411	" A. Sleet	8th R.B.
662	" J. A. Whaley	8th R.B.
1961	Bugler W. J. Farmer	8th K.R.R.C.
7231	Rifleman M. Haggerty	7th R.B.
2173	" J. Wilson	7th R.B.
3847	Private A. J. Fuller	D.L.O.Y.
51336	Driver J. Toonoy	B/49th Bde. R.F.A.

APPENDIX VI.

A. P. M.
(Surplus to establishment)

B.2.	930 Rifleman	J. McGarry	9th R.B.
B.1.	11514 Corporal	R. Carter	9th K.R.R.C.
B.1.	10059 A/C.S.M.	H. Duncan	10th Durham L.I.
B.1.	24047 Rfn.	A. Scales	9th R.B.
B.1.	4232 Rifleman	W. Wint	9th R.B.
B.1-	18581 Rifleman	G. Graham	9th R.B.

D. A. D. O. S.

10563 Rifleman	A. Howells	9th K.R.R.C.
6654 Rifleman	W. Scarlett	8th K.R.R.C.
23241 Private	J. Dean	6th K.O.Y.L.I.
17941 Private	J. Hartsonne	5th K.S.L.I.
9567 Private	G. Russell	5th Ox & Bucks.L.I.
12742 Rifleman	D. Stocks	9th R.B.

C. R. E.

33807 Rifleman	A. Bull.	7th K.R.R.C.
3018 L/Corporal	A. Kenyon	9th K.R.R.C.
1531 Rifleman	A. Samples	9th R.B.
932 Rifleman	T. Cooper	5th Ox & Bucks.L.I.
32703 Private	P.R. Howard	6th D.C.L.I.
22399 Private	G.R. P6well	5th K.S.L.I.
20099 Private	W. Boatwright	

APPENDIX VII

N. C. O's on the Establishment of the D. E. C.

SERGEANTS.

7929	Sgt. C. Owen.	6th Som. L.I.	Bandmaster.
20733	Sgt. F. Mawston	10th D.L.I.	Salvage Coy.
11473	Sgt. O. W. Taylor	6th D.C.L.I.	Div'l Bomb Store
11114	Sgt. E. Turner	5th K.S.L.I.	Div. H.Q.

CORPORALS

192905	Cpl. W.J. Cook	Labour Corps	D.E.C.
20748	Cpl. E. Sykes	10th D.L.I.	Cinema Band
17096	Cpl. G. Salmon	11th K. L'pools.	Salvage Coy.
31606	Cpl. T. Culley	6th D.C.L.I.	Baths & Laundries Laundry
18007	Cpl. C.A. Bean	8th R.B.	Div. H.Q.
A.491	Cpl. D. Sinclair	7th K.R.R.C.	41st I.B. H.Q.

LANCE CORPORALS

15856	L/Cpl H.J. Smart	8th K.R.R.C.	Canteen
S/10204	L/Cpl L. Rogers	7th R.B.	Salvage Coy. Baths
18596	A/Cpl W.C. Lutz	9th R.B.	42nd I.B. H.Q.
20404	L/Cpl M.R. Robson	10th D.L.I.	43rd I.B. H.Q. 41st I.B. Loader 42nd I.B. Loader 43rd I.B. Loader
192914	L/Cpl C. Morsey	Labour Corps	Div. Troops Loader
192844	L/Cpl M. McHugh	Labour Corps	Spare
192842	Corpl. A.J. Nunn	Labour Corps	O.R. Clerk
192841	C.Q.M.S. G.R. Reynolds	Labour Corps	Q.Q.M.S.

APPENDIX VIII

DISTRIBUTION OF TRAIN LOADERS

Div'l Hd. Qtrs.	1	
TOTAL	1	1

DIV'L TROOPS.

D.A. H.Q.	1	
C. R.E.	1	
14th Signal Coy.	1	
D.A. Brigades	10	
D.A.C.	5	
Field Coys R.E.	3	
Field Ambulances	3	
Mobile Vety. Section	1	
Pioneers	2	
M.G.Coy.	1	
D.A. Extra Forage	6	
D.A.C. -do-	3	
Spare	1	
TOTAL	38	38

INFANTRY BDES.

Battalions	24	
Headquarters	3	
M.G.Coys	3	
Extra Forage	3	
Spare	3	
TOTAL	36	36
	TOTAL	75

Army Form C. 2118.

WAR DIARY
or
INTELLIGENCE SUMMARY

(Erase heading not required.)

HQ AQ Q 142 Vol 23

Place	1917 Date	Hour	Summary of Events and Information	Remarks and references to Appendices
St Jans Capel	Aug 1		Division under orders to move at 1 hours notice. No put into effect.	
	2		Reconnoitred site for transport lines in 15th Div: area.	
	3		Heard that Division is to move shortly to the CAESTRE area. Went to see Area Commandant Caestre re accommodation.	
	4		Orders issued for move to CAESTRE area on 6th inst. Drew up table of location of billets in new area and in acc'd. with G operation orders.	
	5		Issued administrative orders for move to new area. 14 Army Sub Park, 50 lorries, placed at disposal of division for the move.	
CAESTRE	6		Moved to CAESTRE area. Accommodation rather cramped owing to influx of refugees from HAZEBROUCK due to German shelling of that town.	
	7		Pioneer and Artillery warned to move shortly to II Corps	

Army Form C. 2118.

WAR DIARY
or
INTELLIGENCE SUMMARY
(Erase heading not required.)

Instructions regarding War Diaries and Intelligence Summaries are contained in F. S. Regs., Part II. and the Staff Manual respectively. Title Pages will be prepared in manuscript.

Place	Date	Hour	Summary of Events and Information	Remarks and references to Appendices
CAESTRE	8		11th Kings Liv. Regt. moved by march to II Corps. 14 Division affiliated to II Corps but to remain in CAESTRE area for the present under administration of II Corps.	
	9		Gun detachment of 46th Bde RFA joined II Corps. Railhead for supply of all 14th Dn. opened at RENING HELST. Train Ration cleared by lorries, refilling at Camp 4 N° 1 A Train. Ration delivered to wagon line by lorry. N° 1 Co. Train & delivered supply wagons of 14 DA rejoined units after refilling.	
	10		Normal routine	
	11-12		Packing trials of T.M. Battery with 42nd T.M.B. Result that 2 limbered G.S. wagons appear most suitable form of transport.	
	13		Division warned to move tomorrow to II Corps. Went to Corps and 18th Division to make arrangements.	
	14.		Administration order not out till after midnight. Advanced billeting parties sent on by lorry in afternoon.	

2449 Wt. W14957/M90 750,000 1/16 J.B.C. & A. Forms/C.2118/12.

Army Form C. 2118.

WAR DIARY
or
INTELLIGENCE SUMMARY

(Erase heading not required.)

Instructions regarding War Diaries and Intelligence Summaries are contained in F.S. Regs., Part II. and the Staff Manual respectively. Title Pages will be prepared in manuscript.

Place	Date	Hour	Summary of Events and Information	Remarks and references to Appendices
RENINGHELST	15		Division moved into II Corps area. H.Q. at Reninghelst. Administrative orders attached App II	App II
	16		Ruilhad WIPPEN HOEK from 16th. Orders issued for move of Division to forward area tomorrow. Div Contalment to started as part of Div Depot Batt?	
	17		A1 & A2 Bdes moved into bin 43 in reserve. SS 135 parties sent back to OUDERZEELE and transport there. Administrative instruction issued as in App III	App III
DICKEBUSCH	18		HQ Div. moved at Dickebusch in relief of 58th Div. Some difficulty in fitting transport him into Waterloo camps owing to strength of division. Grenade dumps taken over, but not in a good state.	App IV App V.
	19		Instructions for reliefs issued. See App IV Relief of A1 by A3rd Bde ordered. Administrative orders as in App V. 70 horses of Div Train killed or wounded by bombs.	
	20		Orders issued for Stragglers posts on Ven Canal and Prisoners collecting post at Half Way House.	

WAR DIARY or INTELLIGENCE SUMMARY

Army Form C. 2118.

Place	Date	Hour	Summary of Events and Information	Remarks and references to Appendices
Dickebusch	21		One Company of Pioneer Co of 56" Div attached to 14 Div for work under CRE.	
	22		Attack by 42" and 43" Inf Bdes at 7. a.m. Objectives practically reached. Estimated casualties 600 in 43" and 200 in 42". Heavy barrage by enemy up to about 4 p.m. preventing motor ambulances from going East of Birr X Roads on the Menin Road. Only 3 stragglers stopped on stragglers line. No difficulty with rations + ammunition.	
	23		German counter attack repulsed during the night. Estimated casualties of 42nd Bde increased to 700. Sent division of Annex cent to Rapheel Task.	
	24		41. Bde moved up by bus. Estimated strong German Counter attack. Casualties up to 12 noon 62 Officers 2,000 other ranks. Administration arrangements communicated to 23rd Div. who are to relieve us.	App VI
	25		Issued administration instructions App VII for move of division to areas round Renninghelst. 83rd Inf Bde moved to Dominion area.	App VII

2449 Wt. W14957/M90 750,000 1/16 J.B.C. & A. Forms/C.2118/12.

WAR DIARY
or
INTELLIGENCE SUMMARY

(Erase heading not required.)

Army Form C. 2118.

Place	Date	Hour	Summary of Events and Information	Remarks and references to Appendices
REMINGHELST	27		Div'l H.Q'rs to Reninghelst. 42nd Inf Bde to WIPPENHOEK area. 41st Inf Bde left in line under 23rd Div. Total estimated casualties now amount to 117 Officers 2000 Other ranks.	
	28		Issued administrative orders for move to BERTHEN area. Some difficulty in allotting billeting areas as the tents had been scattered over the area to avoid casualties from aeroplane raids.	App VIII
BERTHEN	29		Division (less Inf Bde & Artillery) moved to Berthen area. 41st Inf Bde by bus from Dickebusch.	
	30		B.Gen. Wood Comdg 43 Inf Bde appointed to Command 33 Div.	
	31		Went to see A.A.Q.M.G. & Ant Div. about taking over the area. Issued Administrative instructions App IX	App IX

F. Nunn Lt./Nt.
App A.Q.M.G.
14th (light) Div.

App 1

War Diary

Copy No...... 24

SECRET.

O.C/50/9.

Reference 14th Division O.O.No.131 of 4/8/17.

1. Handing over.

(a). The Camp Commandant will hand over the Chateau at ST. JANS CAPPEL to a caretaker from the 19th Division on the morning of 6/8/17.

(b). Camps will be handed over on the morning of 6/8/17 to such caretakers as may be detailed by the 19th Division for this purpose.

(c). The 19th Division will take over the laundry at ST. JANS CAPPEL on 8/8/17. Until this date the personnel of the laundry will remain at St. JANS CAPPEL to complete work and will rejoin the Division under orders to be issued later.

(d). A.P.M. will arrange to hand over by 8 p.m. on August 5th all Traffic Control posts and Water Guards in

    Areas 13 and 16 to ....37 th Division
    " 11, 14, and 15 to ...19th "

2. Salvage.

The Divisional Scheme issued under this office number Q.373/1 of 15/7/17 will be carried out on 6th August 1917 with the following modifications:

(a). Men will not be left in charge of Unit Dumps as laid down in para. 6.

(b). Three lorries will be placed at the disposal of O.C. Salvage Company on August 6th. These lorries will be used to collect all stores and salvage left by Units in their Unit Dumps. The Salvage will be taken to the Corps Salvage Depot at HAEGEDOORNE Siding S.e.d.4.5.

(c). The lorries will then be used to take the Salvage Company to their new billets at CAESTRE.

(d). The whole of the above will be completed on August 6th.

3. Huts and Tents.

No tents, tent shelters, tent boards, or huts are to be moved out of the Divisional Area. On a Unit moving out of camp, tents, tent shelters, and tent boards will be left standing.

4. Move of Units not mentioned in O.O.131.

(a). Div'l Train. March at 12 noon to CAESTRE.
Nos. 2, 3 and 4 Companies after drawing rations (see para. 5) will march via BAILLEUL and FLETRE to

Continued.

their billets in the new area. They will pass BAILLEUL after 10.30 a.m. and before noon.

(b). Div'l Supply Column less that portion required to accompany Div'l Artillery will after clearing pack train (see para. 5) proceed to CAESTRE and park on the road between CAESTRE and CAESTRE Station. The Column will not pass BAILLEUL before 1.0 p.m.

(c). Staff of Div'l Depot Battalion will march under) orders of G.O.C. 41st Infantry Brigade.

5. Supply. Supply railhead while the Division is in the CAESTRE Area will be at HAEGEDOORNE. Div'l Train will draw on 6th August from reserve rations held by Div'l Supply Column rations for consumption on August 7th. These rations will be delivered to Units in the new Area on the arrival of the Train Companies.

Div'l Supply Column will clear the Pack Train on August 6th and move loaded to the new Area.

On August 7th Div'l Supply Column will dump rations by 7 a.m. at refilling points to be notified later. Div'l Train will refill at 7.0 a.m. and deliver to Units.

Div'l Supply Column will, after dumping, proceed to Railhead to clear Pack Train.

The same procedure will be continued while the Division is in the CAESTRE Area.

6. Water.

Drinking water in the CAESTRE Area will be drawn by water carts from the water points at HAZEBROUCK Station or CAESTRE Station.

7. Area Commandant is at CAESTRE. There are no Town Majors or Sub-area Commandants in the Area.

8. D.A.D.O.S. Stores will be at CAESTRE.

9. Railhead for personnel will be HAZEBROUCK from 6th inst. onwards. The R.T.O. has been instructed to send reinforcements direct to their Units.

Trains run as follows:-

WESTWARDS.

```
CAESTRE......dep. 11.13.
HAZEBROUCK...arr. 11.45.
   ditto   ...dep. 12.03.
ST. OMER.....arr. 12.48.
BOULOGNE.....arr. 15.55.
```
EASTWARDS.
```
BOULOGNE.....dep.  0.54.
HAZEBROUCK...arr.  4.50.
   ditto   ...dep.  5.15.
CAESTRE......arr.  5.25.
```

Continued.

-3-

10. **Billets.**

The following amendments should be made to Table "B" of O.O. 131.

41st Infantry Brigade Group.

	Location.	Accomodation.
"A" Battn. Delete.	P.27.c.9.4.	100
	P.27.d.3.6.	200
and Substitute	P.33.d.9.2.	200
	P.33.c.9.8.	100
	P.34.d.1.5.	200
	P.34.d.1.2.	50

"B" Battn. Add the following to list of billets:

	P.29.c.4.2.	100

42nd Infantry Brigade Group.

"D" Battn. Add the following to list of billets:-

	V.11.d.6.4.	100

11. **Lorries.**

The following detail of lorries from No. 14 Ammunition Sub-Park are allotted for the move. They will be available for double journeys if necessary but must be free to return to ST. JANS CAPPEL before midnight on 6/7th August.

Div'l Hd.Qrs.	6 lorries
C. R.E.	3 "
41st Infantry Bde.	5 "
42nd Infantry Bde.	5 "
43rd Infantry Bde.	2 "
11th King's Liverpool R.	2 "
A. P. M.	2 "
Salvage Company	3 "
Depot Battalion	2 "
Total	30 "

Time and place of reporting will be notified separately.

R. Lewis Lt.W.
A.A.& Q.M.G.
14th(Light)Division.

August 5th 1917.

Copies to:- No. 1. C.R.A.
2. C.R.E.
3. 41st Infantry Bde.
4. 42nd Infantry Bde.
5. 43rd Infantry Bde.
6. 'G'.
7. 14th Signal Coy.
8. 11th K.Liverpool R.
9. 14th Div'l Train.
10. S.S.O.
11. 14th Div'l Supply Col.
12. 14th Am. Sub-Park.
13. A.D.M.S.
14. D.A.D.V.S.
15. D.A.D.O.S.
16. A. P. M.
17. 14th.Div.Depot Battn.
18. Camp Commandant.
19. Salvage Coy.
20. IX Corps.
21. 19th Division.
22. 37th Division.
23)
24) War Diary.
25. File.

Reference para. 5.

Refilling will be at 8.30.a.m. on 7th August and onwards while Division is in the CAESTRE area.

Refilling points will be as follows :-

Headquarter Group.　)　　　　Q.32.c.6.4. on the
43rd Brigade Group.　)　　　　CAESTRE - CASSEL road.

42nd Brigade Group.　　　　　W.19.d.0.5. the Square
　　　　　　　　　　　　　　　　　　　　in BORRE.

41st Brigade Group.　　　　　V.11.a.4.8. on the ST.SYLVESTRE -
　　　　　　　　　　　　　　　HAZEBROUCK road, just South of
　　　　　　　　　　　　　　　the X roads at La BREARDE.

Supply lorries will dump rations at these points by 7.0.a.m. each morning and Supply Sections of the Divisional Train will refill and deliver to units.

　　　　　　　　　　　　　　　　　　　　　　　R. Lewis
　　　　　　　　　　　　　　　　　　　　　　　A.A.& Q.M.G.

5/8/17.　　　　　　　　　14th (Light) Division.

App 1   War Diary

Copy No. 23

SECRET.

O.C/50/9.

Reference 14th Division O.O.No.131 of 4/8/17.

1. Handing over.

(a). The Camp Commandant will hand over the Chateau at ST. JANS CAPPEL to a caretaker from the 19th Division on the morning of 6/8/17.

(b). Camps will be handed over on the morning of 6/8/17 to such caretakers as may be detailed by the 19th Division for this purpose.

(c). The 19th Division will take over the laundry at ST. JANS CAPPEL on 8/8/17. Until this date the personnel of the laundry will remain at St. JANS CAPPEL to complete work and will rejoin the Division under orders to be issued later.

(d). A.P.M. will arrange to hand over by 8 p.m. on August 5th all Traffic Control posts and Water Guards in

    Areas 13 and 16 to ....37 th Division
      " 11, 14, and 15 to ...19th   "

2. Salvage.

The Divisional Scheme issued under this office number Q.373/1 of 15/7/17 will be carried out on 6th August 1917 with the following modifications:

(a). Men will not be left in charge of Unit Dumps as laid down in para. 6.

(b). Three lorries will be placed at the disposal of O.C. Salvage Company on August 6th. These lorries will be used to collect all stores and salvage left by Units in their Unit Dumps. The Salvage will be taken to the Corps Salvage Depot at HAEGEDOORNE Siding S.9.d.4.5.

(c). The lorries will then be used to take the Salvage Company to their new billets at CAESTRE.

(d). The whole of the above will be completed on August 6th.

3. Huts and Tents.

No tents, tent shelters, tent boards, or huts are to be moved out of the Divisional Area. On a Unit moving out of camp, tents, tent shelters, and tent boards will be left standing.

4. Move of Units not mentioned in O.O.131.

(a). Div'l Train. March at 12 noon to CAESTRE.
Nos. 2, 3 and 4 Companies after drawing rations (see para. 5) will march via BAILLEUL and FLETRE to

Continued.

-2-

their billets in the new area. They will pass BAILLEUL after 10.30 a.m. and before noon.

(b). Div'l Supply Column less that portion required to accompany Div'l Artillery will after clearing pack train (see para. 5) proceed to CAESTRE and park on the road between CAESTRE and CAESTRE Station. The Column will not pass BAILLEUL before 1.0 p.m.

(c). Staff of Div'l Depot Battalion will march under orders of G.O.C. 41st Infantry Brigade.

5. Supply. Supply railhead while the Division is in the CAESTRE Area will be at HAEGEDOORNE. Div'l Train will draw on 6th August from reserve rations held by Div'l Supply Column rations for consumption on August 7th. These rations will be delivered to Units in the new Area on the arrival of the Their Companies.

Div'l Supply Column will clear the Pack Train on August 6th and move loaded to the new Area.

On August 7th Div'l Supply Column will dump rations by 7 a.m. at refilling points to be notified later. Div'l Train will refill at 7.0 a.m. and deliver to Units.

Div'l Supply Column will, after dumping, proceed to Railhead to clear Pack Train.

The same procedure will be continued while the Division is in the CAESTRE Area.

6. Water.

Drinking water in the CAESTRE Area will be drawn by water carts from the water points at HAZEBROUCK Station or CAESTRE Station.

7. Area Commandant is at CAESTRE. There are no Town Majors or Sub area Commandants in the Area.

8. D.A.D.O.S. Stores will be at CAESTRE.

9. Railhead for personnel will be HAZEBROUCK from 6th inst. onwards. The R.T.O. has been instructed to send reinforcements direct to their Units.

Trains run as follows:-

WESTWARDS.

```
CAESTRE......dep. 11.13.
HAZEBROUCK...arr. 11.45.
   ditto   ...dep. 12.03.
ST. OMER.....arr. 12.48.
BOULOGNE.....arr. 15.55.
```
EASTWARDS.
```
BOULOGNE.....dep.  0.54.
HAZEBROUCK...arr.  4.50.
   ditto   ...dep.  5.15.
CAESTRE......arr.  5.25.
```

Continued.

-3-

10. **Billets.**

The following amendments should be made to Table "B" of O.O. 131.

41st Infantry Brigade Group.

	Location.	Accomodation.
"A" Battn. Delete.	P.27.c.9.4.	100
	P.27.d.3.6.	200
and Substitute	P.33.d.9.2.	200
	P.33.c.9.8.	100
	P.34.d.1.5.	200
	P.34.d.1.2.	50

"B" Battn. Add the following to list of billets:

| | P.29.c.4.2. | 100 |

42nd Infantry Brigade Group.

"D" Battn. Add the following to list of billets:-

| | V.11.d.6.4. | 100 |

11. **Lorries.**

The following detail of lorries from No. 14 Ammunition Sub-Park are allotted for the move. They will be available for double journeys if necessary but must be free to return to ST. JANS CAPPEL before midnight on 6/7th August.

Div'l Hd.Qrs.	6 lorries
C. R.E.	3 "
41st Infantry Bde.........	5 "
42nd Infantry Bde.........	5 "
43rd Infantry Bde.........	2 "
11th King's Liverpool R...	2 "
A. P. M.	2 "
Salvage Company	3 "
Depot Battalion	2 "
Total....	30 "

Time and place of reporting will be notified separately.

E. Lewis Lt.Col.
A.A.& Q.M.G.
14th(Light)Division.

August 5th 1917.

Copies to:- No. 1. C.R.A.
2. C.R.E.
3. 41st Infantry Bde.
4. 42nd Infantry Bde.
5. 43rd Infantry Bde.
6. 'G'.
7. 14th Signal Coy.
8. 11th K.Liverpool R.
9. 14th Div'l Train.
10. S.S.O.
11. 14th Div'l Supply Col.
12. 14th Am. Sub-Park.
13. A.D.M.S.
14. D.A.D.V.S.
15. D.A.D.O.S.
16. A. P. M.
17. 14th.Div.Depot Battn.
18. Camp Commandant.
19. Salvage Coy.
20. IX Corps.
21. 19th Division.
22. 37th Division.
23)
24) War Diary.
25. File.

Reference para. 5.

Refilling will be at 6.30.a.m. on 7th August and onwards while Division is in the CAESTRE area.

Refilling points will be as follows :-

Headquarter Group.)   Q.32.c.6.4. on the
43rd Brigade Group.)   CAESTRE - CASSEL road.

42nd Brigade Group.   W.19.d.0.5. the Square
                                         in BORRE.

41st Brigade Group.   V.11.a.4.8. on the ST.SYLVESTRE -
                             HAZEBROUCK road, just South of
                             the X roads at La BREARDE.

Supply lorries will dump rations at these points by 7.0.a.m. each morning and Supply Sections of the Divisional Train will refill and deliver to units.

P. Lewis
Lt.Col.
A.A.& Q.M.G.

5/8/17.   14th (Light) Division.

TO BOULOGNE.

POPERINGHE	dep.	10.07.
ABEELE	"	10.34.
HAZEBROUCK	"	12.03.
ST. OMER	arr.	12.48.
DO.	dep.	13.03.
BOULOGNE	arr.	15.55.

FROM BOULOGNE.

BOULOGNE	dep.	0.54.
ST. OMER	arr.	3.45.
DO.	dep.	4.00.
HAZEBROUCK	"	5.15.
ABEELE	"	5.53.
POPERINGHE	arr.	6.05.

TO CALAIS.

POPERINGHE	dep.	1.35.
ABEELE	"	1.48.
ST. OMER	arr.	3.45.
DO.	dep.	3.48.
CALAIS	arr.	4.50.

FROM CALAIS.

CALAIS	dep.	10.50.
ST. OMER	arr.	11.55.
DO.	dep.	12.00.
ABEELE	"	13.54.
POPERINGHE	arr.	14.08.

R. Lewis

A.A. & Q.M.G.,
14TH (LIGHT) DIVISION.

15/8/17.

COPIES to :

1. C.R.A.
2. C.R.E.
3. 41st Infantry Brigade.
4. 42nd Infantry Brigade.
5. 43rd Infantry Brigade.
6. 'G'.
7. Camp Commandant.
8. 14th Signal Coy.
9. 11th Bn. K. L'pool R.
10. 14th Div'l Train.
11. S.S.O.
12. 14th Div'l Supply Col.
13. A.D.M.S.
14. D.A.D.V.S.
15. D.A.D.O.S.
16. A.P.M.
17. 14th Div'l Depot Battn.
18. 249 Machine Gun Coy.
19. 14th Div'l Salvage Coy.
20. II Corps.
21. IX Corps.

App II *War Diary*

S E C R E T.   Q.409/4.
           COPY No. .....

ADMINISTRATIVE ARRANGEMENTS,

REFERENCE 14th DIVISION WARNING ORDER No. 132.

1. SUPPLY.   Railhead from 16th August, inclusive - WIPPENHOEK.

   15th instant. Train Companies will march loaded after refilling and deliver to units on arrival in new area.
   D.S.C. after drawing at HAEGEDOORNE will move loaded to new area, dump at Railhead WIPPENHOEK and return to CAESTRE.

   16th instant. Train will draw in detail from park Train at Railhead and deliver to units.

2. ATTACHED TROOPS. will be retained by 18th Division for the present.

3. TRAFFIC CONTROL.   A.P.M. will arrange with A.P.M., II Corps to take over the traffic control posts and patrols from 18th Division by 12. 0 noon, August 16th.

4. BATHS.   The Baths at RENINGHELST will be taken over by 14th Division on 15th instant and allotment will be notified by Officer i/c Baths and Laundries.

5. AREA STORES.   Units taking over Camps from 18th Division will render to Divisional Headquarters, list of tentage and other Area Stores taken over, as soon as handing over is completed.

6. D.A.D.O.S.   Stores will be at RENINGHELST.

7. I.O.M. No. 55 MOBILE WORKSHOP.   1½ miles from RENINGHELST on the ABEELE Road.

8. DIVISIONAL DEPOT BATTALION will move to MILLAM by Lorry on the morning of 16th instant, taking with them rations for consumption on 17th.

9. REINFORCEMENTS, from 15th instant, inclusive, will be disposed of as follows :-

   (a) All Infantry and Pioneer reinforcements will be sent direct to the Divisional Depot Battalion, MILLAM : their arrival will be reported to units by wire from this Office and the same daily State as previously used will be sent to all units direct by O.C. Divisional Depot.

   (b) Reinforcements for all other units in the Division will be sent to POPERINGHE and their arrival notified in the usual way.

10. LEAVE TRAIN SERVICE. The present arrangement will hold good until the 20th instant : on this day, all vacancies allotted to the Division will be by boats sailing from CALAIS.
    TIME TABLE is as follows :-

                                                OVER.

App II

War Diary

SECRET.   Q.409/4.
                                                    COPY No. .....
            ADMINISTRATIVE ARRANGEMENTS,
        REFERENCE 14th DIVISION WARNING ORDER No. 132.

1. **SUPPLY.** Railhead from 16th August, inclusive — WIPPENHOEK.

   15th instant. Train Companies will march loaded after refilling and deliver to units on arrival in new area.
   D.S.C. after drawing at HAEGEDOORNE will move loaded to new area, dump at Railhead WIPPENHOEK and return to CAESTRE.

   16th instant. Train will draw in detail from pack Train at Railhead and deliver to units.

2. **ATTACHED TROOPS.** will be retained by 18th Division for the present.

3. **TRAFFIC CONTROL.** A.P.M. will arrange with A.P.M., II Corps to take over the traffic control posts and patrols from 18th Division by 12.0 noon, August 16th.

4. **BATHS.** The Baths at RENINGHELST will be taken over by 14th Division on 15th instant and allotment will be notified by Officer i/c Baths and Laundries.

5. **AREA STORES.** Units taking over Camps from 18th Division will render to Divisional Headquarters, list of tentage and other Area Stores taken over, as soon as handing over is completed.

6. **D.A.D.O.S.** Stores will be at RENINGHELST.

7. **I.O.M. No. 55 MOBILE WORKSHOP.** 1½ miles from RENINGHELST on the ABEELE Road.

8. **DIVISIONAL DEPOT BATTALION** will move to MILLAM by Lorry on the morning of 16th instant, taking with them rations for consumption on 17th.

9. **REINFORCEMENTS,** from 15th instant, inclusive, will be disposed of as follows :—

   (a) All Infantry and Pioneer reinforcements will be sent direct to the Divisional Depot Battalion, MILLAM : their arrival will be reported to units by wire from this Office and the same daily State as previously used will be sent to all units direct by O.C. Divisional Depot.

   (b) Reinforcements for all other units in the Division will be sent to POPERINGHE and their arrival notified in the usual way.

10. **LEAVE TRAIN SERVICE.** The present arrangement will hold good until the 20th instant : on this day, all vacancies allotted to the Division will be by boats sailing from CALAIS.
    TIME TABLE is as follows :—

                                                    OVER.

TO BOULOGNE.			FROM BOULOGNE.		
POPERINGHE	dep.	10.07.	BOULOGNE	dep.	0.54.
ABEELE	"	10.34.	ST. OMER	arr.	3.45.
HAZEBROUCK	"	12.03.	DO.	dep.	4.00.
ST. OMER	arr.	12.48.	HAZEBROUCK	"	5.15.
DO.	dep.	13.03.	ABEELE	"	5.53.
BOULOGNE	arr.	15.55.	POPERINGHE	arr.	6.05.

TO CALAIS.			FROM CALAIS.		
POPERINGHE	dep.	1.35.	CALAIS	dep.	10.50.
ABEELE	"	1.48.	ST. OMER	arr.	11.55.
ST. OMER	arr.	3.45.	DO.	dep.	12.00.
DO.	dep.	3.48.	ABEELE	"	13.54.
CALAIS	arr.	4.50.	POPERINGHE	arr.	14.08.

R. Lewis Lt-Col.

A.A. & Q.M.G.,

14TH (LIGHT) DIVISION.

15/8/17.

COPIES to :

1. C.R.A.
2. C.R.E.
3. 41st Infantry Brigade.
4. 42nd Infantry Brigade.
5. 43rd Infantry Brigade.
6. 'G'.
7. Camp Commandant.
8. 14th Signal Coy.
9. 11th Bn. K. L'pool R.
10. 14th Div'l Train.
11. S.S.O.
12. 14th Div'l Supply Col.
13. A.D.M.S.
14. D.A.D.V.S.
15. D.A.D.O.S.
16. A.P.M.
17. 14th Div'l Depot Battn.
18. 249 Machine Gun Coy.
19. 14th Div'l Salvage Coy.
20. II Corps.
21. IX Corps.

SECRET.　　　　　　　　　　　　　　　　　　　　　　Q.416.

ADMINISTRATIVE INSTRUCTIONS.

REFERENCE 14TH (LIGHT) DIVISION O.O. No.133.

1. AMMUNITION.

    The Divisional Ammunition Dump for S.A.A., Grnades etc. is at BRIDGE DUMP, H.23.c.9.1.
    This will be taken over by 14th Div'l Bomb Officer at 10 A.M. on 18th instant.

2. TRANSPORT LINES and QUARTERMASTER'S STORES.

    41st Inf. Brigade   ...   Canal Reserve Camp.
    　　　　　　　　　　　　　　　(North of DICKEBUSCH).
    42nd Inf. Brigade   ...   New DICKEBUSCH Camp.
    　　　　　　　　　　　　　　　(H.33.b.6.6.)
    43rd Inf. Brigade   ...   Canal Reserve Camp.

3. MOVES.

    Salvage Company. Will move to Div'l Salvage Dump near DICKEBUSCH, on morning of 19th instant.
    26th Mobile Vet'y Section. Will move into RENINGHELST and take over lines vacated by M.V.S. of the 56th Division when that unit moves out. Meanwhile, the 26th M.V.S. remains at L.24.c.3.9 and will establish an advanced Veterinary Post at DICKEBUSCH on the morning of 18th instant.
    215th Div'l Employment Coy. Remains at RENINGHELST.
    Div'l Depot Battalion. Remains at MILLAM.
    Div'l Supply Column. Moves to-day to 27.L.32.d.9.9.
    Div'l Train. On 18th instant :-
    　　　　　　Hd.Qtrs. to Canal Reserve Camp.
    　　　　　　Nos. 2, 3 and 4 Companies to H.27.c.central.
    　　　　　　On 19th instant :-
    　　　　　　No. 1 Company to H.27.c.central.
    D.A.D.O.S. Remains at RENINGHELST.

4. SUPPLY.

    Railhead - 18th instant, RENINGHELST,
    　　　　　　19th instant
    　　　　　　and onwards, DICKEBUSCH.
    Train Companies will draw from Railhead and deliver to Brigade Transport Lines.
    Refilling Points at Railhead.

5. PRISONERS OF WAR.

    A Collecting Post for Prisoners of War consisting of 1 N.C.O. and 26 men will be established in the vicinity of HALF-WAY HOUSE. This party will be found, when ordered, by the Infantry Brigade in reserve.
    All Prisoners of War will be taken by Infantry Brigades to this Post, whence they will be escorted to the Corps Prisoners' Cage at DICKEBUSCH.

6. STRAGGLERS.

    The general line of Straggler Posts is the YSER CANAL.
    The following Posts will be found, when ordered, by the Infantry Brigade in reserve :-

    　　I. 26. c. 3. 5)
    　　I. 25. b. 9. 4)   1 N.C.O., 12 men.
    　　I. 25. b. 8. 8)

    　　　　　　　　　　　　　　　　　　　　　　　　CONTINUED.

Stragglers will be brought from this line to a Straggler Collecting Post at DICKEBUSCH, under the arrangements of the A.P.M., and from there they will either be taken to Unit Transport Lines or Formations will be directed to send an escort for them.

[signature]

A.A. & Q.M.G.,

14TH (LIGHT) DIVISION.

1W/8/17.

COPIES to :

1. C.R.A.
2. C.R.E.
3. 41st Infantry Brigade.
4. 42nd Infantry Brigade.
5. 43rd Infantry Brigade.
6. 'G'.
7. Camp Commandant.
8. 14th Signal Company.
9. 11th Bn. King's Liverpool Regt.
10. 14th Div'l Train.
11. S.S.O.
12. Div'l Supply Column.
13. A.D.M.S.
14. D.A.D.V.S.
15. D.A.D.O.S.
16. A.P.M.
17. 14th Div'l Depot Battalion.
18. 249th Machine Gun Company.
19. 14th Div'l Salvage Coy.
20. 56th Division.
21. II Corps.

SECRET.   App III   Q.416.   War Diary

ADMINISTRATIVE INSTRUCTIONS.

REFERENCE 14TH (LIGHT) DIVISION O.O. No.133.

1. AMMUNITION.

    The Divisional Ammunition Dump for S.A.A., Grnades etc. is at BRIDGE DUMP, H.23.c.9.1.
    This will be taken over by 14th Div'l Bomb Officer at 10 A.M. on 18th instant.

2. TRANSPORT LINES and QUARTERMASTER'S STORES.

    41st Inf. Brigade   ...   Canal Reserve Camp.
                                  (North of DICKEBUSCH).
    42nd Inf. Brigade   ...   New DICKEBUSCH Camp.
                                  (H.33.b.6.6.)
    43rd Inf. Brigade   ...   Canal Reserve Camp.

3. MOVES.

    Salvage Company. Will move to Div'l Salvage Dump near DICKEBUSCH, on morning of 19th instant.
    26th Mobile Vet'y Section. Will move into RENINGHELST and take over lines vacated by M.V.S. of the 56th Division when that unit moves out. Meanwhile, the 26th M.V.S. remains at L.24.c.3.9 and will establish an advanced Veterinary Post at DICKEBUSCH on the morning of 18th instant.
    215th Div'l Employment Coy. Remains at RENINGHELST.
    Div'l Depot Battalion. Remains at MILLAM.
    Div'l Supply Column. Moves to-day to 27.L.32.d.9.9.
    Div'l Train. On 18th instant :-
                Hd.Qtrs. to Canal Reserve Camp.
                Nos. 2, 3 and 4 Companies to H.27.c.central.
            On 19th instant :-
                No. 1 Company to H.27.c.central.
    D.A.D.O.S.   Remains at RENINGHELST.

4. SUPPLY.

    Railhead - 18th instant, RENINGHELST,
               19th instant
                 and onwards, DICKEBUSCH.
    Train Companies will draw from Railhead and deliver to Brigade Transport Lines.
    Refilling Points at Railhead.

5. PRISONERS OF WAR.

    A Collecting Post for Prisoners of War consisting of 1 N.C.O. and 26 men will be established in the vicinity of HALF-WAY HOUSE. This party will be found, when ordered, by the Infantry Brigade in reserve.
    All Prisoners of War will be taken by Infantry Brigades to this Post, whence they will be escorted to the Corps Prisoners' Cage at DICKEBUSCH.

6. STRAGGLERS.

    The general line of Straggler Posts is the YSER CANAL.
    The following Posts will be found, when ordered, by the Infantry Brigade in reserve :-

        I. 26. c. 3. 5)
        I. 25. b. 9. 4)   1 N.C.O., 12 men.
        I. 25. b. 8. 8)

CONTINUED.

Stragglers will be brought from this line to a Straggler Collecting Post at DICKEBUSCH, under the arrangements of the A.P.M., and from there they will either be taken to Unit Transport Lines or Formations will be directed to send an escort for them.

E. Lewis Lt.W.

A.A. & Q.M.G.,
14TH (LIGHT) DIVISION.

17/8/17.

COPIES to :

1. C.R.A.
2. C.R.E.
3. 41st Infantry Brigade.
4. 42nd Infantry Brigade.
5. 43rd Infantry Brigade.
6. 'G'.
7. Camp Commandant.
8. 14th Signal Company.
9. 11th Bn. King's Liverpool Regt.
10. 14th Div'l Train.
11. S.S.O.
12. Div'l Supply Column.
13. A.D.M.S.
14. D.A.D.V.S.
15. D.A.D.O.S.
16. A.P.M.
17. 14th Div'l Depot Battalion.
18. 249th Machine Gun Company.
19. 14th Div'l Salvage Coy.
20. 56th Division.
21. II Corps.

App IV   Sent to all recipients of OROs

A.221/30.

....

The Divisional Burials Staff having been collected, the following points with regard to their work and responsibilities are issued for the guidance of all concerned :-

1.   Under ordinary conditions, the responsibility of burying their dead rests entirely with units : the only occasions on which units are absolved of this responsibility is when an advance has been made which carries units off the ground on which their dead are lying : under such conditions the collection and burial of the dead will be arranged for by the Division.

2.   The Divisional Burials Party is intended to assist units in the following ways :-

(a) By relieving units of the duty of rendering burial Returns, of disposing of effects, of the marking of graves and of co-operation with the Graves Registration Unit ;

(b) By assisting units in the collection and burial of dead in addition to the duties mentioned in (a) when the tactical situation permits and circumstances demand, i.e., when the situation is something between normal trench warfare and an actual advance and neither labour nor time is available for the ordinary course to be taken.

(c) To arrange for the identification and burial of dead which a unit has been unable to deal with before leaving the ground it has been occupying. This would be done by co-operation with the Burial Staff of the relieving troops.

3.   The following procedure will, therefore, be adopted :-

(a) Units will collect and bring the dead in the area occupied by each unit. Whenever possible, the dead should be taken to the nearest cemetery and buried there by the unit which collects them. The unit will also collect the effects and forward them to the Divisional Burials Officer, with a brief report of the burial, giving the following particulars :-
    NAME and UNIT of the man,
    The RED DISC of the man,
    MAP REFERENCE of the grave.

(b) Whenever it is not possible for tactical reasons for units to bury their dead, a notification should be sent to the Burials Officer, giving the location of the bodies. It must, however, be borne in mind that it is neither practicable nor desirable to send burial parties on to the ground actually held for fighting purposes and that, if units cannot bury their dead, every effort should be made to collect them at some place accessible to transport, where they can be taken over by the Burials Officer.

(c) The occasion may arise when the work of burying or removing the dead may be too great to be carried out by the fighting troops without impairing their morale and efficiency and when the work must be carried out quickly for reasons of health or morale. In these circumstances, Brigades should apply to Div'l Hd.Qtrs. for special burial parties to clear the ground.

R. Lewis Lt.W.
A.A. & Q.M.G.,
14th (Light) Division.

19/8/17.

App IV

A.221/30.

....

The Divisional Burials Staff having been collected, the following points with regard to their work and responsibilities are issued for the guidance of all concerned :-

1. Under ordinary conditions, the responsibility of burying their dead rests entirely with units : the only occasions on which units are absolved of this responsibility is when an advance has been made which carries units off the ground on which their dead are lying : under such conditions the collection and burial of the dead will be arranged for by the Division.

2. The Divisional Burials Party is intended to assist units in the following ways :-

(a) By relieving units of the duty of rendering burial Returns, of disposing of effects, of the marking of graves and of co-operation with the Graves Registration Unit ;

(b) By assisting units in the collection and burial of dead in addition to the duties mentioned in (a) when the tactical situation permits and circumstances demand, i.e., when the situation is something between normal trench warfare and an actual advance and neither labour nor time is available for the ordinary course to be taken.

(c) To arrange for the identification and burial of dead which a unit has been unable to deal with before leaving the ground it has been occupying. This would be done by co-operation with the Burial Staff of the relieving troops.

3. The following procedure will, therefore, be adopted :-

(a) Units will collect and bring the dead in the area occupied by each unit. Whenever possible, the dead should be taken to the nearest cemetery and buried there by the unit which collects them. The unit will also collect the effects and forward them to the Divisional Burials Officer, with a brief report of the burial, giving the following particulars :-
  NAME and UNIT of the man,
  The RED DISC of the man,
  MAP REFERENCE of the grave.

(b) Whenever it is not possible for tactical reasons for units to bury their dead, a notification should be sent to the Burials Officer, giving the location of the bodies. It must, however, be borne in mind that it is neither practicable nor desirable to send burial parties on to the ground actually held for fighting purposes and that, if units cannot bury their dead, every effort should be made to collect them at some place accessible to transport, where they can be taken over by the Burials Officer.

(c) The occasion may arise when the work of burying or removing the dead may be too great to be carried out by the fighting troops without impairing their morale and efficiency and when the work must be carried out quickly for reasons of health or morale. In these circumstances, Brigades should apply to Div'l Hd.Qtrs. for special burial parties to clear the ground.

R. Lewis Lt.Wr.

A.A. & Q.M.G.,
14th (Light) Division.

19/8/17.

App V

War Diary

SECRET.   O.C./10/12.

Reference 14th Divisional Warning Order No. 134 of 18/8/17 : para. 7 :-

1. The following Camps are allotted on relief of 41st Infantry Brigade by 43rd Infantry Brigade :-

   41st INFANTRY BRIGADE.

41st Bde. Hd.Qtrs.	DICKEBUSCH Huts,	28.H.20.c.9.1.
'A' Battalion	New DICKEBUSCH Camp,	28.H.26.b.4.9.
'B' "	Canal Reserve Camp.	28.H.33.a.7.1.
'C' "	Do.	Do.
'D' "	CHATEAU SEGARD No.2,	28.H.30.a.9.0.
41st M.G. Coy.	New DICKEBUSCH Camp,	28.H.27.b.central.
41st T.M. Bty.	DICKEBUSCH Huts,	28.H.20.c.9.1.
Transport Lines (no change),	...	28.H.27.b.5.4.

   43rd INFANTRY BRIGADE.

   Transport Details, New DICKEBUSCH Camp, 28.H.27.b.central,
   present Camp of 6th K.O.Y.L.I.

2. 41st Infantry Brigade will send 30 men under an Officer belonging to 'D' Battalion to report to Area Commandant, CHATEAU SEGARD, at 9.0 A.M. on 20th instant, at 28.H.30.a.2.8 to draw shelters and corrugated iron for the Camp at 28.H.30.a.9.0. This party will pitch the Camp and leave a Guard on it till the Battalion marches in.

3. 41st Infantry Brigade will arrange to send advanced parties to take over the Camps for their other units from 43rd Infantry Brigade before the latter march out.

                                              E. Lewis Lt.W.
                                              A. A. & Q.M.G.,
19/8/17.   14TH (LIGHT) DIVISION.

            COPIES TO :
                41st Infantry Brigade.
                43rd Infantry Brigade.
                14th Signal Coy.
                14th Div'l Train.
                S.S.O.
                A.D.M.S.
                D.A.D.O.S.
                'G'.

SECRET.   App V   O.C./10/12.

Reference 14th Divisional Warning Order No. 134 of 18/8/17 : para. 7 :-

1. The following Camps are allotted on relief of 41st Infantry Brigade by 43rd Infantry Brigade :-

   41st INFANTRY BRIGADE.

41st Bde. Hd.Qtrs.	DICKEBUSCH Huts,	28.H.20.c.9.1.
'A' Battalion	New DICKEBUSCH Camp,	28.H.26.b.4.9.
'B' "	Canal Reserve Camp.	28.H.33.a.7.1.
'C' "	Do.	Do.
'D' "	CHATEAU SEGARD No.2,	28.H.30.a.9.0.
41st M.G. Coy.	New DICKEBUSCH Camp,	28.H.27.b.central.
41st T.M. Bty.	DICKEBUSCH Huts,	28.H.20.c.9.1.
Transport Lines (no change),	...	28.H.27.b.5.4.

   43rd INFANTRY BRIGADE.

   Transport Details, New DICKEBUSCH Camp, 28.H.27.b.central, present Camp of 6th K.O.Y.L.I.

2. 41st Infantry Brigade will send 30 men under an Officer belonging to 'D' Battalion to report to Area Commandant, CHATEAU SEGARD, at 9.0 A.M. on 20th instant, at 28.H.30.a.2.8 to draw shelters and corrugated iron for the Camp at 28.H.30.a.9.0. This party will pitch the Camp and leave a Guard on it till the Battalion marches in.

3. 41st Infantry Brigade will arrange to send advanced parties to take over the Camps for their other units from 43rd Infantry Brigade before the latter march out.

E. Lewis
Lt.Col.

A. A. & Q.M.G.,

19/8/17.   14TH (LIGHT) DIVISION.

COPIES TO :

41st Infantry Brigade.
43rd Infantry Brigade.
14th Signal Coy.
14th Div'l Train.
S. S. O.
A.D.M.S.
D.A.D.O.S.
'G'.

App. VI

14th (LIGHT) DIVISION ADMINISTRATIVE ARRANGEMENTS.

1. **AMMUNITION.**

    The Divisional Ammunition Dump for S.A.A., Grenades etc. is "BRIDGE DUMP", at 28.H.23.c.9.1.

    There are also Sub-dumps at :

        WOOD DUMP   ...   28.H.26.b.7.6.
        BEDFORD HOUSE   28.I.26.a.5.1.

    Brigade Dumps are as follows :-

        LEFT Brigade   HOOGE CRATER.
                             HALF-WAY HOUSE.

        RIGHT Brigade   DORMY HOUSE.

    Contents of Ammunition Dumps are shown on the attached tables.

    S.A.A. and Grenades are obtained by wiring Corps Ammunition Park (repeated II Corps 'Q') who deliver direct to Ammunition Dump.

    The following must be demanded through 'G', IInd Corps :-

    Flares.
    S.O.S. (Grenades Rifle).   Chemical Grenades.
    Rockets.   Single Smoke Cases.
    V. P. A. Red and Green.   Wire Breakers and Cutters.
    "P" Bombs.   Hedging Gloves.

    One Officer and 30 men are required at BRIDGE DUMP. There is telephone connection with the Dump Office.

2. **MEDICAL.**

    R. A. P.'s.

        LEFT Brigade   HOOGE TUNNEL, J.13.a.
        RIGHT Brigade   CLAPHAM JUNC. J.13.d.9.9.
                             STIRLING CASTLE, J.13.d.4.0.

    Adv. Dressing Post.

                             HOOGE TUNNEL, J.13.a.

    Cases from A.D.P. are carried by bearers to Ambulances to BIRR Cross-roads (or if the Ambulances can get as far, to HOOGE CRATER) to be taken to A.D.S.

    Advanced Dressing Station.   ...   ... I.9.c.9.6.

    Cases are cleared from A.D.S. by relays of Ambulances to Corps Main Dressing Station, at H.27.c.

    Cases from Support Battalions are sent to COW FARM, I.22.b.6.4, whence they are carried by horsed Ambulances to WOODCOTE HOUSE, I.20.c.5.2. From WOODCOTE HOUSE, cases are evacuated by Motor Ambulances to Corps M.D.S.

    Bearer Posts. HALF-WAY HOUSE and COW FARM.

    Walking Wounded are directed to the A.D.S. along the MENIN road or to WOODCOTE HOUSE if in that locality. In ordinary times they are sent from these places by Motor Ambulances to Corps M.D.S. During active operations, they are evacuated by lorries detailed for this purpose or by the light railway from I.15.b.3.3.

3. VETERINARY.

Mobile Veterinary Section at RENINGHELST,
Advanced Veterinary Post at DICKEBUSCH.

4. PRISONERS OF WAR.

Collecting Post at HALF-WAY HOUSE, of 1 N.C.O. and 16 men, with Sub-post at BIRR Cross-roads.

All prisoners of war are taken by Infantry Brigades to this Post, whence they are escorted to CAFE BELGE. At CAFE BELGE they are taken over by a detachment of Yeomanry, by whom they are escorted to the Joint Divisional Cage at DICKEBUSCH.

5. STRAGGLERS.

The general line of Straggler Posts is along the YSER Canal. Divisional Posts of 1 N.C.O. and 12 men are at :

I.26.c.3.5.
I.25.b.9.4.
I.25.b.8.8.

There is also a Post at the A.D.S. for walking wounded.

Stragglers are brought from this line to a Straggler Collecting Post near the Prisoners of War Cage at DICKEBUSCH, under the A.P.M. and from there sent to Unit Transport Lines.

6. SUPPLY. Railhead, DICKEBUSCH.

The system in force is to clear the pack train in detail, one group at a time, direct on to supply wagons of Divisional Train, which deliver the same day to Qr.Mstr.Stores at First Line Transport Lines, for consumption 2 days later.

4 lorries from the D.S.C. are stationed permanently at Railhead.

Fuel Dump in Camp of No. 1 Coy., Divisional Train, at 28.H.27.d.5.1.

2,000 Iron Rations are held in reserve in the Dug-outs at HALF-WAY HOUSE and handed over by Brigades on relief. They are for use in emergency if the pack transport fails to bring up rations in time to distribute to Battalions in Line.

7. BATHS and LAUNDRY.

The Laundry at RENINGHELST is shared with the Division occupying RENINGHELST.

Baths exist at :

RENINGHELST	for details at RENINGHELST.
CORNWALL CAMP (G.30.a.9.9)	small and insanitary ; used by units round OUDERDOM.
VIJUERHOEK (H.29.c.26) ...	used fully by Division on right.

A new Bath with 12 sprays is in course of erection at H.29.a.5.2. This when completed will be sufficient to bathe a Battalion in a day of 8 hours.

Divisional Clean Clothes Store is at the Laundry at RENINGHELST and issues are made to units on returning an equivalent number of soiled articles.

8. D.A.D.O.S. Stores are at RENINGHELST.

9. R. E. DUMPS.

    Advanced Dump ... ... THE CULVERT, 28.I.18.a.3.8.
    Divisional Dump ... ... KRUISSTRAAT, 28.H.18.d.2.2.
    IInd Corps Dump ... ... DICKEBUSCH.

10. SALVAGE.

The Headquarters and Camp of the Divisional Salvage Company is at 28.H.28.d.7.5.

The Divisional Salvage Dump is at the same place.

IInd Corps Salvage Dump is at REMINGHELST.

O.C. Salvage Company demands daily the lorries he requires for the day following. These lorries take up the salvage parties to the Forward Areas at day-break and return loaded with the salvage obtained, which is sent off to the Corps Dump for sorting.
    Serviceable S.A.A. is sent to Divisional Grenade Dump.
    Bombs and other ammunition are de-detonated and sent to Corps Salvage Dump.

11. CEMETERIES.

A list of Cemeteries in use is attached. Those for which the Division is responsible for looking after are marked with a cross.

12. ROUTES OF SUPPLY are shown in attached table. Best time for Transport to go up is between 5 A.M. and 8 A.M.
    Points where hostile barrage is usually heavy are ZILLEBEKE and HOOGE.
    Water tins are filled in Transport Lines.

13. LOCATION OF UNITS.

See Table attached.

14. TRACKS.

A map showing tracks in Forward Area is attached.

                                              A. A. & Q.M.G.,

24 - 8 - 17.   14th (Light) Division.

DESTINATION.	ROUTES.	TRANSPORT.	LIMIT of TRANSPORT.	
			WET WEATHER.	DRY WEATHER.
OBSERVATORY RIDGE	Shrapnel Corner - Corduroy road along North of Lake - ZILLEBEKE - I.22.d.8.7 - Track to Ridge. Return from ZILLEBEKE by track South of Lake.	Limbers. Pack.	I.22.d.8.7. OBSERVATORY RIDGE.	RUDKIN HOUSE. JEFFERY RESERVE.
STIRLING CASTLE	As above to ZILLEBEKE - I.16.d.7.1 - track past Yeomanry Post - I.24.b.2.5.	Limbers. Pack.	I.16.d.7.1. I.24.b.2.5.	I.16.d.7.1. STIRLING CASTLE.
CLAPHAM JUNCTION	As above to ZILLEBEKE - Menin R^d I.16.b.0.5 - corduroy track to MENIN road - CLAPHAM JUNCTION OR KRUISSTRAAT - YPRES - MENIN road.	Limber. Pack.	I.18.a.8.6. CLAPHAM JUNC.	I.18.a.8.6. CLAPHAM JUNC.

App VI

14th (LIGHT) DIVISION ADMINISTRATIVE ARRANGEMENTS.

1. **AMMUNITION.**

    The Divisional Ammunition Dump for S.A.A., Grenades etc. is "BRIDGE DUMP", at 28.H.23.c.9.1.

    There are also Sub-dumps at :

        WOOD DUMP ... 28.H.26.b.7.6.
        BEDFORD HOUSE 28.I.26.a.5.1.

    Brigade Dumps are as follows :-

        LEFT Brigade   HOOGE CRATER.
                                 HALF-WAY HOUSE.

        RIGHT Brigade   DORMY HOUSE.

    Contents of Ammunition Dumps are shown on the attached tables.

    S.A.A. and Grenades are obtained by wiring Corps Ammunition Park (repeated II Corps 'Q') who deliver direct to Ammunition Dump.

    The following must be demanded through 'G', IInd Corps :-

    Flares.
    S.O.S. (Grenades Rifle).   Chemical Grenades.
    Rockets.   Single Smoke Cases.
    V. P. A. Red and Green.   Wire Breakers and Cutters.
    "P" Bombs.   Hedging Gloves.

    One Officer and 30 men are required at BRIDGE DUMP. There is telephone connection with the Dump Office.

2. **MEDICAL.**

    R. A. P.'s.

        LEFT Brigade   HOOGE TUNNEL, J.13.a.
        RIGHT Brigade   CLAPHAM JUNC. J.13.d.9.9.
                                  STIRLING CASTLE, J.13.d.4.0.

    Adv. Dressing Post.

                                  HOOGE TUNNEL, J.13.a.

    Cases from A.D.P. are carried by bearers to Ambulances to BIRR Cross-roads (or if the Ambulances can get as far, to HOOGE CRATER) to be taken to A.D.S.

    Advanced Dressing Station. ... ... I.9.c.9.6.

    Cases are cleared from A.D.S. by relays of Ambulances to Corps Main Dressing Station, at H.27.c.

    Cases from Support Battalions are sent to COW FARM, I.22.b.6.4, whence they are carried by horsed Ambulances to WOODCOTE HOUSE, I.20.c.5.2. From WOODCOTE HOUSE, cases are evacuated by Motor Ambulances to Corps M.D.S.

    Bearer Posts. HALF-WAY HOUSE and COW FARM.

    Walking Wounded are directed to the A.D.S. along the MENIN road or to WOODCOTE HOUSE if in that locality. In ordinary times they are sent from these places by Motor Ambulances to Corps M.D.S. During active operations, they are evacuated by lorries detailed for this purpose or by the light railway from I.15.b.3.3.

3. **VETERINARY.**

Mobile Veterinary Section at RENINGHELST,
Advanced Veterinary Post at DICKEBUSCH.

4. **PRISONERS OF WAR.**

Collecting Post at HALF-WAY HOUSE, of 1 N.C.O. and 16 men, with Sub-post at BIRR Cross-roads.

All prisoners of war are taken by Infantry Brigades to this Post, whence they are escorted to CAFÉ BELGE. At CAFÉ BELGE they are taken over by a detachment of Yeomanry, by whom they are escorted to the Joint Divisional Cage at DICKEBUSCH.

5. **STRAGGLERS.**

The general line of Straggler Posts is along the YSER Canal. Divisional Posts of 1 N.C.O. and 12 men are at :

I.26.c.3.5.
I.25.b.9.4.
I.25.b.8.8.

There is also a Post at the A.D.S. for walking wounded.

Stragglers are brought from this line to a Straggler Collecting Post near the Prisoners of War Cage at DICKEBUSCH, under the A.P.M. and from there sent to Unit Transport Lines.

6. **S U P P L Y.**   Railhead, DICKEBUSCH.

The system in force is to clear the pack train in detail, one group at a time, direct on to supply wagons of Divisional Train, which delivers the same day to Qr.Mstr.Stores at First Line Transport Lines, for consumption 2 days later.

4 lorries from the D.S.C. are stationed permanently at Railhead.

Fuel Dump in Camp of No. 1 Coy., Divisional Train, at 28.H.27.d.5.1.

2,000 Iron Rations are held in reserve in the Dug-outs at HALF-WAY HOUSE and handed over by Brigades on relief. They are for use in emergency if the pack transport fails to bring up rations in time to distribute to Battalions in Line.

7. **BATHS and LAUNDRY.**

The Laundry at RENINGHELST is shared with the Division occupying RENINGHELST.

Baths exist at :

RENINGHELST	for details at RENINGHELST.
CORNWALL CAMP (G.30.a.9.9)	small and insanitary ; used by units round OUDERDOM.
VIJVERHOEK (H.29.c.26) ...	used fully by Division on right.

A new Bath with 12 sprays is in course of erection at H.29.a.5.2. This when completed will be sufficient to bathe a Battalion in a day of 8 hours.

Divisional Clean Clothes Store is at the Laundry at RENINGHELST and issues are made to units on returning an equivalent number of soiled articles.

8. **D. A. D. O. S.**   Stores are at RENINGHELST.

9. R. E. DUMPS.

   Advanced Dump   ...   ...   THE CULVERT, 28.I.18.a.3.8.
   Divisional Dump   ...   ...   KRUISSTRAAT, 28.H.18.d.2.2.
   IInd Corps Dump   ...   ...   DICKEBUSCH.

10. SALVAGE.

   The Headquarters and Camp of the Divisional Salvage Company is at 28.H.28.d.7.5.

   The Divisional Salvage Dump is at the same place.

   IInd Corps Salvage Dump is at RENINGHELST.

   O.C. Salvage Company demands daily the lorries he requires for the day following. These lorries take up the salvage parties to the Forward Areas at day-break and return loaded with the salvage obtained, which is sent off to the Corps Dump for sorting.
   Serviceable S.A.A. is sent to Divisional Grenade Dump.
   Bombs and other ammunition are de-detonated and sent to Corps Salvage Dump.

11. CEMETERIES.

   A list of Cemeteries in use is attached. Those for which the Division is responsible for looking after are marked with a cross.

12. ROUTES OF SUPPLY are shown in attached table. Best time for Transport to go up is between 5 A.M. and 8 A.M.
   Points where hostile barrage is usually heavy are ZILLEBEKE and HOOGE.
   Water tins are filled in Transport Lines.

13. LOCATION OF UNITS.

   See Table attached.

14. TRACKS.

   A map showing tracks in Forward Area is attached.

24 - 8 - 17.

A. A. & Q.M.G.,
14th (Light) Division.

DESTINATION.	ROUTES.	TRANSPORT.	LIMIT of TRANSPORT.	
			WET WEATHER.	DRY WEATHER.
OBSERVATORY RIDGE	Shrapnel Corner - Corduroy road along North of Lake - ZILLEBEKE - I.22.d.8.7 - Track to Ridge. Return from ZILLEBEKE by track South of Lake.	Limbers. Pack.	I.22.d.8.7. OBSERVATORY RIDGE.	RUDKIN HOUSE. JEFFERY RESERVE.
STIRLING CASTLE	As above to ZILLEBEKE - I.16.d.7.1 - track past Yeomanry Post - I.24.b.2.5.	Limbers. Pack.	I.16.d.7.1. I.24.b.2.5.	I.16.d.7.1. STIRLING CASTLE.
CLAPHAM JUNCTION	As above to ZILLEBEKE - Menin Rd. I.16.b.0.5 - corduroy track to MENIN road - CLAPHAM JUNCTION O R KRUISSTRAAT - YPRES - MENIN road.	Limber. Pack.	I.18.a.8.6. CLAPHAM JUNC.	I.18.a.8.6. CLAPHAM JUNC.

App VII
O.O./50/11.

ADMINISTRATIVE INSTRUCTIONS.

Reference 14th (Light) Division O.O. 138 of Aug.25th, 1917.

1. **G R O U P S.**

    Units will, on 26th instant, be grouped for Supply purposes as follows :-

    <u>41st Brigade Group.</u>
    41st Infantry Bde.
    62nd Field Coy. R.E.
    44th Field Ambulance.
    No. 2 Coy. Divisional Train.

    <u>42nd Brigade Group.</u>
    42nd Infantry Bde.
    89th Field Coy. R.E.
    43rd Field Ambulance.
    No. 3 Coy. Divisional Train.
    26th Mobile Vet'y Section.
    249 Machine Gun Company.

    <u>43rd Brigade Group.</u>
    43rd Infantry Bde.
    61st Field Coy. R.E.
    No. 4 Coy. Divisional Train.
    Divisional Headquarters.
    14th Div'l Signal Company.
    215th Div'l Employment Company.
    14th Div. M. M. P.
    Hd. Qtrs. Divisional R.E.
    Hd. Qtrs. Divisional Train.

    <u>Divisional Troops Coy.</u>
    14th Divisional R.A.
    42nd Field Ambulance.
    14th Div'l Salvage Company.

2. **M O V E S.**

    On 26th instant, of Units not referred to in Operation Orders.

UNIT.	TO AREA.	ADVANCED PARTY TO REPORT TO AREA COMMANDANT AT
43rd Field Amb'ce	WIPPENHOEK.	27.L.21.c.4.4.
Hd.Qtrs., Div.Train	RENINGHELST.	-
No.4 Coy. Div.Train	DOMINION.	28.G.23.b.central.
No.3 " " "	WIPPENHOEK.	27.L.21.c.4.4.

    The following Units remain at their present locations till further orders :-
    42nd Field Ambulance.
    44th "   "
    No. 1 Coy. Div'l Train.
    No. 2 "   "   "
    14th Div'l Salvage Company.
    14th Div'l Supply Column.
    215th Div'l Employment Coy.
    Div'l Depot Battalion.
    D.A.D.O.S.

3. **S U P P L Y.**

    Railhead, from 27th instant, inclusive - RENINGHELST.

    On 26th instant, Train Companies will march loaded after refilling at DICKEBUSCH and deliver to units.

    CONTINUED.

On 27th instant, Train Companies will draw from Railhead, refill at Train Company Camps and deliver to units.

4. **BATHS.**

The Baths at RENINGHELST will be taken over by the 14th Division on 26th instant and allotment will be notified by Officer i/c Baths and Laundries.

The Baths are allotted to 43rd Infantry Brigade for the whole of 26th instant.

5. **ADVANCED REINFORCEMENT CAMP.**

The Details of 42nd Infantry Bde. will rejoin their units on 27th instant : those of the 41st Infantry Bde. on 28th instant.

Brigades concerned will arrange transport.

6. **COAL DUMP.**

Will be at 28.G.15.c.2.6, near WARATAH CAMP.

R. Lewis Lowe.
A.A. & Q.M.G.,
14TH (LIGHT) DIVISION.

25/8/17.

COPIES to :

1. C. R.A.
2. C. R.E.
3. 41st Infantry Bde.
4. 42nd Infantry Bde.
5. 43rd Infantry Bde.
6. 'G'.
7. Camp Commandant.
8. 14th Signal Company.
9. 11th Bn. K. L'pool Regt.
10. 14th Div'l Train.
11. S. S. O.
12. 14th Div'l Supply Column.
13. A.D.M.S.
14. D.A.D.V.S.
15. D.A.D.O.S.
16. A.P.M.
17. 14th Div'l Depot Battn.
18. 249 Machine Gun Company.
19. 14th Div'l Salvage Coy.
20. O.C. IInd Corps Advd. Reinft. Camp,, OUDEZEELE.
21. 23rd Division.
22. IInd Corps.

On 27th instant, Train Companies will draw from Railhead, refill at Train Company Camps and deliver to units.

4. **BATHS.**

The Baths at RENINGHELST will be taken over by the 14th Division on 26th instant and allotment will be notified by Officer i/c Baths and Laundries.

The Baths are allotted to 43rd Infantry Brigade for the whole of 26th instant.

5. **ADVANCED REINFORCEMENT CAMP.**

The Details of 42nd Infantry Bde. will rejoin their units on 27th instant : those of the 41st Infantry Bde. on 28th instant.

Brigades concerned will arrange transport.

6. **COAL DUMP.**

Will be at 28.G.15.c.2.6, near WARATAH CAMP.

R. Lewis Lt.ur.
A.A. & Q.M.G.,
14TH (LIGHT) DIVISION.

25/8/17.

COPIES to :

1. C.R.A.
2. C.R.E.
3. 41st Infantry Bde.
4. 42nd Infantry Bde.
5. 43rd Infantry Bde.
6. 'G'.
7. Camp Commandant.
8. 14th Signal Company.
9. 11th Bn. K. L'pool Regt.
10. 14th Div'l Train.
11. S.S.O.
12. 14th Div'l Supply Column.
13. A.D.M.S.
14. D.A.D.V.S.
15. D.A.D.O.S.
16. A.P.M.
17. 14th Div'l Depot Battn.
18. 249 Machine Gun Company.
19. 14th Div'l Salvage Coy.
20. O.C. IInd Corps Advd. Reinft. Camp,, OUDEZEELE.
21. 23rd Division.
22. IInd Corps.

App VII   War diary
O.C./50/11.

ADMINISTRATIVE INSTRUCTIONS.

Reference 14th (Light) Division O.O. 138 of Aug.25th, 1917.

1. **G R O U P S.**

    Units will, on 26th instant, be grouped for Supply purposes as follows :-

    <u>41st Brigade Group.</u>   41st Infantry Bde.
    62nd Field Coy. R.E.
    44th Field Ambulance.
    No. 2 Coy. Divisional Train.

    <u>42nd Brigade Group.</u>   42nd Infantry Bde.
    89th Field Coy. R.E.
    43rd Field Ambulance.
    No. 3 Coy. Divisional Train.
    26th Mobile Vet'y Section.
    249 Machine Gun Company.

    <u>43rd Brigade Group.</u>   43rd Infantry Bde.
    61st Field Coy. R.E.
    No. 4 Coy. Divisional Train.
    Divisional Headquarters.
    14th Div'l Signal Company.
    215th Div'l Employment Company.
    14th Div. M. M. P.
    Hd. Qtrs. Divisional R.E.
    Hd. Qtrs. Divisional Train.

    <u>Divisional Troops Coy.</u> 14th Divisional R.A.
    42nd Field Ambulance.
    14th Div'l Salvage Company.

2. **M O V E S.**

    On 26th instant, of Units not referred to in Operation Orders.

UNIT.	TO AREA.	ADVANCED PARTY TO REPORT TO AREA COMMANDANT AT
43rd Field Amb'ce	WIPPENHOEK.	27.L.21.c.4.4.
Hd.Qtrs., Div.Train	RENINGHELST.	-
No.4 Coy. Div.Train	DOMINION.	28.G.23.b.central.
No.3 " " "	WIPPENHOEK.	27.L.21.c.4.4.

    The following Units remain at their present locations till further orders :-

    42nd Field Ambulance.
    44th   "   "
    No. 1 Coy. Div'l Train.
    No. 2 "   "   "
    14th Div'l Salvage Company.
    14th Div'l Supply Column.
    215th Div'l Employment Coy.
    Div'l Depot Battalion.
    D.A.D.O.S.

3. **S U P P L Y.**

    Railhead, from 27th instant, inclusive - RENINGHELST.

    On 26th instant, Train Companies will march loaded after refilling at DICKEBUSCH and deliver to units.

    CONTINUED.

App VIII

SECRET

OC/50/12

28/8/17.

ADMINISTRATIVE INSTRUCTIONS

Move to BERTHEN AREA.

Copy No.....

1. SUPPLY.

Railheads to August 30th inclusive RENINGHELST
FROM " 31st " STEENWERCK

On 29th inst. Nos. 3 and 4 Companies Div'l. Train will move loaded with their Brigade Groups to the new area and deliver rations on arrival for consumption on 30th.

No. 2 Company will draw from Railhead, stand loaded overnight, move loaded to new area on 30th and deliver to units on arrival for consumption on 31st. Divisional Supply Column will deliver to No. 3 Company on 29th inst. the rations they now hold for 11th King's Liverpool Regt for consumption on 31st inst.

On 29th inst. Divisional Supply Column will draw for 42nd and 43rd Brigade Groups from Railhead, stand loaded overnight and deliver to Nos. 3 and 4 Companies Divisional Train at refilling points on 30th inst. Time and place of refilling points will be notified later. Nos. 3 and 4 Companies will then deliver to Units on 30th for consumption on 31st.

On 30th inst and following days Divisional Supply Column will draw from Railhead for the whole Division, less Artillery. Train Coys. will refill on following days and deliver to Units.

2. GROUPS.

Will be as follows from 29th inst. Changes in Groups notified in OC/50/11 of 25/8/17 are marked with a star.

41st Brigade Group.
    41st Infantry Bde.
  (a) 62nd Field Coy R.E.
  * 42nd Field Ambulance
    No.2 Coy. Div'l Train.
  * H.Q., Div'l Train
  (b) Div'l Depot Battln.

  (a) with 43rd Brigade Group for 29th inst. only.
  (b) from 30th inst.

42nd Brigade Group.
    42nd Infantry Bde.
    89th Field Coy. R.E.
    43rd Field Ambulance
    No. 3 Coy. Div'l Train
    26th Mob. Vet. Section.
    249th Machine Gun Coy.
  * 11th King's Liverpool Regt.

43rd Brigade Group.
    43rd Infantry Bde
    61st Field Coy. R.E.
  * 44th Field Ambulance
    No. 4 Coy. Div'l Train
    Div'l H.Qrs.
    14th Div'l Signal Coy. R.E.
    215th Div'l Employment Coy.
    14th Div. M.M.P.
    H.Qrs. Div'l R.E.
  * 14th Div'l Salvage Coy.

Divisional Troops.   14th Div'l R.A.
                          No. 1 Coy. Div'l Train.

3. Railheads for personnel will be as follows for the groups detailed in para 2.
   - 41st Brigade Group. ... ... BAILLEUL.
   - 42nd Brigade Group. ... ... CAESTRE.
   - 43rd Brigade Group. ... ... -do-
   - Divisional Troops ... ... POPERINGHE.

4. Advanced Billeting parties from 42nd and 43rd Brigade Groups as ordered in G warning order, will report to Area Commandant BERTHEN at 3.P.M. this afternoon where they will be met by the D.A.A.G. and allotment of billetting areas will be made.

5. Handing over. Units of 42nd and 43rd Brigade groups will hand over their camps as they took them over to the advanced parties of the 7th Division to-morrow.

6. Area Commandant is at BERTHEN.
   There are no sub area Commandants or Town Majors in the area.

7. Baths. Divisional Baths are at LA BESACE FARM 27.X.9.a.2.7. Allotment will be notified by Officer i/c Baths & Laundries.

8. D.A.D.O.S. stores will be at BERTHEN.

9. Divisional Depot Battalion will move to the new area on the 30th inst and join the 41st Brigade Group under instructions to be notified later. They will bring with them rations for the 31st inst.

10. Traffic Control A.P.M. will arrange with A.P.M. 7th Division for the relief of Traffic Control personnel in the present area on the 31st inst.

11. Leave   The present allotments hold good. Time Table of trains is as follows.

TO CALAIS			FROM CALAIS.		
Poperinghe	dep.	1-35.	Calais	dep.	10-50.
Caestre	"	2-15.	St.Omer	arr.	11-55.
St.Omer	arr.	3-45.	"	dep.	12-00.
"	dep.	3-48.	Caestre	arr.	13-28.
Calais	arr.	4-50.	Poperinghe	"	14-08.

P. Lewis Lt.
A.A. & Q.M.G.,
14th (Light) Division.

28/8/17.

App VIII

War Diary

SECRET

OC/50/12

28/8/17.

ADMINISTRATIVE INSTRUCTIONS

Move to BERTHEN AREA.

Copy No.____

1. SUPPLY

Railheads to August 30th inclusive RENINGHELST
FROM " 31st " STEENWERCK

On 29th inst. Nos. 3 and 4 Companies Div'l. Train will move loaded with their Brigade Groups to the new area and deliver rations on arrival for consumption on 30th.

No. 2 Company will draw from Railhead, stand loaded overnight, move loaded to new area on 30th and deliver to units on arrival for consumption on 31st. Divisional Supply Column will deliver to No. 3 Company on 29th inst. the rations they now hold for 11th King's Liverpool Regt for consumption on 31st inst.

On 29th inst. Divisional Supply Column will draw for 42nd and 43rd Brigade Groups from Railhead, stand loaded overnight and deliver to Nos. 3 and 4 Companies Divisional Train at refilling points on 30th inst. Time and place of refilling points will be notified later. Nos. 3 and 4 Companies will then deliver to Units on 30th for consumption on 31st.

On 30th inst and following days Divisional Supply Column will draw from Railhead for the whole Division, less Artillery. Train Coys. will refill on following days and deliver to Units.

2. GROUPS.

Will be as follows from 29th inst. Changes in Groups notified in OC/50/11 of 25/8/17 are marked with a star.

41st Brigade Group.
                41st Infantry Bde.
(a) 62nd Field Coy R.E.
* 42nd Field Ambulance
    No. 2 Coy. Div'l Train.
* H.Q., Div'l Train
(b) Div'l Depot Battln.

(a) with 43rd Brigade Group for 29th inst. only.
(b) from 30th inst.

42nd Brigade Group.
    42nd Infantry Bde.
    89th Field Coy. R.E.
    43rd Field Ambulance
    No. 3 Coy. Div'l Train
    26th Mob. Vet. Section.
    249th Machine Gun Coy.
* 11th King's Liverpool Regt.

43rd Brigade Group.
    43rd Infantry Bde
    61st Field Coy. R.E.
* 44th Field Ambulance
    No. 4 Coy. Div'l Train
    Div'l H.Qrs.
    14th Div'l Signal Coy. R.E.
    215th Div'l Employment Coy.
    14th Div. M.M.P.
    H.Qrs. Div'l R.E.
* 14th Div'l Salvage Coy.

Divisional Troops.   14th Div'l R.A.
                            No. 1 Coy. Div'l Train.

3. **Railheads for personnel** will be as follows for the groups detailed in para 2.
   - 41st Brigade Group. ... ... BAILLEUL.
   - 42nd Brigade Group. ... ... CAESTRE.
   - 43rd Brigade Group. ... ... -do-
   - Divisional Troops ... ... POPERINGHE.

4. **Advanced Billeting parties** from 42nd and 43rd Brigade Groups as ordered in G warning order, will report to Area Commandant BERTHEN at 3.P.M. this afternoon where they will be met by the D.A.A.G. and allotment of billetting areas will be made.

5. **Handing over.** Units of 42nd and 43rd Brigade groups will hand over their camps as they took them over to the advanced parties of the 7th Division to-morrow.

6. **Area Commandant** is at BERTHEN.
   There are no sub area Commandants or Town Majors in the area.

7. **Baths.** Divisional Baths are at LA BESACE FARM 27.X.9.a.2.7. Allotment will be notified by Officer i/c Baths & Laundries.

8. **D.A.D.O.S.** stores will be at BERTHEN.

9. **Divisional Depot Battalion** will move to the new area on the 30th inst and join the 41st Brigade Group under instructions to be notified later. They will bring with them rations for the 31st inst.

10. **Traffic Control** A.P.M. will arrange with A.P.M. 7th Division for the relief of Traffic Control personnel in the present area on the 31st inst.

11. **Leave** The present allotments hold good. Time Table of trains is as follows.

TO CALAIS			FROM CALAIS		
Poperinghe	dep.	1-35.	Calais	dep.	10-50.
Caestre	"	2-15.	St.Omer	arr.	11-55.
St.Omer	arr.	3-45.	"	dep.	12-00.
"	dep.	3-48.	Caestre	arr.	13-28.
Calais	arr.	4-50.	Poperinghe	"	14-08.

                                                                           R. Lewis Lt.
                                                                    A.A. & Q.M.G.,
                                                                14th (Light) Division.

28/8/17.

App IX War Diary

SECRET.   O.C./50/13.
                                                           31/8/17.

Administrative Instructions

Reference 14th Division O.O.142 of 31/8/17.
****

1. Location of units of Brigade in RAVELSBERG Area:

Unit.	Camp Name	Camp Location.	Transport Lines.
Bde H.Q.	WATERLOO	S.18.c.8.5.	S.18.c.8.2.
A Battn.	Do.	S.12.c.8.8.	S.12.c.5.5.
B Battn.	do	S.12.b.5.4.	S.12.b.2.3.
C Battn.	ALDERSHOT	T.19.b.9.1.	T.20.c.1.9.
D Battn.	WHEAL	T.14.d.5.4.	T.9.a.5.1.
M.G.Coy.	HILLSIDE	T.14.c.5.4.	T.14.c.5.4.
T.M.Bty.	HILLSIDE	T.14.c.95.30	—

2. AMMUNITION.

   Divisional S.A.A. & Grenade Dump.
        KENNEBAK   T.3.b.3.0.

   Brigade Dumps.
        MIN DE L'HOSPICE   U.2.a.7.9
        SCHNITZEL FARM   U.3.c.8.2.

3. Move of Units not mentioned in O.O.142 :

   26th Mobile Vet.Sect. S.29.a.2.4 Buller Lines
        move with 43rd Infantry Bde at date to be notified later.

   D.A.D.O.S. Stores : T.14.b.9.8.
        move on 1st September under separate instructions.

   14th Div.Salvage Coy. T.15.a.0.5.
        move on 4th September under separate instructions.

4. Baths & Laundry.

   Palmer Baths S.26.a.0.8.
   The Officer i.c Baths & Laundries will arrange to take over the baths & laundry from 4th Austrln Divn on 3rd Sept. Allotment will be made by him to units from that date.

5. Y.M.C.A. Neuve Eglise S.12.a.8.2.

6. Area Commandant. Divisional Area, is at Divisional Hd.Qrs.

7. Railhead, for personnel - BAILLEUL.

                                                     Continued.

5. SUPPLY. Railhead - STEENWERCK.

As Groups move into the new Area their Companies of the Divisional Train will move with them loaded and deliver to Units on arrival.

Groups in the new area will on the day after arrival draw from Railhead by Supply Wagons of Train.

Refilling will be in Div'l Train Company lines and supply wagons will deliver to Unit's transport lines.

[signature]
A.A. & Q.M.G.
14th (Light) Division.

Copies to :-

1. C.R.A.
2. C.R.E.
3. 41st Inf. Bde.
4. 42nd Inf. Bde.
5. 43rd Inf. Bde.
6. "G".
7. Camp Commandant.
8. 14th Signal Coy.
9. 11th K.Liverpool R.
10. 14th Div'l Train.
11. S.S.O.
12. 14th Div'l Supply Column.
13. A.D.M.S.
14. D.A.D.V.S.
15. D.A.D.O.S.
16. A.P.M.
17. 14th Div'l Depot Battn.
18. 249th Machine Gun Coy.
19. 14th Div'l Salvage Coy.
20. IInd Anzac Corps.
21. 4th Australian Divn.
22. Area Commandant, RAVELSBERG AREA.

App IX

SECRET.   O.C./50/13.
                                                           31/8/17.

Administrative Instructions

Reference 14th Division O.O.142 of 31/8/17.

1. **Location** of units of Brigade in RAVELSBERG Area:

Unit.	Camp Name	Camp Location.	Transport Lines.
Bde H.Q.	WATERLOO	S.18.c.8.5.	S.18.c.8.2.
A Battn.	Do.	S.12.c.8.8.	S.12.c.5.5.
B Battn.	do	S.12.b.5.4.	S.12.b.2.3.
C Battn.	ALDERSHOT	T.19.b.9.1.	T.20.c.1.9.
D Battn.	WHEAL	T.14.d.5.4.	T.9.a.5.1.
M.G.Coy.	HILLSIDE	T.14.c.5.4.	T.14.c.5.4.
T.M.Bty.	HILLSIDE	T.14.c.95.30	—

2. **AMMUNITION.**

   Divisional S.A.A. & Grenade Dump.
       KENNEBAK   T.3.b.3.0.

   Brigade Dumps.
       MIN DE L'HOSPICE   U.2.a.7.9
       SCHNITZEL FARM   U.3.c.8.2.

3. **Move of Units** not mentioned in O.O.142 :

   26th Mobile Vet.Sect. S.29.a.2.4 Buller Lines
       move with 43rd Infantry Bde at date to be notified later.

   D.A.D.O.S. Stores : T.14.b.9.8.
       move on 1st September under separate instructions.

   14th Div.Salvage Coy. T.15.a.0.5.
       move on 4th September under separate instructions.

4. **Baths & Laundry.**

   Palmer Baths S.26.a.0.8.
   The Officer i.c Baths & Laundries will arrange to take over the baths & laundry from 4th Austrln Divn on 3rd Sept. Allotment will be made by him to units from that date.

5. **Y.M.C.A.**   Neuve Eglise S.12.a.8.2.

6. **Area Commandant.** Divisional Area, is at Divisional Hd.Qrs.

7. **Railhead**, for personnel - BAILLEUL.

Continued.

-2-

5. SUPPLY. Railhead - STEENWERCK.

As Groups move into the new Area their Companies of the Divisional Train will move with them loaded and deliver to Units on arrival.

Groups in the new area will on the day after arrival draw from Railhead by Supply Wagons of Train.

Refilling will be in Div'l Train Company lines and supply wagons will deliver to Unit's transport lines.

A.A. & Q.M.G.
14th (Light) Division.

Copies to :-

1. C.R.A.
2. C.R.E.
3. 41st Inf. Bde.
4. 42nd Inf. Bde.
5. 43rd Inf. Bde.
6. "G".
7. Camp Commandant.
8. 14th Signal Coy.
9. 11th K. Liverpool R.
10. 14th Div'l Train.
11. S.S.O.
12. 14th Div'l Supply Column.
13. A.D.M.S.
14. D.A.D.V.S.
15. D.A.D.O.S.
16. A.P.M.
17. 14th Div'l Depot Battn.
18. 249th Machine Gun Coy.
19. 14th Div'l Salvage Coy.
20. IInd Anzac Corps.
21. 4th Australian Divn.
22. Area Commandant, RAVELSBERG AREA.

WAR DIARY

ADMINISTRATIVE BRANCH

14th LIGHT DIVISION

SEPTEMBER 1917

Army Form C. 2118.

WAR DIARY
or
INTELLIGENCE SUMMARY
(Erase heading not required.)

Instructions regarding War Diaries and Intelligence Summaries are contained in F.S. Regs., Part II. and the Staff Manual respectively. Title Pages will be prepared in manuscript.

Place	Date	Hour	Summary of Events and Information	Remarks and references to Appendices
RAVELSBERG 28 S 17 actual	Sept 1		Div Hd Qrs and 42nd Inf Bde moved to RAVELSBERG area. Camps of huts & tents taken over standing with ample accommodation. Brig Gen TEMPEST took over command of 43rd Inf Bde.	
	2.		41st Inf Bde moved to RAVELSBERG area in relief of 42nd & 13. who moved into line. Orders received for 43 Bde to move to La Creche – Vieuxland area on Sept 4th. Reconnoitred this area and selected camps for units.	
	3		Conference at Corps Hd Qrs with reference to future arrangements. Took over ammunition dumps from 4 Aust Div.	
	4		Drew up scheme of winter hutting for the area & took it to Corps for discussion. It is however not yet decided whether division will be on one or two Bde front.	
	5.		Reconnoitred area for accommodation of Div who move in tomorrow.	

Army Form C. 2118.

WAR DIARY
or
INTELLIGENCE SUMMARY
(Erase heading not required.)

Instructions regarding War Diaries and Intelligence Summaries are contained in F. S. Regs., Part II. and the Staff Manual respectively. Title Pages will be prepared in manuscript.

Place	Date	Hour	Summary of Events and Information	Remarks and references to Appendices
RAVELSBERG	6		Quarterly audit board on divisional funds. Issued instructions for working of tramways.	App I.
	7.		Quarterly audit board still sitting. Arranged for future work on divisional Tramways. Issued instructions for Salvage App II.	App II
	8.		Arranged for move of 7: R.B. to Shrapnell Hut. Quarterly audit board still sitting.	
	9.		Quarterly audit board completed their audit, found all correct but suggested that no credit should be given to units dealing with Div: Canteen as this leads to complicated accounts. Drew up hutting scheme for winter based on 2 brigades in line.	
	10		Reconnoitred area with view to divisional winter hutting.	
	11.		Conference at VIII Corps on winter hutting and other subjects. Agreed that 8" Div: should hand on to us the Kortepyp Bde area on Sept 18th.	
	12.		Drew up scheme for winter hutting and submitted to Corps. Requirements of 291 Nissen huts to comp lete accommodation.	App III

2449 Wt. W14957/M90 750,000 1/16 J.B.C. & A. Forms/C.2118/12.

Army Form C. 2118.

WAR DIARY or INTELLIGENCE SUMMARY

(Erase heading not required.)

Place	Date	Hour	Summary of Events and Information	Remarks and references to Appendices
RAVENSBERG	13		Inspected Coys of Divl Train at La Crèche. Camps require careful drainage. Materials satisfactory.	
	14		Issued scheme for forward clothes stores, foot rubbing cream & gum boot drying rooms. App 17	App 17
	15		Discussed the above with 41st Inf Bde & finer provisional sites. Reconnoitred sites for new baths at Wulverghem. Moved in structure and detail for camp caretakers. 42nd Inf Bde moved to Berquin area.	
	16		Reconnoitred sites for 42nd Bde Transport lines, found the existing ones too low lying and selected others. Decided with CRE on site for Wulverghem baths. Erection of winter huttings begun.	
	17		Started Divisional Coal dump at Neuve Eglise from withdrawals of units. Winter kit came up by rail from SAULTY kit store. Initial baths at Bailleul, Oudezeele & Poperinghe.	
	18		Normal routine.	
	19		42nd Bde moved into KORTEPYP area. Erection of horse standings begun.	

WAR DIARY
or
INTELLIGENCE SUMMARY
(Erase heading not required.)

Army Form C. 2118.

Place	Date	Hour	Summary of Events and Information	Remarks and references to Appendices
RAVERSBERG	20		Inspected Baths, huttin' & Transport Lines with CRE with a view to further improvements. Selected sites for Cook houses, Latrines & Ablution places in Shankill Camp and Bde Transport Lines.	
	21			
	22		Normal routine	
	23		SA & AMG VIII Corps visited site of Camps & horse lines. Corps Commander suggested withdrawal of 42" Bde Tram line to west of Neuve Eglise. Selected site for 42" Bde Tram lines just north of Hillside Camp.	
	24		Some difficulty with owner of field required for 42" Bde lines. Allotment of 61 horses, & 91 mention notified by telephone for the New Years dispatch. Issued divisional allotment. Made plans for Conference of brigadiers under G.O.C.	App V
	25			
	26		Conversion of existing drying room at Palmer Baths into an Officers' Club.	

Army Form C. 2118.

WAR DIARY
or
INTELLIGENCE SUMMARY

(Erase heading not required.)

Instructions regarding War Diaries and Intelligence Summaries are contained in F. S. Regs., Part II. and the Staff Manual respectively. Title Pages will be prepared in manuscript.

Place	Date	Hour	Summary of Events and Information	Remarks and references to Appendices
RAYESBERG	27		Went round transport lines with O.R.E. Horse standings getting on well.	
	28		Spent all day on honours list for New Year's dispatch. Divisional allotment being 61 honours 91 mentions.	
	29			
	30		Planned improvements for divisional Rest Station & submitted them to Corps.	

J. Aminister
Moda mm

App¹

Q/371/5.

REGULATIONS
FOR 14TH DIVISIONAL TRENCH TRAMWAYS.

1. 2/Lieut. S.C. DAVEY, 11th King's Liverpool Regt. is appointed 14th Divisional Trench Tramways Officer (T.T.O.)

2. Headquarters of the T.T.O. will be at WULVERGHEN, T.5.c.55.95.

3. The T.T.O. is responsible for the Traffic Management and line maintenance of the tramways in the Divisional area.
   He will have under him a party of about 9 R.E. and 20 Pioneers for maintenance and control.

4. Units using the tramways will provide their own working parties for loading, unloading and hauling and, for the present, their own mules for haulage.

5. Daily indents for rolling stock for the day following should normally be in the T.T.O's office by 6.0.p.m. Units will be notified by 10.0.p.m. whether their requirements can be met. On emergency, indents can be submitted at any time, but 6. hours' notice should be given before the trucks are required.
   Battalions and batteries will indent through their Staff Captains, R.E. Coys. and Pioneers direct to the T.T.O.

6. The indent will show :-

   (a) The material to be carried.
   (b) Time and place of loading.
   (c) Destination.

7. On taking delivery of trucks the Senior N.C.O. or man will sign a receipt for the trucks received, showing the respective number of each truck.
   The unit of the N.C.O. or man who signs a receipt for trucks will be held responsible that the same trucks are returned in good condition to the point from which they were issued, or to a point on the return journey ordered by the T.T.O.
   A break in the line due to shell fire or other cause will not be accepted as an excuse for the non-return of trucks as they are sufficiently light to be easily manhandled round the break.

8. All traffic will give way to wounded being brought down the line. Empty trucks will give way to full ones in the absence of crossings. If there are crossing places, the empty trucks must wait at the nearest till the line is clear. Trucks removed from the line must not be capsized, but lifted carefully off the line with the platform uppermost.

- 2 -

9.　In the event of a truck becoming damaged during transit the truck will be taken off the line and the T.T.O. or his representative informed of the spot where it has been left on return of the party in charge of it.

10.　Preference as regards provision of trucks when the demands exceed the rolling stock available, will be given as follows :-

    (a) Ammunition.
    (b) Wounded.
    (c) Rations.
    (d) R.E. material.

except in cases of emergency when the T.T.O. will use his discretion.

11.　A plan of the tramway system is attached.

12.　Any alterations or improvements suggested in these regulations for the working of the Trench Tramways will be sent in to the T.T.O. who will submit them with his remarks to Divisional Headquarters for consideration.

R. Lewis Lt.W.
A.A.& Q.M.G.

6/9/17.　　　　　　　　　　14th (Light) Division.

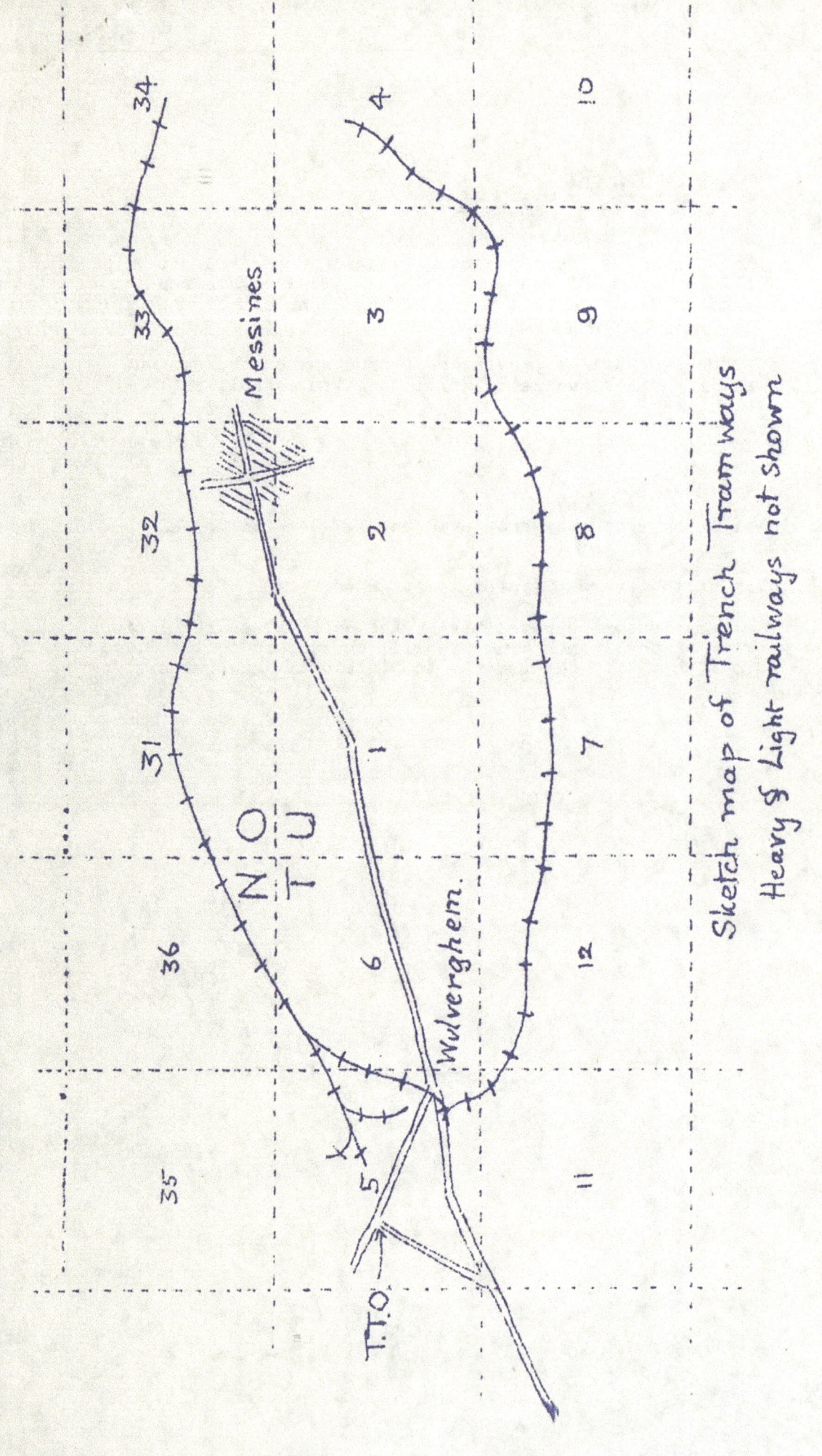

App II

Q/34/56.

SALVAGE.

1. Headquarters, 14th Salvage Company and main Divisional Salvage Dump is at NEUVE EGLISE T.14.b.9.8.
   A forward Divisional Salvage Dump will be formed at WULVERGHEM, with one section of the Salvage Company in charge.

2. East of MESSINES the brigade in line will be responsible for salvage.
   Salvage dumps for the brigade in line have been formed at

   MOULIN d' HOSPICE   U. 2. a. 7. 9.
   SCHNITZEL FARM   U. 3. c. 8. 2.

   Salvage from these dumps will be evacuated under brigade arrangements by wagon or tram to the Brigade Transport lines or to the forward divisional dump at WULVERGHEM.

3. The Divisional Salvage Company will be responsible for salvage in the area West of a North and South line through MESSINES as far as and including the road DRANOUTRE - NEUVE EGLISE - T.20. central.
   Salvage in the area between WULVERGHEM and MESSINES will be collected by the Salvage Company in temporary dumps near the tramway. A man of the forward Section will be left with each of these dumps to stop trucks returning empty and to put the salvage on the trucks.
   All parties in charge of empty trucks going to WULVERGHEM will be warned to stop and take up salvage from these temporary salvage dumps en route.

4. O.C. Salvage Company will indent daily on VIII Corps for the lorries he requires to clear the forward dump. Salvage lorries will not go East of WULVERGHEM by day.
   Salved R.E. material in the forward area will not be taken to the salvage dump but will be collected in the advanced R.E. dumps at

   O. 31. c. 1, 6.
   U. 8. a. 5. 5.

   which are situated at the junction of the Light Railway and the tramways.

5. From NEUVE EGLISE westwards each unit will be responsible for collecting into unit dumps all salvage in or near their own lines.
   The position of their unit dumps will be selected by each unit and notified forthwith to Divisional Headquarters and to the O.C. Salvage Company. One dump should be shared by adjoining units.
   O.C. Salvage Company will be responsible for clearing these unit dumps periodically into the main divisional dump.

(over)

6. The remaining area outside unit camps West of the road DRANOUTRE - NEUVE EGLISE - T.20. central will be divided into two areas by CLAPHAM and VICTORIA Roads.
The salvage of these areas will be carried out -

I In the N.E. area by the Brigade in Support.

II In the S.W. area by the Convalescent Company of the Divisional Depot Battalion.

Parties detailed by the above will be sent out daily to collect salvage in their area into the nearest unit dump.

7. The importance of an efficient system is becoming greater every day and all ranks should be impressed with the necessity of salving every article that could possibly be made use of.
Besides the more obvious articles of salvage such as arms, ammunition, equipment and R.E. material, there is a great demand at home for all articles made of Wool and Tin and all such articles must be carefully salved.

R. Lewis
A... & Q.M.G.

7/9/1917.   14th (Light) Division.

App III

14th (Light) DIVISION.   Q435.

Scheme for Winter Hutting with 2 Brigades in Line.

UNIT	CAMP	MAP REFERENCE	ACCOMMODATION Available O. O.R. H.	Required.
Div. H.Q.	RAVELSBURG	S.17.Central	30 800 40	-
A.Inf.B.H.Q.	NEUVE EGLISE	T.14.b.95.75		-
A. Battn.	ALDERSHOT	T.19.d.9.9.	30 800 -	-
B. "	NEUVE EGLISE	T.15.a.0.5.)		Repairs to houses to increase accom'r to 2 Battns.
C. "	" "	T.15.a.0.5.)		
D. "	SHANKILL	T.15.b.4.4.	6 190 -	57 huts.
M.G. Coy.	TROIS ROIS	T.20.c.4.5.)		
T.M. Bty.	" "	T.20.c.4.5.)	6 210 -	Horse standgs.
B.Inf. Bde.	In the line.			
C.Inf. Bde.	In the line.			
Pion'r Bn.		Nr. WULVERGHEM		Camp of 60 huts.
Depot Bn.	VAUXHALL	S.18.d.1.2.	9 282 6	22 huts.
Div.M.G.Co.	MAHUTONGA	T.19.b.6.5.	4 152 84	
A Fld. Amb.	RAVELSGURG R.S.	S.16.c.2.3.	- 495 -	
B " ")	WESTHOF A.D.S.	T.19.b.5.4.		
C " ")	A.D.S.	T.10.b.6.7		
A Fld. Coy.	WHEAL	T.14.d.5.5.	4 120 -	Standings for horses & 5 huts.
B " "		T.16.b.2.9.		14 huts.
C " "		T.16.a.7.8.		14 huts.
Div. Train	LA CRECHE.			
Div.Sup.Col.	STEENWERCK.			
Gas School		S.15.d.1.3.	3 36 30	
Mob.Vet.Sec.	BULLER	S.29.b.1.2.	3 130 84	
A Bde. Trans.		T.9.d.8.4.		23 huts & Standings.
B " "		T.20.b.0.0.		11 huts.
C " "	HILLSIDE	T.14.c.	6 200 -	12 huts & standings.

(Con'd)

UNIT.	CAMP.	MAP REFERENCE.	Accommodation Available. O. O.R. H.	Required.
1st F.A.Bde H.Q.		S.12.Central.	Nil	4 huts.
A Battery		S.23.a.8.5.	150 200	
B "	INKERMAN.	S.12.a.9.6.	25 100	9 huts.
C "		S.12.a.8.1.		10 huts & horse standings.
D "	KEERSEBROM.	S.11.c.Central.	90 102	5 huts.
2nd F.A.Bde. H.Q.	RAWSON.	T.20.a.8.0.	) 6 220 200	
A Battery	"	T.20.a.8.0.	)	
B "	GARDEN FARM	B.1.b.1.7.	3 100 170	
C "	KENT.	T.25.d.2.3.	) 8 360	Horse standings.
D "	"	T.25.d.2.3.	)	
D.A.C.Hd.Qrs.		T.1.d.6.9.		
A Echelon.)		(T.8.c.5.6.		
B ")		(T.7.d.5.5.		41 huts and horse standings.
		(T.14.a.3.9.		
Trench Mortar Batteries.	LEE FARM	S.22.a.2.0.	2 100 100	4 huts.

App IV

9455/4.

C. R. A.
C. R. E.
41st Infantry Bde.
42nd Infantry Bde.
43rd Infantry Bde.
11th K. Liverpool R.
Div'l M.G. Officer.
A. D. M. S.
D. A. D. O. S.
Officer i.c. Baths & Laundries.

================================

1. The Brigade in Line will select sites suitable for foot rubbing rooms, gum boot drying rooms and small forward clothing store and drying room.
   The sites selected will be notified to Div'l Headquarters and to the other Brigades.
   The actual rooms for these purposes should be above ground but dugout accommodation in close proximity will be required for personnel in charge and men waiting to use the rooms.
   Estimates of material for sheds, etc., required for these purposes should be sent in to C. R. E. and will have precedence over demands for material for the back areas.

2. As soon as the forward clothing store and drying room is ready for use arrangements will be made by which the Brigade in Line will hold 200 spare S.D. suits, shirts, pants and socks in their forward clothing store. This is to enable a man who gets thoroughly wet to obtain an immediate complete dry change. His own S.D. suit would then be dried and returned to him and the underclothing sent to the Laundry and exchanged for clean.
   The S.D. suit lent to the man will be returned by him when his own suit has been dried. The S.D. suits held for issue on loan will be marked with a triangular piece cut out of the centre of the back of the collar of the jacket or between the centre and right hand brace button of the trousers.

3. A baths will be erected under Divisional arrangements near WULVERGHEM for the use of the units in the forward area.
   At the baths a supply of dry S.D. suits and underclothing will be held for providing a change of clothing as in para.2 for men of the Artillery, Engineers, Infantry, and Pioneers in the neighbourhood.

4. Notification will be made to all concerned when the above arrangements are in working order.

Sept. 14th 1917.

P. Lewis Lt.W.
A. A. & Q. M. G.,
14th (Light) Division.

O.C. 213/1.

CONFIDENTIAL.

....

With reference to this Office O.C. 213 of 18/9/17, recommendations will reach this Office not later than last D.R. on September 27th, 1917.

The following are the numbers of names to be submitted :-

	HONOURS.	MENTIONS.
14th Divisional Artillery	10	13
14th Divisional Engineers	4	5
14th Divisional Signal Co.	1	1
41st Infantry Brigade ...	11	16
42nd Infantry Brigade ...	11	16
43rd Infantry Brigade ...	11	16
11th Bn. King's Liverpool R.	3	5
14th Divisional Train ...	2	3
R. A. M. C.	3	5
A. V. C.	-	1
A. O. C.	-	1
Chaplains	-	1

R. Lewis Lt.Col.
A.A. & Q.M.G.,
14th (Light) Division.

25/9/17.

CONFIDENTIAL.   O.C. 213.

NEW YEAR'S HONOURS GAZETTE.

1. The period to be covered will be from 26th February to 20th September 1917 inclusive.
   Recommendations must reach Divisional Headquarters not later than September 25th 1917. The allotment of Honours and Mentions will be notified as soon as received from G.H.Q., probably on September 22nd.

2. Attention is specially directed to the instructions contained in the revised Circular Letter S.S.477A dated 4th August 1917, copies of which have been sent to all concerned.
   The system of forwarding recommendations will be that laid down in paras. 21 & 28 of the above circular i.e. Infantry Brigades will submit separate lists for each Unit in the Brigade in the order recommended by the Officer Commanding that Unit: C.R.A. will submit separate lists for each Brigade of Artillery, for the D.A.C., for T.M. personnel and for D.A. Headquarters Staff. C.R.E., A.D.M.S., O.C. Train, and Officers Commanding other Units of Divisional troops will submit one list, Officers and other ranks separately, for all personnel belonging to these units.
   In the case of Services or Departments the channel for recommendations will be as follows:-

Signal Service	through	O.C. Signal Coy.
Transport and Supply Service	"	O.C. Divisional Train.
Medical Service	"	A.D.M.S.
Veterinary Service	"	D.A.D.V.S.
Ordnance Service	"	D.A.D.O.S.
Army Chaplains Department	"	Senior Chaplain C. of E. or Non-C. of E.

   Postal Service direct to Divisional Headquarters.

3. Services rendered subsequent to September 20th 1917, or previous to 26th February 1917 should not be brought to notice for the New Year's Honours Gazette, but previous good service may be referred to in order to support the recommendation.

4. Commanders of Units and formations will be responsible for the submission of recommendations concerning all those who were under their command or administered by them at midnight 20/21st September 1917.

5. The proportion this time will be 2 Honours to 3 mentions (as against 1 to 3 for the King's Birthday Gazette 1917). This increase in the number of Honours is made so that "other ranks" may receive more consideration.

6. Should a Commander wish to recommend any Officer or man who has left his command to join another formation in this Country prior to 20th September 1917 he should forward his recommendations to the Officer who was the immediate superior of that Officer or man on 20th September 1917. Should there be any difficulty in ascertaining who this was the recommendation should be forwarded to the Military Secretary, G.H.Q.

(1)

7. The following should be accepted as a general guide regarding the class of decoration and promotion for which Officers and W.Os should be recommended:-

D.S.O.   Lieut.Colonels and Majors holding the temporary rank of Brig. General, or Commanding Battalions, and such other Officers whose services have earned reward.

PROMOTION TO BREVET LIEUT. COLONEL.   Battalion Commanders and Officers holding equivalent appointments whose names have been noted on the G.H.Q. list for Command of a Brigade.

PROMOTION TO BREVET MAJOR.   No restrictions if the Officer is Commanding a Battalion or holding an equivalent appointment. In other cases a minimum of 5 years service is required.

M.C.   Captains, Subalterns and W.Os for gallant service in action, or for such services as are specified in War Office 0137/3077 (M.S.3.) of 8/3/17.

8. QUARTERMASTERS.   Recommendations for accelerated promotion cannot be submitted in connection with an honours despatch.

Recommendations for advancement to higher rate of pay for distinguished service in the Field may be submitted in connection with an honours despatch but will be restricted to Quartermasters who have completed

(a) 3 years commissioned service on full pay as an honorary Lieutenant.

(b) 5 years commissioned service on full pay as an honorary Captain.

(c) 5 years commissioned service on full pay as an honorary Major.

A Quartermaster who has received a step in honorary rank under Art. 80 or 331 of the Royal Warrant and who accordingly has been advanced to the next higher rate of pay (see Art.241) is not eligible for recommendation for higher rate of pay under (a), (b), or (c) above, so long as he remains in that rank.

9. In the event of any notification having been received by Headquarters of formations that recommendations for immediate reward were not approved, but that they would be considered for various awards in a general despatch, such recommendations will not count against any allotment.

10. The general allotment will be made on a more liberal scale this time and it is hoped that Commanders will consider it sufficient to meet all requirements.

R. Lewis Lo.Col.
A.A. & Q.M.G.
14th (Light) Division.

Sept. 18th 1917.